Educational Values and Sustainable Development

Educational Values and Sustainable Development

Kamaleswar Talwar

ADHYAYAN

ADHYAYAN PUBLISHERS & DISTRIBUTORS

NEW DELHI (INDIA)

Published by
ADHYAYAN PUBLISHERS & DISTRIBUTORS
4378/4B, 105, J.M.D. House, Murari Lal Street
Ansari Road Darya Ganj, New Delhi - 110002
Ph.: 011-23263018, 011-23277156, Fax: 011-23280028
Email: adhyayanpublishers@yahoo.com

Educational Values and Sustainable Development

Edition 2011
ISBN 978-81-8435-229-0

Printed in India

Published by Harish Chandra Yadav for Adhyayan Publishers & Distributors, Laser Typeseting at A.V. Rao and Printed at Tarun Offset Printers, Delhi

Preface

Sustainable development is a vision of development that encompasses populations, animal and plant species, ecosystems, natural resources and that integrates concerns such as the fight against poverty, gender equality, human rights, education for all, health, human security, intercultural dialogue, etc. Sustainable development is seeking to meet the needs of the present without compromising those of future generations. We have to learn our way out of current social and environmental problems and learn to live sustainably.

Education for sustainable development aims to help people to develop the attitudes, skills and knowledge to make informed decisions for the benefit of themselves and others, now and in the future, and to act upon these decisions. Education enables us to understand ourselves and others and our links with the wider natural and social environment. Along with a sense of justice, responsibility, exploration and dialogue, education aims to move us to adopting behaviours and practices which enable all to live a full life without being deprived of basic. Education alone is unlikely to inculcate values of this kind—if that were the case, the world would already be much father down the road towards the practices of sustainable development.

The present book introduces a focus on values and ethics, and on new challenges for multi-disciplinary and inter-disciplinary dialogue, teaching and research. It encourages educational institutions to enhance their role in shaping society's future, and in seeking solutions to environmental and developmental challenges. It gives a broad orientation to the concept of sustainable development, and introduces university teachers and managers to the range of possibilities for action that exist in teaching, research, community engagement and management.

Kamaleswar Talwar

Contents

1

Education and Values

Values are defined in literature as everything from eternal ideas to behavioural actions. As used here values refer to criteria for determining levels of goodness, worth or beauty. Values are affectively-laden thoughts about objects, ideas, behaviour, etc. that guide behaviour, but do not necessarily require it. The act of valuing is considered an act of making value judguments, an expression of feeling, or the acquisition of and adherence to a set of principles as part of the affective system. However, once they are developed they provide an important filter for selecting input and connecting thoughts and feelings to action, and thus could also be included in a discussion of the regulatory system.

Some of the values important for workers in the information age are responsibility, self-esteem, sociability, integrity and honesty. An additional set of important values suggested by the writings of futurists or behavioural scientists as important for life success are: autonomy, benevolence, compassion, courage, courtesy, honesty, integrity, responsibility, trustworthiness and truthfulness. Other lists of core values have been developed. For example, a group of educators, character education experts, and leaders of youth organisations meeting under the sponsorship of the Josephson Institute of Ethics developed the following list: respect, responsibility, trustworthiness, caring, justice and fairness, and civic virtue and citizenship.

The Council for Global Education asserts that the following set of values are also to be considered: compassion, courtesy, critical inquiry, due process, equality of opportunity, freedom of thought and action, human worth and dignity, integrity, justice, knowledge, loyalty, objectivity, order, patriotism, rational consent, reasoned argument, respect for other's rights, responsibility, responsible citizenship, rule of law, tolerance and truth. Despite the debate over exactly what are the core values that ought to be taught in schools, the Association for Supervision and Curriculum Development suggests it is possible for communities to reach a consensus on a set of values that would be appropriate for inclusion in the school curriculum. Once a community has done so, the next issue is how should one go about the process of teaching values.

1.1. Importance of Value Education

Education is a methodical effort towards learning basic facts about humanity. And the core idea behind value education is to cultivate essential values in the students so that the civilization that teaches us to manage complexities can be sustained and further developed. It begins at home and it is continued in schools. Everyone accepts certain things in his/her life through various mediums like society or government.

Value education is important to help everyone in improving the value system that he/she holds and put them to use. Once, we understand our values in life, we can examine and control the various choices we make in our lives. It's our duty to uphold the various types of values in life such as cultural values, universal values, personal values and social values.

Thus, value education is always essential to shape a student's life and to give him an opportunity of performing himself on the global stage. The need for value education among the parents, children, teachers etc, is constantly increasing as we continue to witness increasing violent activities, behavioral disorder and lack of unity in society.

The family system in India has a long tradition of imparting value education right from the ancient practice of the gurukul system. But with modern developments and a fast changing role of the parents, it has not been very easy for the parents to impart relevant values in their wards. Therefore many institutes today conduct various value education programs that meet the rising needs of modern society w.r.t. code of conduct and values. These activities concentrate on the development of the children, young adults etc. focusing on areas like happiness, humility, cooperation, honesty, simplicity, love, unity, peace etc.

Value education is education in values and education towards the inculcation of values. Implicit in this definition is the conviction that value education is a universal phenomenon intrinsic to all learning and education, whether at home or in an institution. It is not. Neither teaches us to be critical thinkers or to regard ourselves as proactive beings in relation to ourselves, our community and humanity at large. Unwittingly and through habit we accept most things handed out to us by the media, the government and the polity. Unfortunately when there is so much talk about individual capabilities and potentialities, there is so little confidence on the part of the individual about his own power to make a difference. Our educational system is of little help. We are not trained to be proactive thinkers because we are told so little of the life values that are the basis for creative thinking.

What really is education? It is not literacy, nor information. Education is a systematic attempt towards human learning. All learning is subjective and self-related. Educational activity starts with the individual—Who am I? Where am I going? Where have I come from? It is only with an understanding of the Self that we can begin to understand our relationships with others and the environment.

Knowledge should not be made remote from individual reality and irrelevant to the individual. Knowledge can never be 'learned'. Knowledge is the fruit of experience and experience is the sensation of the individual. Individual experience is an internal happening and is the function of awareness. And one of the processes of knowing ourselves, of raising our awareness, is to be able to identify and clarify our values. Education in values is essential in helping each one of us directly encounter the values that we hold, understand them completely, so that we may order our relationships to the environment that lies outside us. Once we are clear about values we shall be better able to sift and control information of the natural world, make wise choices and be creative in our mental processes.

'Know thyself' is what each of us needs to do, yet modern life moves at such a pace that we seldom take the time to examine ourselves. We become strangers to our own selves. We follow the dictates of others blindly. Why should any debate be left to a few 'experts'? Why is not critical thinking an integral part of everyday life? It must be so if we are to create a sane society.

For this to happen we must be equipped to examine our values. These are our internal guideposts. Much of the great literature of the world—from Bhagavad Gita to Socrates to Hamlet—has dwelled on value choices and moral dilemmas that are bound to occur when your values are clearly defined. Values do conflict. Making value choices is not easy, but it is this very thing we must confront and make part of our lives if we are to be truly creative human beings. Moral dilemmas are only possible for those who have strongly held principles and it is through these moral dilemmas that new and revolutionary thought processes emerge and character develops.

Value conflicts are the strongest test of character. Yet, today, moral dilemmas are considered a waste of time, a domain for 'losers'. Ultimately we declare all value assertions unscientific and relative, hence dispensable. We do not realize that value conflict is healthy, necessary and by eliminating it we are also erasing all conviction. Confucius once said: "If a man carefully cultivates values in his conduct, he may still err a little but he won't be far from the standard of truth."

1.2. Categories of Values

It is time to clarify these values that we speak of. It is up to each one of us to determine the society we will create by deciding upon the values we will emphasize today. But first, let us be clear about the categories of values. These are three-universal, cultural or ethnic and individual or personal values.

1.2.1. Universal Values

Universal values reveal the essence of the human condition. These arise out of the fundamental questions-Who am I? What is my essence? Who am I when I remove myself from my social and cultural environment? Is there anything in me that cannot be explained by heredity, environment and society? It is universal values that indicate the essence of the human condition. It is through universal values that we link ourselves with humanity and the cosmos, it is through these that all barriers of time, place and ethnicity are eliminated.

These values are not manifest. They must be experienced, as one experiences a sunrise, the beauty of a flower, as one experiences joy, pleasure, bliss, awe, serenity. These values cannot be contained by words. That the Upanishads and the Bible have remained relevant today as they were centuries ago, tells us that at the core, there are some constants in human condition, that time has not changed. That we are still moved by the wonder of the Taj Mahal, the music of Mozart, the life of Hamlet, the perennial philosophy of the Bhagavad Gita speaks volumes about the mystery and timelessness of universal values.

Universal values can be experienced as life, joy, brotherhood, love, compassion, service, bliss, truth and eternity.

1.2.2. Cultural Values

Cultural values are speculative and there is nothing wrong with speculating. But it becomes wrong when speculation becomes 'truth', when opinion becomes 'fact' and when prejudice becomes the 'cause'. When cultural values are elevated to the status of universal values, there is the risk of intolerance, oppression, demagoguery, brutality and aggression. A cultural value may serve a function in a particular situation and circumstance, but in no way can it be seen as the only or the best way of doing things. A spoon can serve the function of lifting food but so can a fork, a knife, a spatula or bare fingers. A cultural value similarly has limited relevance and the fact that it serves a particular function in a given society does not imply that it is the only or best way of doing so.

When seen in this light, cultural values have the advantage of becoming a source of insight into a time and society. Creative development of ideas often emerges out of an interaction of different cultural values and an understanding and respect for differences. Much of what we find exciting and interesting has in fact come from a meeting of cultures. The Renaissance came about from a meeting of the ancient Greek and medieval European cultures. Jazz is African-European music and the American Transcendentalists studied the Indian Vedas and Upanishads. The East heavily influenced writers such as Aldous Huxley, Somerset Maugham and Carl Jung. Gandhi drew inspiration from Tolstoy, and Martin Luther King Jr. was in turn, deeply affected by Gandhi.

If all one knows is one's own culture, there is narcissism. The study of other cultures gives us a wider frame of reference. And the study of other cultures is through its sacred (poetic, mythic, religious) traditions and not only through studying history. Cultural values are reflected in language, ethics, social hierarchy, aesthetics, education, law, economics, philosophy and social institutions of every kind.

1.2.3. Individual Values

Individual values are our private principles, the result of individual personality and individual experiences. Parents, teachers and one's peer group shape individual values. Personal values determine the differing reactions of people to similar events. A crisis may dim one person's enthusiasm and land him in depression, while another may be propelled into greater action.

Individual values are reflected in individual goals, vows, relationships, commitments and personal preferences. These are often colored by memories of the past and therefore there are differences in the meaning attributed to a common experience. To one person children denote happiness and strength, to another they may denote bondage. Individual values are malleable, often contained in a time and memory warp. They can transform themselves into universal values when you practise awareness and living in the moment.

After clarifying our values, we must determine which of the three are most meaningful for us after considering the relative priority of each category, so that we may be able to confront these and understand our own psychological and social conditioning.

Beyond our ego (sense of self) and identity (sense of belonging to a group) that dictates what we know, think, feel and how we act lies the universal identity. Dissonance between ego and identity can create anxiety and alienation but acting upon universal values will not, for here it is authentic action emanating from an authentic Self. Universal values are at the top of the list. The others have their place but it is through universal values that we experience a sense of oneness with the human race.

Universal values must be our foundation if we are to enjoy a rich, profound and fulfilling life. Our personal and cultural biases limit and distort our perception of the universal wonder that is life. Even as the hands of a clock are powered from the center that remains ever still, so the universal values remain ever at the center of human life, no matter where the hands of time are pointing—past, present or future.

1.3. Basic Approach to Value Education

Value education is an explicit attempt to teach about values and/or valuing. There are five basic approaches to values education: inculcation, moral development, analysis, values clarification, and action learning.

1.3.1. Inculcation

Most educators viewing value education from the perspective of inculcation see values as socially or culturally accepted standards or rules of behaviour. Valuing is therefore considered a process of the student identifying with and accepting the standards or norms of the important individuals and institutions within his society. The student "incorporates" these values into his or her own value system. These educators take a view of human nature in which the individual is treated, during the inculcation process, as a reactor rather than as an initiator. Extreme advocates believe that the needs and goals of society should transcend and even define the needs and goals of the individuals. However, advocates who consider an individual to be a free, self-fulfilling participant in society tend to inculcate values as well, especially values such as freedom to learn, human dignity, justice and self-exploration. Both the social- and individualistic-oriented advocates would argue the notion that certain values are universal and absolute. The source of these values is open to debate. On the one hand some advocates argue they derive from the natural order of the universe; others believe that values originate in the omnipotent Creator.

1.3.2. Moral Development

Educators adopting a moral development perspective believe that moral thinking develops in stages through a specific sequence. It is assumed that students invariantly progress developmentally in their thinking about moral issues. They can comprehend one stage above their current primary stage and exposure to the next higher level is essential for enhancing moral development. Educators attempt to stimulate students to develop more complex moral reasoning patterns through the sequential stages.

In this perspective the person is viewed as an active initiator and a reactor within the context of his or her environment; the individual cannot fully change the environment, but neither can the environment fully mold the individual. A person's actions are the result of his or her feelings, thoughts, behaviours and experiences. Although the environment can determine the content of one's experiences, it cannot determine its form. Genetic structures already inside the person are primarily responsible for the way in which a person internalises the content, and organises and transforms it into personally meaningful data.

The moral development technique most often used is to present a hypothetical or factual value dilemma story which is then discussed in small groups. Students are presented with alternative viewpoints within these discussions which is in hypothesized to lead to higher, more developed moral thinking. There are three critical variables that make a dilemma appropriate:

1. The story must present a real conflict for the central character, include a number of moral issues for consideration, and generate differences of opinion among students about the appropriate response to the situation.
2. A leader who can help to focus the discussion on moral reasoning.
3. A classroom climate that encourages students to express their moral reasoning freely.

There is an assumption that values are based on cognitive moral beliefs or concepts. This view would agree with the inculcation assumption that there are universal moral principles, but would contend that values are considered relative to a particular environment or situation and are applied according to the cognitive development of the individual.

1.3.3. Analysis Approach

The analysis approach to values education was developed mainly by social science educators. The approach emphasizes rational thinking and reasoning. The purpose of the analysis approach is to help students use logical thinking and the procedures of scientific investigation in dealing with values issues. Students are urged to provide verifiable facts about the correctness or value of the topics or issues under investigation. A major assumption is that valuing is the cognitive process of determining and justifying facts and beliefs derived from those facts. This approach concentrates primarily on social values rather than on the personal moral dilemmas presented in the moral development approach.

The rationalist and empiricist views of human nature seem to provide the philosophical basis for this approach. Its advocates state that the process of valuing can and should be conducted under the total authority of facts and reason' and 'guided not by the dictates of the heart and conscience, but by the rules and procedures of logic.

The teaching methods used by this approach generally centre around individual and group study of social value problems and issues, library and field research, and rational class discussions. These are techniques widely used in social studies instruction.

A variety of higher-order cognitive and intellectual operations are frequently used. These include:

1. stating the issues;
2. questioning and substantiating in the relevance of statements;
3. applying analogous cases to qualify and refine value positions;
4. pointing out logical and empirical inconsistencies in arguments;
5. weighing counter arguments; and
6. seeking and testing evidence.

1.3.4. Values Clarification

The values clarification approach arose primarily from humanistic psychology and the humanistic education movement as it attempted to implement the ideas and theories of Gordon Allport, Abraham Maslow, Carl Rogers, and others. The central focus is on helping students use both rational thinking and emotional awareness to examine personal behaviour patterns and to clarify and actualise their values. It is believed that valuing is a process of self-actualisation, involving the subprocesses of choosing freely from among alternatives, reflecting carefully on the consequences of those alternatives, and prizing, affirming, and acting upon one's choices.

Whereas the inculcation approach relies generally on outside standards and the moral development and analysis approaches rely on logical and empirical processes, the values clarification approach relies on an internal cognitive and affective decision making process to decide which values are positive and which are negative. It is therefore an individualistic rather than a social process of values education.

From this perspective, the individual, if he or she is allowed the opportunity of being free to be his or her true self, makes choices and decisions affected by the internal processes of willing, feeling, thinking and intending. It is assumed that through self-awareness, the person enters situations already pointed or set in certain directions. As the individual develops, the making of choices will more often be based on conscious, self-determined thought and feeling. It is advocated that the making of choices, as a free being, which can be confirmed or denied in experience, is a preliminary step in the creation of values.

Within the clarification framework a person is seen as an initiator of interaction with society and environment. The educator should assist the individual to develop his or her internal processes, thereby allowing them, rather than external factors, to be the prime determinants of human behaviour; the individual should be free to change the environment to meet his or her needs.

Methods used in the values clarification approach include large- and small-group discussion; individual and group work; hypothetical, contrived and real dilemmas; rank orders and forced choices; sensitivity and listening techniques; songs and artwork; games and simulations; and personal journals and interviews; self-analysis worksheet. A vital component is a leader who does not attempt to influence the selection of values. Like the moral development approach, values clarification assumes that the valuing process is internal and relative, but unlike the inculcation and developmental approaches it does not posit any universal set of appropriate values.

A sixfold process describing the guidelines of the values clarification approach is as follows;

1. choosing from alternatives;
2. choosing freely;
3. prizing one's choice;
4. affirming one's choice;
5. acting upon one's choice; and
6. acting repeatedly, over time.

1.3.5. Action Learning

The action learning approach is derived from a perspective that valuing includes a process of implementation as well as development. That is, it is important to move beyond thinking and feeling to acting. The approach is related to the efforts of some social studies educators to emphasize community-based rather than classroom-based learning experiences. In some ways it is the least developed of the five approaches. However, a variety of recent programs have demonstrated the effectiveness of the techniques advocated by this approach.

Advocates of the action learning approach stress the need to provide specific opportunities for learners to act on their values. They see valuing primarily as a process of self-actualisation in which individuals consider alternatives choose freely from among those alternatives; and prize, affirm, and act on their choices. They place more emphasis on action-taking inside and outside the classroom than is reflected in the moral development, analysis, and values clarification processes.

Values are seen to have their source neither in society nor in the individual but in the interaction between the person and the society; the individual cannot be described outside of his or her context. The process of self-actualisation, so important to the founders of the values clarification approach, is viewed as being tempered by social factors and group pressures. In this way it is more related to Maslow's level of transcendence which he discussed towards the end of his career.

A problem-solving/decision making model and related techniques that can serve as a sound beginning for this approach is as follows:

a) *Input Phase*—a problem is perceived and an attempt is made to understand the situation or problem

1. Identify the problem(s) and state it (them) clearly and concisely
2. State the criteria that will be used to evaluate possible alternatives to the problem as well as the effectiveness of selected solutions; state any identified boundaries of acceptable alternatives, important values or feelings to be considered, or results that should be avoided
3. Gather information or facts relevant to solving the problem or making a decision

b) *Processing Phase*—alternatives are generated and evaluated and a solution is selected

4. Develop alternatives or possible solutions
5. Evaluate the generated alternatives vis-a-vis the stated criteria
6. Develop a solution that will successfully solve the problem diagnose possible problems with the solution and implications of these problems; consider the worst that can happen if the solution is implemented; evaluate in terms of overall "feelings" and "values"

c) *Output Phase*—includes planning for and implementing the solution

7. Develop plan for implementation (sufficiently detailed to allow for successful implementation)
8. Establish methods and criteria for evaluation of implementation and success
9. Implement the solution

d) *Review Phase*—the solution is evaluated and modifications are made, if necessary

10. Evaluating implementation of the solution
11. Evaluating the effectiveness of the solution
12. Modifying the solution in ways suggested by the evaluation process

Many of the teaching methods of similar to those used in analysis and values clarification. In fact, the first two phases of Huitt's model are almost identical to the steps used in analysis. In some ways the skill practice in group organisation and interpersonal relations and action projects is similar to that of Kohlberg's "Just School" program that provides opportunities to engage in individual and group action in school and community.

1.4. Value Development through Education

If we give good education to the present day children, the future of the next generations will be well. My opinion education is the solution for all types of the problems. Now we are living in the modern century. If we use science and technology in the proper way it is not difficult for us to solve all the problems of the non-moral and value things.The main object of the study is to inculcate moral and value based education in schools and colleges and to know the attitude of intermediate students towards moral values. Gandhiji advised the inmates of Sabarmati Ashram on the practice of the following values in their day-to-day life:

1. Ahimsa
2. Non-stealing
3. Non-possession
4. Swadeshi
5. Manual work
6. Fearlessness
7. Truth
8. Chastity
9. Equality of religion
10. Removal of untouchability
11. Control of palate

1.5. Life Goals and Personal Characteristics

Life goals and Personal characteristics are very necessary for all types of persons in the society.

1.5.1. Life Goals

— A world at peace (free of war and conflict)
— Freedom (independence, free choice)
— Wisdom (a mature understanding of life)
— Happiness (contentedness)
— An exciting life (a stimulating, active life)
— Equality (brotherhood, equal opportunity for all)
— A comfortable life (a prosperous life)
— Self-respect (self-esteem, feeling good about yourself)
— Salvation (religiously saved, eternal life)
— Mature love (sexual and spiritual intimacy)
— Social recognition (respect, admiration)
— A sense of accomplishment (having made a lasting contribution)
— Family security (taking care of loved ones)
— True friendship (close companionship)
— A world of beauty (beauty of nature and the arts)
— Inner harmony (freedom from inner conflict)
— Pleasure (an enjoyable, leisurely life)
— National security (protection from attack)

1.5.2. Personal Characteristics

— Self-controlled (thinks first, restrained, self-disciplined)
— Honest (sincere, truthful, disclosing)
— Loving (affectionate, tender, caring)
— Ambitious (hard working, aspiring)
— Cheerful (lighthearted, joyful)
— Responsible (dependable, reliable)
— Independent (self-reliant, sufficient)
— Broad-minded (open-minded, able to see other viewpoints)
— Polite (courteous, well mannered)
— Forgiving (willing to pardon others)

— Intellectual (intelligent, reflective, knowledgeable)
— Helpful (working for the welfare of others)
— Obedient (dutiful, respectful)
— Capable (competent, effective, skilful)
— Logical (consistent, rational, aware of reality)
— Clean (neat, tidy)
— Imaginative (daring, creative)
— Courageous (standing up for your beliefs, strong)

It is believed that moral behaviour is determined by five factors:

— *Socialisation*: becoming aware as a child of society's and parents' rules of conduct for being good.
— *Moral judgement:* learning to think reasonably about our own ethics and deliberately deciding on our own moral standards.
— *Moral feelings*: the internalisation of our moral beliefs to the degree that we feel shame and guilt when we fail to do what we "should."
— *Empathy:* the awareness of other people's situation, feelings, and needs so that one is compelled to help those in need.
— *Confidence and knowledge*: knowing the steps involved in helping others and believing that one is responsible for and capable of helping.

Today we facing so many problems, like terrorism, poverty and population problem. It is necessary to inculcate moral values in curriculum. Education is an effective weapon. Education is a weapon, whose effect depends on who holds it in his hands and at whom it is aimed.

1.6. Curricular Activities

Due to liberalisation, industrialisation and globalisation rapid changes are occurring in almost all social sciences. The value possessed and their attitudes according to the changes should be known up to date vast changes are occurring in the education. So by called philosophical foundations of India are declining day today, and with the country in a state of social turbulence, the goals and functions of formal education need to be reassessed and updated. Through education we can change the world:

a) by giving a place for moral values in the curriculum.

b) by explaining moral values through stories and illustrations.

c) by inculcating moral values in the students through poetry, novel and stories.

d) by role playing of a good story in the lesson.

e) by educating students through posters, advertisements and dramatisations; these are all a part of the curriculum.

f) by introducing a course on moral values as a part of its Master Degree in Developmental Administration.

g) by giving course training to students to develop moral values in the society.

h) by educating citizen through direct contact by setting up local offices across the religion.

i) by first of all educating women in the society. A mother is the first teacher. Motivate every woman to know about moral values through special course like "Gandhian Studies.

References

Clarke, J. 1975. *Beginning Values Clarifications*, Pennat Press.

Damon, William. 1988. *The Moral Child: Nurturing Children's Natural Moral Growth*. The Free Press, New York.

Kirschenbaum, M. 1977. *Advanced Value Clarification*. California University Associates.

Rath, R.E., Harmin. M. and Simon, S.B. 1978. *Values and Teaching: Working with values in Classroom*, Columbus, Charles E, Merrill.

2

Value Education in India

The educational system in India has faced a basic dilemma ever since its introduction by the British. The essence of this problem was summed up by Mahatma Gandhi in his historic statement at Chatham House, London, in 1931:

> The British administrators when they came to India, instead of taking hold of things as they were, began to root them out. They scratched the soil and began to look at the root and left the root like that and the beautiful tree perished. The village schools were not good enough for the British administrator so he came out with his own programme. Every school must have so much paraphernalia, building and so forth. Well, there were no such schools at all — ancient schools have gone by the board — and the schools established after the European pattern were too expensive to fulfil a programme of compulsory primary education of these inside of a century. This very poor country of mine is ill able to sustain such an expensive method of education.

Free India did not have the will to fulfil Mahatma Gandhi's dream of reviving the ancient tradition of the village schoolmaster, supported by the community, his status and survival as a guru being embedded within the culture and ecology of his immediate environment. Instead the government chose to continue with efforts to educate the masses through a vast, centralised machinery and superstructure of staff, infrastructure and resources. Successive efforts at universalisation of primary education, ranging from Operation Blackboard to DPEP and Education For All, have only reinforced the strength of the challenge posed by Mahatma Gandhi in his statement at Chatham House. The Adult Literacy Campaign and, more recently, the investment thrust on primary education to produce the literate child, carries within itself the hidden suspicion that the goal of universal education for the masses may even be quietly set aside one day, planners having perhaps finally realised that the goal is unattainable within the present system.

2.1. Quality Education System

As pointed out by the Mahatma, the success of this system depends solely on expenses and affordability. It thus gives rise to a situation where a mass of underprivileged and under-educated children face a largely urban elite population of privileged school children. Needless to say, it is the latter who get into the universities. While the tax-payer pays for both government schools as well as universities, the poor man pays for both but benefits from neither. The per capita public cost of university education is exorbitant when compared with school education. In the words of Ivan Illich, the school is a perfect system of regressive taxation where the privileged graduates ride on the back of the entire paying public.

Every poor Indian who can manage to make both ends meet thus strives to join the ranks of far better schools, because only these can form the gateway to subsidised higher education. The past two decades have seen a phenomenal growth of two types of private schools outside the system of government schools. These are the so-called elite schools where education is sold to the highest bidder, and the plethora of petty teaching shops against which it is fashionable for the educated elite to occasionally raise a hue and cry. In between there do exist a large number of institutions, often run by charitable or religious organisations, which seek to make as many compromises as possible within the given system.

2.1.1. Kendriya Vidyalayas

It is not surprising that the government of a democratic state would also be compelled to join this race for providing more expensive schools for quality education. The Kendriya Vidyalayas, Sainik Schools, Railway Schools, Tibetan Schools and Navodaya Vidyalayas are responses to the basic dilemma facing the existing system. The KVs and NVs together run about 1,200 schools. The KVs, which were set up to cater to children of government servants having All-India transfer liability, have now increasingly opened their doors to the children of upwardly mobile, less privileged urban families. While 'political pressure' is ostensibly to blame, the trend basically reflects a sensible popular response of the underprivileged. In the public perception, the system of mass government-sponsored education appears to have failed to deliver the goods, increasing expansion having led apparently to decreasing quality. Hence the upwardly mobile social classes are aggressively latching on to whatever better education is available at public cost.

2.1.2. Navodaya Vidyalayas

As regards rural India, it needed a statesman like Rajiv Gandhi to visualise that the day was not far off when the rural elite would also grow restive and clamour for expensive quality education at par with quality schools set up in urban areas serving predominantly urban populations. Hence Navodaya Vidyalayas were set up as residential schools with 75 per cent reservations for rural candidates, all candidates being selected on the basis of a nation-wide talent test. No doubt the Navodaya system has made the best possible compromises within the given contradictions of the existing social system. There is a 30 per cent reservation for girls and reservation for scheduled castes and scheduled tribes commensurate with their population strength in the district. Elitism of merit is the hallmark of the system. While the talent test is open to all rural children studying in Class V of rural schools, the admissions are also structured so as to ensure that all geo-economic regions within the district are proportionately and equitably represented and no single region dominates.

Navodaya Vidyalayas have sometimes been sarcastically described as the Doon School alternative for rural areas. But this can mean different things to different people. From the urban point of view it is often a derisive comment implying that by the very nature of the socio-economic set-up of the country, Doon Schools can hardly be relevant for country bumpkins. For the rural elite it is viewed as an optimistic statement, since they would naturally like to have the best for themselves, the urban elite invariably furnishing the role model.

There is a third point of view put forth by planners and educationists who feel that these rural elite schools are being set up at the cost of improvements in mass universal education. Such expensive schools set up in the rural environment only bring into focus the deprivation suffered by the rural masses. Setting aside expenditure on construction, which is quite heavy, the average cost per Navodaya student comes to about Rs. 9,900 per annum. Is such heavy investment on as few as 500-odd students per district justified? These are the questions raised by the Acharya Ramamurti Report, as also by the CPI(M) government of West Bengal, which has steadfastly refused to introduce the Navodaya Vidyalaya Scheme in its state purely for ideological reasons.

The Acharya Ramamurti Report indicts the NV Scheme on the grounds that it is very costly, it caters to a microscopic minority of the total school population and perpetrates an exclusive system inconsistent with the long cherished common school system of public education. These educationists, however, seem to have overlooked the main problem pointed out by Mahatma Gandhi with the 'cherished system of public education', namely, that if at all schools are to be established after the European pattern they will inevitably be too expensive for the people. If rural areas are not to follow the pattern of more and more exclusive and expensive schooling mushrooming in urban areas, rural talent will never get a chance to compete for higher education unless it migrates to the urban environment. This is a hard fact of life which this point of view does not face but which could be realised. By initiating the Navodaya Vidyalaya Scheme, the government simply brought the process of handling contradictions inherent within the system to its logical climax. To the urban elite, however, what is sauce for the goose is definitely not sauce for the gander.

In the trend towards exclusive and increasingly expensive education the residential school stands at the apex of the school system and is sought to be duplicated for educationally underprivileged and rural children by the Navodaya Vidyalayas. As regards day schools, it is no secret that home tuition is embedded in the system of even the best public schools today. Both schools as well as parents find themselves unable to cope with the existing syllabus as well as an increasingly competitive environment without the aid of home tuitions, which today comprise a flourishing business. In government schools the underprivileged may also suffer since the temptation to earn more as a side business tends to retard optimum contribution of government teachers within school.

Thus even the expensive day school has ended up in total dependence on a parallel and equally expensive system of home coaching. A recent development in the private sector has now led to the opening of even more exclusive elite schools which restrict the number of students per class. While sixty students are replaced by twenty students only in these super schools, the costs of sixty are naturally paid for by the twenty privileged families. School has, therefore, become a flourishing and money-guzzling industry. Children exist for schools, not schools for children, and this is as true for private paying schools as it is for government schools.

2.2. Maladies of the School System

2.2.1. Seeds of Alienation

While the seeds of spiralling expenses have grown into monstrous weeds, the seeds of alienation spread in a more subtle manner. The residential school is an apt symbol of alienation not only from its cultural and social environment but also from society itself. It stands at the apex of a system which rests on this artificial separation that seeks to inculcate values of exclusivity and elitism. Within the day schools the system alienates the teacher from the taught through the weight of sheer numbers and the cumulative burden of learning and measuring up to academic standards. It also alienates the student community as a whole from the socio-cultural matrix which surrounds it. The accent on competition and the constant stress on the individual as against the group and the community further alienates children from one another.

Seeds of alienation are embedded in the examination system, which lays a premium on a system of marking that is the sole determinant of individual achievement, the costs of which are paid for by the under-achievers. In its mildest form the under-achievers pay for it by being relegated to 'non-ability' as against 'ability' sections in public schools, alienation from one's immediate peers being thus glorified and institutionalised. At its worst, the system is scarred by student suicides.

2.2.2. Ragging in Educational Institutions

Universities like Takshashila and Nalanda flourished and attained international acclaim. In the ancient systems of learning the guru invariably utilised the older boys to teach the younger ones. Their roles were supportive, not exploitative. How unlike the system of public schools, where the exploitation of younger boys by older boys is dubbed respectably as ‘ragging’. While the school tie and similar indicators of superior status may still hold them together at school, these tenuous bonds no longer operate in the universities. University students in India in particular are in essence a mob, whether it be a passive mob or a mob on the rampage.

There are often deaths of students in which their peers are indirectly or directly involved through ragging. It is not a mere coincidence that these incidents have generally occurred in professional institutions for engineering or medical students. While at first glance this phenomenon may appear to be incomprehensible, once the seeds of alienation present in the whole system are exposed it could also be seen as an offshoot of the system itself. The idea and essence of peace and universal harmony, of oneness with nature and association with the earth, of education as a pursuit in the arts of living in an interconnected universe is entirely missing from the system. Instead to the fore are values of individual achievement, branding and typing young persons as bright, mediocre, elite, poor, underprivileged.

That this system is giving rise to problems entirely of our own making is being realised in many parts of the world. Radical thinkers, sociologists and educationists have raised voices in protest. Everett Reimer in *School Is* Dead and Ivan Illich in *Deschooling Society* have asked some of the profoundest questions about education today. They have recognised that most countries in the world can only afford to give their children the barest minimum of education while the costs of schooling are rising everywhere faster than enrolments and faster than national incomes. While regarding schools as institutional props for privilege for most people, Everett Reimer also recognises the fact that they are at the same time major instruments of social mobility. But he questions the cost in terms of true learning, true creativity and true democracy.

The search for alternatives in education has already begun. Some, like Everett Reimer, search for alternatives in terms of content, organisation and finance. At the other end of the spectrum, *Letter to a Teacher*, written by eight young Italian village boys from the school of Barbiana, is a minor classic which reveals with devastating clarity how the school system oppresses and marginalises the rural poor by divorcing them completely from their ecological base and their cultural environment. It also presents a radical alternative.

2.2.3. Emergence of Non-formal Schools

In India today, the government's and NGOs' search for alternatives has led to greater support and funding for non-formal schools, the most dramatic example being that of the Charvaha Schools of Bihar. However, this experiment suffers from all the general weaknesses of the state system. In Bihar there are other alternatives developed with more success, such as the model 'Sidh', started by Pawan Kumar Gupta, an NGO, in and around about 15 villages surrounding Kempty, near Mussoorie. Many other examples of rural-based education centres can be documented where the initiative for establishment and management has vested with communities themselves. Craft-oriented training and basic education have been outstanding successes of Dwarko Sundrani's Bodh Gaya Ashram, where schooling on the Gandhian pattern is made available to the poorest of the poor in Bihar. These non-formal schools, being beyond the pale of the state boards, are also free from the usual bureaucratic supervision of school inspectors, but by their very nature they are limited to the Class V level.

2.2.4. Yashpal Committees Recommendations

The Yashpal Committee was set up specifically for suggesting ways to reduce the academic burden on students in recognised schools. The Committee strongly recommended toning down of individual competitiveness and introduction of group activity in schools. Simultaneously it advocated decentralisation of curriculum formation, textbook writing and much greater involvement of teachers in these processes, particularly textbook formation. In general the Yashpal Committee came out strongly against textbooks, syllabi and examinations which together form a system that inflicts upon the children the tyranny of rote memorisation.

The Department of Education has taken up these suggestions for serious review. The CBSE pattern of education will be set aside or modified in the near future. Sir Thomas Munro, who set in motion the process of establishment of schools after a new pattern in Madras Presidency in the 1820s, aptly summarised the aims of the new education as being 'to facilitate the acquisition of wealth or rank'. As long as society accepts these as the aims of schooling, the CBSE syllabus and the emphasis on science and commerce streams will continue regardless of the Yashpal Committee report or any other similar reports. There are a few notable public schools which have departed from the mainstream and yet retained eminence within the general delivery system.

2.2.5. Benefits from Novadaya Vidyalayas

The difficulties of innovating within over 370 government residential schools such as the Navodaya Vidyalayas would be apparent to any educational administrator. Being wholly funded by government, there is an even greater compulsion for these schools to deliver and perform as per the marks-oriented examination system laid down by the CBSE. Not only do residential schools allow for more investment in time, but the Vidyalayas themselves, with their resource pool of talented rural students, stand Janus-like between two worlds - with one hand they can reach out to grasp the best of scientific and technical skills, while with the other they can gather easily the ancient wisdom of the east enshrined in the oral tradition and rituals of their immediate cultural environment. Hence the Navodaya Vidyalaya Samiti has started a small venture to give schooling a human face through a carefully planned programme of Art in Education, based firmly on the indigenous guru-shishya tradition of learning.

Workshops in theatre, folk music, folk arts, epics and ballad singing can very easily slip into the groove of consumerism and assembly-line production that has come to characterise our school system. Again, overemphasis on achievement and the accent on the individual could vitiate the cathartic experience, the flowering of creativity, the realisation of a deep harmony between man and nature which these workshops should generate. Hence every workshop in

Navodaya Vidyalayas is designed around an activity with a cluster of groups working on the theme in accordance with their own particular talent.

Thus a Pandawani workshop held in Durg was an experience in which the literary group interviewed Teejan Bai, wrote up reports and poems, while the visual art group was busy drawing and painting the scenes she depicted. Those who had talent for dramatic performances learnt the art and performed on the stage, but it was a holistic experience through which the Chhattisgarhi children of Durg moved towards a joyous self-attainment, a recognition of an abiding and ancient identity which was derived from sources that stand apart from and are superior to their school and their schoolmasters.

The richness of rural roots and traditions gave them a sense of pride and psychological reassurance which no success in examinations could ever give. By honouring notable rural artists in this fashion the Samiti was able to bridge the gulf between teacher and taught, urban and rural, so-called literate and so-called illiterate. To put it in the works of Dharampal, the present system "has kept most educated Indians not only ignorant of the society they live in, the culture which sustains this society and their fellow beings, but yet more tragically, for over a century it has induced a lack of confidence and loss of bearing amongst people of India in general".

It is ultimately left to each one of us in the educational field to move one small step forward towards this transformation of vision towards reorientation of values and objectives of education. Not only in India, but in the entire world, education places an overriding value on products over people, on achievement over harmony.

2.3. Concept and Classification of Values

Moral, ethical and spiritual values represent the aspirations of a society and act as its guide. Values are principles, self-imposed rules or the ethical policy we adopt in order to travel through life with a clear conscience. There are many temptations, illusions and negative experiences which prompt us to do wrong. People who practise values develop inner strength to resist otherwise common human weaknesses. The values in a person's life reveal their character and determine their moral and ethical choices.

Since moral and spiritual values are abstract and hard to conceptualise, they are contrasted with material values which tend to disable moral, ethical and spiritual values. Human values are derived from universal ideals. They are personal, their definitions are subjective and everyone has their own set of human values.

Values are expressed in interpersonal relationships. The more we identify with the inner self, the easier it is to relate to others on the basis of moral and spiritual values. When we are influenced by materialism, spiritual values are corrupted and material values become dominant. Recognition of our spiritual identity is necessary to develop values because all values dwell in the mental, emotional and spiritual self and not in matter.

Values are often confused with desires, which is one cause of the crisis in values today. A lack of clear definitions creates contradictions and confusion, then something unethical gets cleverly described as a value to justify actions that are contrary to values. It is important to give greater priority to universal values than temporal ones when making ethical choices. The universal reference point for values is the Divine.

Both internal and external challenges obstruct us from practising our values. Internal challenges arise from character weaknesses, while external challenges arise from the people and situations around us. It requires strength of character to perform ethically pure actions to uphold a principle, especially in the face of opposition. Truth is lived by morally strong people.

Values are integral parts of a well-adjusted holistic personality and are linked to our moral conscience. The attempt to live according to our principles brings us face to face with challenges that force us to recognise and confront our weaknesses. Any social context requires us to adjust and harmonise with one another. Any discrepancy between our thoughts, words and actions implies self-deception and a tendency to deceive others.

Harmonious relations are based on honesty, open communication, trust and generosity. Our interdependence with the natural environment also demands our respect and love for the habitat of animals and plants to ensure the future sustenance of the world's natural resources.

2.4. Need for Value Education

Values and spirituality are central to the moral philosophy of human civilisation and its legal institutions. Values and spirituality are traditionally considered to be the prerogatives of the religions and they are viewed as being embodied in the family unit. Yet for 25 centuries, the great and the lesser-known civilisations have been struggling with the issues of human frailty. Our collective inability to live up to our espoused values and moral principles, with the exception of a few outstanding individuals, has paved the way for a long, slow moral decline. Today we face a values crisis.

The aim of the Diploma of Education in Values and Spirituality is to inspire participants to re-examine their ideas and beliefs about values and spirituality. It covers a wide range of subjects where clarity about values and spirituality is important. Subjects for exploration include, for example, the emotional and psychological impact of archaic social attitudes, gender bias, economic and social stress, human rights, addiction and environmental issues. In addition, the Diploma provides definitions of values, methods of meditation, and explains how to develop critical thinking, negotiation skills and structured conversation.

Conventional education in the present economic framework has become oriented toward acquiring specialised skills and knowledge for the purpose of obtaining remunerative work. Competition has become so intense that higher education has either chosen, or been forced, to compromise on education that focuses on life, values, culture, integrity, and other skills and on dimensions of understanding that make one a better man or woman who can contribute qualitatively to a civilised world.

Value education aims to supplement conventional education, to supply important information and to teach skills without which a student's chances of experiencing success in their physical, emotional, social and spiritual life are diminished.

When young adults emerges from their educational alma mater it is important that they have the qualifications to facilitate financially rewarding employment. Many other elements, however, are essential as a preparation to meet social challenges and the stresses and expectations of life in the family, community and workplace. If an individual has not had the opportunity to develop character, inner strength and the powers of good judgement and discrimination, then he at a disadvantage in any social and professional environment. Unless individuals take the time to think about their values, to form an ethical policy for themselves, and to determine their priorities, they remain ill-equipped to deal with the tests they will face as the years go by.

Swami Vivekananda once defined education as "The manifestation of the perfection already in man." By using the expression 'perfection', he directed attention to the divinity inherent in everyone. An institution of education becomes truly educational when it turns its attention inward, towards the discovery of the self in relation to the vast, infinite creation of the Divine.

Erosion of values is of concern for India. Commissions and committees set up by the Government of India since Independence have emphasised education in values for people to inculcate truth, peace, love and co-operation. Corruption, bribery and nepotism are prevalent at all levels of society despite laws against them. Greed is at the root of this attitude, which can be prevented only by voluntary self-restraint and inspiring leadership.

Education today is primarily focused on material development and raising economic standards. Indian society is suffering from a loss of human and moral values as a consequence of this focus and the prevalent perception that education in human and moral values is unnecessary. Education in values and spirituality enriches our personality. When it is integrated into education, and provided to both genders equally, it equips people for civic life and helps boost the confidence of socially disadvantaged individuals and inspires them to claim their self-respect.

It is generally thought that only children and youth need education in values. But materialism and egocentricity in adults is setting a weak or negative example to the youth, therefore it is also necessary to teach values to adults. Voluntary self-restraint, education in moral and spiritual values and examples of moral and spiritual rectitude in the leadership are required. The public could be better informed about the dangers of all forms of addiction through education in values. They could also be taught skills to resist peer pressure.

India has always preached the message of non-violence. However, violence is an increasing problem nationwide. Although India is still a predominantly agricultural society, there is a lack of harmony with the environment. Greater awareness is needed to sensitise people to nature and caring for the natural environment.

Many traditional stories disregard the rights of women and encourage prejudiced generalisations. In spite of 150 years of efforts for female emancipation, women are still struggling for their social, political, economic, cultural and religious rights. Traditional stories usually advocate strict adherence to casteism yet it is against Indian law to discriminate on the basis of caste. The power of the oral tradition in forming social attitudes is significantly greater than the laws enacted by governments.

Educationalists and researchers in social development have found that change is successful when brought about at the micro level. Macro level attempts through legislation and development programmes have not been successful. Education in values at the individual level demonstrates the power of each one to influence society through example. People tend to act in an honourable way when presented with an example of high standards.

2.5. Values in Everyday Life

It has been well established that the crisis in values is worldwide. Its intensification is reported in newspapers, magazines and on television and radio. It varies according to cultural conditions: among the greatest challenges are violence, poverty, hypocrisy and archaic social values. In India, as in many other countries, most organisations and institutions concerned with enhancing the use of positive values take the view that it is too late to do anything with the adult population and the older generation, the solution lies in providing education in values for young people.

Integrating values into life is challenging because circumstances oppose the 100 percent application of espoused values in everyday life. One must sustain a commitment to resist temptations and weaknesses. Corruption is endemic in our society but if you resist giving and taking bribes, you develop the strength to remain beyond corruption. This needs balance, and one of the distinguishing characteristics of this is to be pliable when it is a matter of taste and firm when it is a matter of principle.

The principles underlying the Constitution of India are often in stark contrast with Indian folklore. This tension is one of the reasons why the crisis of values in India is more extreme than in other parts of the world. Some archaic values perpetrate a lack of human values because they originate in patriarchy, intellectual arrogance, false assumptions and prejudices against women, children and the weaker sections of society. An important value is social justice. Inequality is a given, but we must try to reduce this by curtailing exploitation and reducing oppression. The challenge of empowerment is that rights must be tempered by a sense of responsibility.

2.6. Necessity of Good Communication

Functionality in human society and organisations is dependent on good communication. We need to talk to each other about problems, determine how to negotiate for our rights, and learn how to define our own responsibilities and those of others. Developing communication skills is a value for society, as it takes us forward toward the goal of understanding common aims.

Good communication skills between parents and children are enhanced by the development of critical thinking. When critical thinking is developed, self-censorship is a natural by-product of a discerning mind. The more an individual is educated to cultivate self-respect, the more they will be drawn towards those images, books, films, websites, etc., which harmonise with that inner self-awareness. Also, when a person has self-esteem and strength of character, then negative values, violence, pornography and commercialism do not find a resonance and so do not bring the individual under their influence.

Critical thinking makes one independent and able to make free choices. Critical thinking enables you to examine the values you have espoused through your upbringing and social background, and develop your own ethical policy based on conscious choice.

Parents are the greatest influence on children and the bearers of values to the next generation. People look for role models and occasionally history offers up individuals of great moral power who inspire others to bring values and ethics into their lives.

The process of adopting more and more values opens the door to a beautiful world of harmonious relationships, mutual trust and love. At the same time, this effort provokes challenges from within yourself and from the outer world. This compels you to delve within to find the values, virtues, powers and qualities you need to help you meet each challenge and progress.

2.7. Principles of Integrity

The principles of integrity encourage you to make choices that generate inner harmony and avoid choices that create discordance within. Having integrity means that you are honest and have strong moral principles. It is a state of being whole and undivided. Integrity means to have internal consistency without corruption. A person of integrity is someone who applies their criteria for right action and refuses double standards and hypocrisy.

The principles of integrity include being fully aware of your criteria for ethically correct or incorrect behaviour; checking that your principles are logically consistent and coherent and that your motivations are congruent with your essential qualities of peace, love, purity, power and bliss; being reflective about your behaviour; continuing to refine your capacity for moral reasoning, and maintaining an open mind.

2.7.1. Adopting a Positive Attitude

Most of the prevailing ideas about positive and negative behaviour are polarised. On one side is the absolutist position, usually based on scriptural references and patriarchal attitudes. On the other side is the relative position often adopted by the legal system whereby decision making is related to precedent. While it is common to refer to precedent, no two situations or circumstances are the same so each moral challenge requires careful consideration and analysis. Many people find this difficult, so they look for formulaic solutions or turn to those who preach moral absolutes because they don't know how to perform moral reasoning.

In cultivating a spiritual perspective a helpful gauge is: what leads to purity, peace and happiness is good, or beneficial; and what leads towards weaknesses and character defects such as arrogance, lust, greed, violence and dependence is bad or harmful. The process of deciding whether an action or incident is positive or negative includes considering it in context and not in isolation. You need to be aware of the traps of creating double standards through bypassing the conscience and applying faulty moral logic by not distinguishing between morality and legality.

From a spiritual perspective, integrity is supported by spiritual qualities and discordance arises through emotions or feelings that are provoked by unfulfilled material desires. Where there is loss of spiritual power there is a tendency to become motivated by material desires, and when spiritual power is restored there is a tendency to be motivated by spiritual values. This is the reason why this programme develops values and spirituality simultaneously.

The philosophy of karma says that physical or mental suffering or disease is one of the consequences of negative action. The healing of physical and mental diseases needs to take place on the physical symptomatic level, the emotional and psychological levels and at the spiritual level. The state of being free from mental or physical illness is a result of positive thought and actions. All actions are initiated by thoughts.

2.7.2. Power of Meditation

Change cannot take place within until there is inner silence. Meditation is an important agent for change because it is a way to reach inner stillness. Meditation is an inner journey. Along the way one encounters two forms of pain. One is the pain one feels when one comes face to face with one's past wrong actions. These are the things that are on one's conscience. The second form of pain surrounds the violations, traumas and bad experiences of one's past, including childhood trauma and experiences of shock and grief.

One discovers that the coping mechanisms and means of psychological survival one used as a child to preserve a semblance of sanity have become character defects in one's adult life. Without getting in touch with one's original pain and finding out why one adopted dysfunctional behaviours or how one acquired irrational fears one cannot change.

A combination of professional therapy and meditation can enable a person to work through their original pain. Meditation becomes an essential element for empowering the soul with love, peace, inner power, and all the missing positive feelings. The source is the Supreme Being who is described as the unlimited ocean of purity, peace, love, mercy, light and other spiritual qualities.

This contact enables a person to strengthen his inner authority and reduce his dependency on the various external moral authorities. The most obvious of these are the religions, the state, parents, traditions, social groupings, folklore and myths. When he puts faith in an external moral authority he allows it to control his behaviour and influence his choices. This diminishes his respect for and acknowledgement of his own ability to lead and control his life.

Materialism views all moral authorities as external, and that it is the prerogative of the religions and the state to define and enforce moral standards. Religions are considered man-made responses to the uncivilised and immoral, or brutish, nature of humanity. Punishment is thought of as a suitable deterrent, and force is the method to keep people in line with socially acceptable behaviour. Studies have repeatedly shown that these methods are ineffectual but these preconceptions remain firmly in place. When laws are made by moral authorities who sometimes live and work as if they are above the law, then the law itself becomes corrupt.

Folklore deals with parenting and the different kinds of characters a person can expect to encounter in life. If the prevailing attitudes of a society are authoritarian, the folklore will reflect that. The conviction persists that it is essential to teach morality and values through threats. There are many fairy tales and mythological scriptures which fill the minds of children with dire consequences if they do not comply with the dictates of moral authorities. These exhortations to blind obedience to the authority figures do not teach young people how to take care of themselves, how to avoid being deceived, how to protect themselves from those who would harm them, including rapists, thieves, molesters, etc. The stories coerce them into being fear-based, easy to intimidate and control, and naïve about realities.

A burgeoning resistance to external moral authorities is one of the reasons why people are becoming interested in spirituality. It is being seen as a viable alternative to the religions as it places emphasis on the inner moral authority. The spiritual world view is holistic, rational and coherent. Coherence refers to wholeness and congruence means that all the elements are in harmony. Challenging mythical notions that society has held sacrosanct for generations is a complex and delicate task. Most people have great respect for concepts that are passed down through the generations and feel uncomfortable and afraid about questioning them.

Certain behaviours and practices are considered to be based in integrity and others are regarded as discordant. Integrity is internal consistency that comes from rigorous honesty and strong moral principles. It involves recognising one as a whole and undivided being. A person experiences that he will cannot be broken, so he is not fear-based. Integrity brings contentment. He is not greedy or worried about scarcity but are naturally generous. He neither gives nor accepts abuse and does not experience emotional upheavals. He has performed the inner work necessary to find his authentic self and his niche.

Lack of integrity is brought about by inner depletion and a discordant relationship with oneself. Spiritual empowerment makes it possible for a person to reclaim his integrity, exercise his freedom of choice, experience empowerment and redress his internal imbalance. Spiritual empowerment is characterised by decision-making that is based on the principles of integrity. The accumulation of spiritual power through meditation feeds his integrity and ensures that he can sustain his principles of being kind, sympathetic, magnanimous, pure and fearless. He is discriminating and a good judge of character and situations because he is sure of what to do and what not to do, and when. His spiritual power enables him to face danger, physical and emotional pain, change and loss with understanding and forbearance. Spiritual empowerment enables him to succeed in doing positive actions and maintaining his integrity.

A person who leads his life on the basis of enlightened self-interest frequently has a deep understanding of the laws of karma. These laws govern the moral life of human beings. The simplest description of these laws is that whatever he does at the level of thought, word or action creates an equal and opposite return. The repercussions of actions are short-term, medium-term and long-term.

Any action based in love, peace, bliss, purity and inner power is positive and brings positive consequences to the doer. Any thought, word or action performed on the basis of the ten weaknesses of greed, lust, anger, arrogance, attachment, jealousy, fear, slander, hatred or laziness is negative and brings negative consequences to the doer. Both positive and negative consequences occur immediately, over the course of the rest of this life and in subsequent lives. When a person lives consciously according to the laws of karma, he experiences happiness. When he defies the laws of karma, he suffer. The more he takes the laws of karma into consideration when he chooses how to think, speak or act, the more he creates a positive future for himself and others around him.

The question of good and bad is connected to the issue of personal responsibility. Accountability is the attitude of taking responsibility for and expecting to be held accountable for the consequences of your actions. A spiritually-minded person knows that he or she is accountable and cannot avoid the consequences of actions, and so places a high value on self-accountability.

Priority must be given to the development of moral reasoning and asserting the validity of the individual conscience in order to reset the balance. The challenge is to intervene in the interaction between the external moral authorities and the individual and to establish a positive relationship. The first step is to transform and strengthen the self.

2.7.3. Constitutional Freedom

Freedom of thought, conscience, expression, choice and the freedom to be authentic are some of the most important forms of freedom that support moral and spiritual values. We have a right to information, to freedom of innovation and the right to ask questions and to express our experience. People benefit from freedom to progress, grow and develop and this allows individuals to experience a sense of achievement. It encourages them to develop further. Societies which guarantee these freedoms benefit from the creativity and innovation of their thinkers in the fields of the arts, science, social development or any other.

It is necessary to distinguish between freedom that implies responsibility, integrity, rational thinking and a clear and dependable conscience from licence. Licence implies that you are free to disregard accepted social conventions, to be irresponsible, antisocial, licentious and unprincipled.

2.8. Character Development

Character development is one of the most ancient concerns of civilisation and a principal aim of the great religions, philosophical traditions and cultures. The problem affects all cultures and has been grappled with at each stage of history. Whether 5,000 years ago or 100 years ago, the same exhortations and advice have been given to people but seem to have had little impact.

Character is a measure of your ability to interact with love and regard towards all and command the love and respect of others. You have the intelligence of wisdom but do not have intellectual arrogance. You value solitude and cultivate introversion because they enable reflection on your character and behaviours. You practise dignity. Your attitude is broad-minded, inclusive, non-prejudiced and your powers of judgement and discernment are stable. Your relationship with yourself determines your morality or your inner purity and integrity. Purity is synonymous with good character. You give importance to honesty and truth. You live simply and humbly within your means. You are free from limited desires and are satisfied and contented regardless of the situation, people in opposition or physical suffering. Anyone who discerns their higher purpose and applies themselves to accomplish it can achieve deeper meaning in their life and even greatness by doing something inspirational and beneficial to many.

Character is also measured by generosity and the depth of sympathy and empathy you have for others and for nature. Character development includes braving danger, facing social censure and other difficulties in order to fulfil your ideals and convictions. A person of good character practises equilibrium in the face of praise and defamation, appreciation and rejection. People in positions of power and responsibility need to develop good character to retain public trust.

Character is developed through self-restraint and an attitude of non-violence. It includes not talking to others harshly or angrily and not being aggressive or confrontational. Character includes being able to protect yourself from getting duped, caught up and damaged by people with dishonest intentions who wish you harm.

Good character means you have no hidden agenda of lust. A man does not insult women or consider them objects of sensual gratification, despite society's compulsion to do so. Women need to refrain from using their sexuality as a weapon against men.

Character defects are antisocial behaviour patterns prompted by material desires. They include jealousy, slander, hatred, resentment, revenge and projection. Arrogance is probably the greatest obstacle to character development because it is so subtle and masquerades as the real you. It also compels a person to deny his faults or mistakes. This is because he finds it too emotionally or psychologically painful to face up to his weaknesses. Arrogance acts as a blindfold that prevents him from seeing where he is acting against his espoused values, morality or principles. The voice of conscience is disregarded and he finds ways to justify his behaviour, blame others for it, lie about it, claim it never happened, etc.

The most important element to bring about good character is an individual's direct connection with the Supreme Soul. To begin with he experiences peace which gives him the confidence that peace is his fundamental inner quality. He gradually gets used to being aware of himself as a soul and begins to absorb power. All the while the contact with the Supreme Soul is purifying him. The more he, the soul, becomes pure, the more he regains his original blissful state of being.

2.9. Educational Reforms in Colonial Period

As part of her struggle for freedom from colonial rule, India needed a fresh approach to educational planning. It was necessary, first of all, to get rid of the educational system that the colonial rulers had imposed on the country after destroying its indigenous traditions and institutions, and second, to design its own educational system for helping to build a genuinely liberated and egalitarian India.

By the middle of the nineteenth century a significant degree of awareness of their own identity had developed among the educated elite of the country. It was the dawn of the period of social reformation and growth of Indian nationalism. There were two distinct ways of looking at the issues of reconstructing the social fabric of the country at that point in time of the freedom struggle. Some of the leaders were of the opinion that to be able to rise to the level of the British rulers Indians must educate themselves in the English system. They established educational institutions which aimed at the particular goal. Although they too were interested in discovering their original roots, they probably felt that the British were able to rule India because of their superiority over us in many ways.

On another level movements grew to motivate people to go back to their Vedic culture, in other words, to discover the classical roots of Indian civilisation. They founded gurukuls and other traditional institutions of learning and teaching. According to them India had become weak because she had drifted away from her classical way of life. Neither of these approaches faced the real issues, issues that were related to the question of real liberation and self-reliance.

India had been severely impoverished and her population demoralised. The Indian masses had lost the taste for freedom almost completely. Until the end of the first half of the nineteenth century, the military might of the whole country, if it could have been put together, was considerable. But during the period after the 1857 sepoy mutiny, the morale of the people had fallen to a very low ebb. Moreover, the British rulers, having realised the tenacity of the Indian soldiers and realising that militarily they could not enslave India permanently, cunningly and systematically disarmed the nation. So much so that the simple farmer could not own an ordinary gun to protect his crops from the menace of wild and stray animals.

The colonial rulers could not have been satisfied only by destroying India's industry, agriculture, administrative and legal institutions and their national defence system. They were hoping to enslave India permanently. The British knew that only material enslavement was not sufficient. Psychological enslavement was the most important and effective mechanism to reach that goal. Thus education became the biggest prey for the Raj.

The colonisers took immediate steps to build a long-term strategy based on 'educational reforms'. They took every possible step to weaken the educational traditions which were deeply ingrained in the culture of the people and were the most powerful instruments that had retained cultural values among the masses for such a long period. We should also note the attitude of the colonisers to the literature of Asian countries. In his famous minutes Lord Macaulay wrote:

> I have no knowledge either of Sanskrit or Arabic, but I have done what I could to form a correct estimate of their value. I have read translations of the more celebrated Arabic and Sanskrit works. I have conversed both here and at home with men distinguished by their proficiency in the Eastern tongues. I am quite ready to take Oriental learning at the valuation of the orientalists themselves. I have never found one among them who could deny that a single shelf of a good European library was worth the whole native literature of India and Arabia.

The Governor General, Lord Bentinck, said:

> I give my entire concurrence to the sentiments expressed in minutes.

In spite of such a calculated onslaught on Indian culture, specially its educational traditions, a significant proportion of institutions had survived until at least 1835. Adams, who was an officer in the Education Department of Bengal, conducted an inquiry into the number of schools in that region at that time. According to his calculations there was a school for every 32 boys and these schools were provided to most of the 150,000 villages. Writing about the Indian educational system of that time, Max-Muuller said:

> There is such a thing as social education and education outside the books; and this education is distinctly higher in India than in any part of Christendom. It is an education not in the so-called three R's, but in humanity.

There are documents prepared by some British officials of that period to show that in several regions of the country literacy was very high - 100 per cent among the male population and not very much lower among females. It is the same country in which literacy had fallen to less than 10 per cent by the end of the last century.

2.9.1. National Awakening

The end of the nineteenth century saw the re-emergence of movements for national awakening, but this time of a different kind — very different from the wars of Tipu Sultan and the Sepoy Mutiny. The emergence of the Arya Samaj, the Prarthana Samaj and the Brahmo Samaj brought about much awareness among the people of their cultural heritage, which gave them a sense of self-identity.

The Indian National Congress, which had a political character, was formed in 1885. Although it started talking of Indian self-rule, Indians' participation in the administrative services, etc., the majority of its leadership was English educated and did not speak the language of the people, who did not understand what the Congress leadership was talking about. As these leaders had no contact with the masses, the Congress could not command a popular following.

During the beginning of the growth of the Indian National Congress the British took advantage of the situation and, to some extent, were able to co-opt some of its leadership to neutralise their effect, if any, on the masses. But this time they could not stop the tide of liberation. They could only slow it down by their classical technique of divide and rule.

2.10. Gandhiji's Efforts at Improving Education in India

Before going into Gandhiji's educational experiments in India we should briefly discuss his educational experiences in South Africa.

After reading *Unto This Last* he said:

> I believe that I discovered some of my deepest convictions reflected in this great book of Ruskin, that is why it so captured me and made me transform my life.

The teachings of the book as he grasped them were: (a) that the good of the individual is contained in the good of all; (b) that a lawyer's work has the same value as the barber's, inasmuch as all have the same right of earning their livelihood from their work; (c) that a life of labour, i.e., the life of the tiller of the soil and the handicraftsman, is the life worth living. This experience put him on to a new track more intensely and with greater commitment to search for a better life.

Gandhiji was also editing and publishing *Indian Opinion* from Durban, which he thought should be moved to a farm, on which everyone should labour, drawing the same living wage, and attending to press work in their spare time. After a discussion with his colleagues about his ideas, with which they all agreed, *Indian Opinion* was moved to Phoenix, 14 miles from Durban. Thus the Phoenix Settlement was started in 1904. It became a well-knit family of committed people trying to live their lives under the guidance of Gandhiji.

He was very conscious about the need for the education of the members of the Phoenix Farm, specially of children. He wrote in his autobiography:

> As the Farm grew, it was found necessary to make some provision for the education of its boys and girls. There were among these, Hindu, Musalman, Parsi and Christian boys and some Hindu girls. It was not possible, and I did not think necessary, to engage a special teacher for them. It was not possible, for qualified Indian teachers were scarce, and even when available, none would be ready to go to a place 21 miles distant from Johannesburg on a small salary.... I did not believe in the existing system of education, and I had a mind to [find] by experience and experiment the true system.

Gandhiji wrote in his autobiography:

> When I landed at Durban in January 1897, I had three children with me. My sister's son aged 10, and my own sons aged 9 and 6. Where was I to educate them? I could have sent them to the school for European children, but only as a matter of favour and exception. For no other Indian children would be allowed. For these there were schools established by Christian missions, but I was not prepared to send my children there, as I did not like the education imparted in those schools. For one thing, the medium of instruction there would be only English, or perhaps incorrect Tamil or Hindi, which too could be arranged not without difficulty. I could not possibly put up with this and other disadvantages. I was making my own attempt to teach them but that was at best irregular and I could not get hold of a suitable Gujarati teacher.... I was at my wits' end....

Gandhiji's struggle continued. On the one hand he totally rejected the existing system of education, but on the other he did not have a clear alternative to replace it. He had no idea of how to go about the task of educating the children of his extended family. However, he was deeply convinced that only that education is desirable which develops a healthy self-image and inculcates certain values in the individual.

After getting the journal well settled he wanted to start a school for Indian children. On 13 January 1905 he wrote a letter to Professor Gokhale asking for his support.

The school eventually had 50 children. He was determined to find out by experience and experiment the true system. He took some time to discover it, specially the kind that could be offered for wider application in a country so large as India, for he knew that his home was India and not South Africa.

Gandhiji eventually realised that it was time for him to return to his home country. He reached Bombay with Kasturba on 9 January 1915. Wise man that he was, Gandhiji decided not to straight away plunge into the politics of the country or even pass any judgment on the situation here. He gave a year to going around the country to see and acquaint himself with the life of the people and their feelings. He wanted to have first-hand knowledge of the rural as well as urban conditions in which the common man and woman lived. This was also the advice given to him by Gopal Krishna Gokhale, who was like a political guru to him. The question of discovering the right kind of educational system, however, remained his primary concern.

Within two or three years Gandhiji had to undertake three major satyagraha campaigns — the Ahmedabad Satyagraha related to the textile mill-hands' strike, the Kheda Satyagraha about the payment of land revenue by farmers, and the Champaran Satyagraha against the exploitation of the indigo farmers by the British plantation owners.

In *Satyagraha in Champaran* Rajendra Prasad wrote:

> He [Gandhiji] was convinced from the very beginning that it was impossible for any outside agency to improve their lot unless their mental and moral condition was improved. This applies to the whole of India but it can be demonstrated beyond contradiction in Champaran.... Mahatmaji had accordingly decided that arrangement for spread of education was as necessary among them as the redress of their grievances. Some time before the Enquiry Committee commenced its work Mahatmaji had written to some friends about it and told them what sorts of volunteers he needed for social work.

He did get some of the most educated people from various parts of India to run the schools which he had managed to start. Unfortunately very few educated people from Bihar joined him. Describing the plan he wrote to a Government official:

> In the schools I am opening, children under the age of 12 only are admitted. The idea is to get hold of as many children as possible and to give them an all round education, i.e. a good knowledge of Hindi or Urdu, [and] through that medium, of arithmetic and the rudiments of history and geography, a knowledge of simple scientific principles and some industrial training. No cut and dried syllabus has yet been prepared because I am going on an unbeaten track. I look upon our present system with horror and distrust. Instead of developing the moral and mental faculties of the little children it dwarfs them....

Five schools started functioning in the area. Some of his closest companions were with him to carry out the plans, about which he wrote:

> I shall endeavour to avoid the defects of the present system. The chief thing aimed at is contact of children with men and women of culture and unimpeachable moral character. That to me is education. Literary training is to be useful merely as a means to that end....

Those schools functioned for a while but were then closed for lack of workers and the vision required for such a pioneering work.

In addition to his preoccupation with national politics there was one subject which occupied his mind all the time. It was education for the masses of India. He knew what 'education' meant in pre-British India. At a conference in Allahabad on 23 December 1916 he gave a talk which was reported in *The Leader* (27.12.1916). The following is an excenpt from that report:

> Mr Gandhi then described the ancient system of education... even elementary education imparted by the village teacher taught the students all that was necessary for their occupation. Those who went in for higher education became fully conversant with the science of wealth, *Artha Shastra*, ethics and religion, *Dharma Shastra*. In ancient times, there were no restrictions on education.... It was due to such a system of education that Indian civilisation had outlived so many vicissitudes through thousands of years.... No doubt the wave of a new civilisation had been passing through India. But he was sure that it was transitory, it would soon pass away and Indian civilisation would be revivified.

Gandhiji was steadily getting closer to his ideal educational system. But he had yet to try many more experiments before he discovered the true system.

2.11. National Education

After the Sabarmati Ashram was well settled, Gandhiji began planning for a national school.

The medium of instruction was to be Gujarati (the mother tongue and local language) right up to the highest stage. The syllabus included the usual subjects such as mathematics, book-keeping, history, geography, chemistry and astronomy. By way of instruction in religion, general ethical principles were to be taught. The aim of that education was that after a few years the student's equipment would approximate to that of a well-informed graduate.

It is obvious that although he was more or less clear about the objectives of his ideal education, he had not yet reached the stage when he could put forward a concrete plan of his system which, by definition, had to be entirely different from the existing one with the structure the British had created.

He was firm about education being imparted through the mother tongue at all its stages. In a speech at the Second Gujarat Educational Conference in October, 1917, he said:

> It should be obvious to everyone that the first thing to do in this connection is to come to a definite decision about the medium of instruction. Unless that is done, all other efforts, I fear, are likely to prove fruitless.

He put equally great stress on the desirability of having a common language for the whole country. He enumerated five requirements of a national language. It should be: (a) easy to learn for government officials; (b) capable of serving as a medium of religious, economic and political contact between all parts of the country; (c) the speech of a large number of Indians; (d) easy for everyone to learn; and (e) chosen without consideration of temporary or passing circumstances. It was evident that English did not fulfil any of these requirements. Gandhiji considered Hindi, eventually Hindustani, to be the language that fulfilled all the requirements.

Gandhiji emphasised the building of character as the major task of education. The third item on which he put emphasis was music and the fourth was physical training. He strongly pleaded for the education of women.

2.11.1. National Universities — Vidyapeeths

After the First World War India waited for a change of heart on the part of the British. Instead she received the Rowlatt Act. The people as a whole resented it. In April 1919 more than a thousand innocent unarmed people were massacred in Jallianwalla Bagh, Amritsar, by the army. This outrage wounded India's pride and she rose in revolt against foreign domination.

The Congress and Gandhiji declared total non-cooperation with the British Government. The call included a total boycott of legislative bodies, Government schools and law courts.

The Gujarat Political Conference held on 27-29 August passed a resolution which meant that title-holders and persons holding medals should renounce the titles and return the medals; lawyers should try to settle disputes privately and should give up practice in law courts; parents should withdraw their children from any school that had any connection with the Government; college students should give up colleges on their own; voters should refuse to vote for any one seeking election to a council and candidates should withdraw their candidature; and every man, woman and child should follow the rule of perfect swadeshi and should spin cotton.

Although it was a solely political campaign, it had a profound impact on the educational scene in the country. With the call for boycotting schools and colleges having any connection with the government, it was necessary to have some alternative institutions. That was the beginning of the establishment of vidyapeeths — national schools and colleges all over the country. In November Gandhiji founded the National University of Gujarat, Gujarat Vidyapeeth. Such national institutions also came up in Calcutta, Patna, Aligarh, Bombay, Banaras and Delhi. The Jamia Millia Islamia — the National Muslim University — was founded through the joint efforts of Gandhiji and Md. Ali.

These institutions made a significant contribution in the fields of both political awakening and educational awareness. Establishing these centres of learning was a step towards the growth of a new approach to education. They created the spirit of freedom, an element essential for the development of a healthy personality. Second, they prepared a cadre of freedom-fighters for the next 'battle for liberation'.

More important, as experimental centres they were useful for Gandhiji to explore the structural side of his educational scheme, basic education, which was started in 1937. By that time institutions like Gujarat Vidyapeeth and Jamia Millia Islamia had fully developed their systemic structures in a way that was favourable for giving a trial to the new scheme.

Between 1920 and 1937 a lot happened in the country. People's awareness of their cultural foundation, their knowledge of the damage done to it by the colonial rulers, and an understanding of the socio-political conditions of the country made it imperative that for building a healthy India mass education in general and education of the individual along with the struggle for freedom were the most important elements. Gandhiji also believed that without gaining freedom, building a new and independent educational programme was not possible.

Most of the revivalist institutions, barring some exceptions, such as Santiniketan and vidyapeeths, had lost their original relevance or had become dependent on government recognition. Some continued catering for the needs of the elite, who looked for government patronage. Santiniketan was deliberately kept apolitical by Tagore, except that some individuals occasionally took active part in the freedom struggle.

2.11.2. Tagore's and Gandhi's Approaches to Education

According to Tagore's scheme there are three centres of education: the mother tongue, not only as the medium of instruction but also as the major means of communication between people; creative activities; and Nature, of which we are an inseparable part.

Gandhiji's scheme as presented to the nation in 1937 also had three similar elements. He was convinced that the medium of instruction in schools and colleges must be the mother tongue or the language of the area. He also insisted that the language of communication between people of various regions ought to be that which most people understood or could easily learn. In other words, it should be an effective tool for community relationships. For most of its needs, physical as well as spiritual, human society depended on Nature. *Nayee talim*, as envisaged by Gandhiji, gave top priority to our relationship with Nature. According to Tagore Nature was the most important source of knowledge, human creativity and livelihood. The highest education is that which does not merely impart information but puts life in harmony with all existence.

The third element is meaningful manual work according to Gandhiji, and creative activities according to Tagore. There is very little difference in the two approaches. Tagore did not talk of the economic side of creative activities. For him it was art, something that caters for all human needs, physical, emotional and spiritual. Gandhiji, on the other hand, placed emphasis on it as a vocation for livelihood and a way of gaining knowledge.

While Gandhiji's approach was obviously egalitarian, Tagore's was elitist. Taking into account the time factor, Gandhiji had the advantage of drawing from Gurudev's educational experience. He not only learned something but he also improved on it.

2.12. Commencement of Basic Education

The fruit which Gandhiji had nurtured for two decades was now nearly ripe. The political situation in India had changed. After the elections for Legislative Assemblies the British Government had to accept the formation of Congress ministries in nine provinces. In addition to whatsoever these Congress Governments were hoping to do, Gandhiji offered them an educational plan to replace the current system of education.

Until then the expenditure on education came from excise (alcohol) revenue. He suggested that the money required for education could be raised by taxing the rich.

In October 1937 Gandhiji called a conference which was attended by many eminent education experts of the country and the Education Ministers of several provinces. He presented his scheme to them. The conference passed a resolution which agreed that free and compulsory education should be provided to every child of seven to 14 years of age; the medium of instruction should be the mother tongue; the process of education throughout this period should centre around some form of manual productive work, and all the other abilities to be developed should be integrally related to the central handicraft chosen, with due regard to the environment of the child; and this system of education would gradually be able to cover the remuneration of the teachers.

A little later the Hindustani Talimi Sangh, an all-India organisation, was formed to develop the Basic Education programme all over the country and to run experimental schools. The first such school was set up in Sevagram, Gandhiji's ashram, which also became the central office of the Sangh with Shri E.W. Aryanayakam as General Secretary. Gandhiji chose Dr. Zakir Hussain, the head of Jamia Millia Islamia, as the Chairman of the Sangh.

A wave of educational reconstruction seemed to pass over the country. Some provinces appointed education reorganisation committees, teacher training and refresher training centres. Some basic schools were opened and some primary schools were converted into basic schools. *New literature on Basic Education* was published for the use of teachers. A seven-year syllabus was prepared by some of the most experienced teachers of their subjects.

In his report of two years of work Aryanayakam wrote that:

> basic education was being carried out as an educational experiment by the Governments of C.P., U.P., Bihar, Orissa, Bombay, and Kashmir and a few non-Government institutions. In all there were twelve training schools and two training colleges, seven Refreshers Training Centres and over five thousand schools carrying out the experiment of basic education.

There was so much enthusiasm that even when the Orissa Government closed its basic schools in the second year of the experiment, the people of the province continued the work on their own. Out of the 15 basic schools, seven continued functioning, which indicates that the system had attracted the interest of the people.

After about two years the Congress Ministries resigned, resulting in the closure of basic schools run by the governments in all the seven provinces. But the ones run by voluntary bodies continued until the launch of the Quit India struggle in 1942, the consequence of which was the arrest of most of the active workers, including those engaged in Gandhiji's constructive programmes. He was the first to be arrested.

The resolution passed by the Second Basic Education Conference held on the campus of Jamia Millia Islamia gives an idea of the results attained by the basic schools during the short period of a little over two years.

This conference records with satisfaction that the reports on the working of basic schools run by the Governments, local bodies and by private enterprise are almost unanimous that general standards of health or behaviour as well as intellectual attainment, are very encouraging. The children in basic schools are more active, cheerful, self-reliant, their power of self-expression is well-developed, they are developing habits of cooperative work, and social prejudices are breaking down. Considering the difficulties inherent in the initial stages of a new scheme of education, involving a new ideology and a new technique, the progress reported holds out the promise that even better results can be expected in future.

2.13. Establishment of *Nayee Talim*

The Quit India movement of 1942 proved a very intense experience for the country, specially in regard to looking back and reviewing the achievements and difficulties faced by the freedom struggle led by Gandhiji.

Gandhiji was in prison for nearly two years. That was probably the hardest period in his life. His two closest life companions died in the same prison — his wife Kasturba and Mahadev Desai, his right hand. When he came out of prison, two of his major concerns were (a) to see the British rule over India end at the earliest, and (b) to plan an educational programme for the people of India which would prepare them for using that freedom to lift themselves up from the conditions they had been pushed into during colonial rule, such as stark poverty, pessimism, ignorance and helplessness.

For the last quarter of a century Gandhiji had led the non-violent war of freedom on political as well as socio-economic grounds. He went on encouraging the people to build alternatives for nearly all aspects of life. The eighteen-point Constructive Programme was for replacing the existing systems and institutions. For instance, development of indigenous industries - textiles, housing, food, basic education, health and sanitation, social equality and cooperative living.

His internment in the Aga Khan Palace, as has been said before, was a time of introspection for Gandhiji. After coming out of prison he said: "I have been thinking hard during the detention over the possibilities of *Nayee Talim* until my mind became restive". He also said:

> We must not rest content with our present achievements. We must penetrate the homes of the children. We must educate their parents. Basic education must become literally education for life.... It had become clear to me that the scope of basic education has to be extended.... A basic school teacher must consider himself a universal teacher. His village is his universe....

A *nayee talim* conference was called in the month of January 1945. In his inaugural speech Gandhiji introduced an entirely revised and enlarged map of the system. Addressing the basic education workers he said:

> Although we have been working for *Nayee Talim* all these years, we have so far been, as it were, sailing in an inland sea which is comparatively safe. We are now leaving the shoals and heading for the open sea. So far our course was mapped out. We have now before us uncharted waters with the Pole Star as our only guide and protection. That Pole Star is village handicrafts.

Our sphere of work now is not confined to *Nayee Talim* of children from seven and fourteen years; it is to cover the whole of life from the moment of conception to the moment of death. This means that our work has increased tremendously. Yet workers remain the same. But that should not worry us. Our guide and companion is Truth which is God. He will never betray us. But Truth will be our help only if we stand by it regardless of everything. There can be in it no room for hypocrisy, camouflage, pride, attachment or anger.

We have to become teachers of villagers; that is to say, we have to become their servants in the true sense. Our reward, if any, has to come from within and not from without. It should make no difference to us whether in our quest for Truth we have any human company or not. Nor does *Nayee Talim* depend on outside financial help. It must proceed on its own way, whatever critics might say. True education must be self-supporting. There is nothing to feel ashamed of in this. It may be a novel idea if we can make good our claim and demonstrate that ours is the only method for the true development of the mind. Those who scoff at *Nayee Talim* today will become our ardent admirers in the end and *Nayee Talim* will find universal acceptance.

Whether this is a mere dream or a practical reality, this is the goal of *Nayee Talim* and nothing short of it. May the God of Truth help us to realise it.

> I want to draw your attention also to another thing. I consider the Sevagram centre to be an ideal centre for conducting the central experiment in *Nayee Talim*, as it is here that the Charkha Sangh (All Indian Spinners' Association) is carrying out its main experiment. Wardha is the centre for the other village industries.... Sevagram does not stand alone; there are nearly 20 villages lying about it in close proximity. Therefore if experiments in *Nayee Talim* in its most natural form can be carried out anywhere, it is here.

The plan he put forward was for the education of everybody in the community. It was divided as follows: (i) Adult education — of the whole community, including the parents of unborn babies; (ii) pre-basic — education of children between two and a half to seven years; (iii) basic education — for children between seven and fourteen years; (iv) post-basic education — 14 to 18 years; (v) university level education — beyond 18 years of age.

The most significant statement from Gandhiji at that time was that after the launching of the new perspective of *nayee talim* every constructive programme must have its orientation. To put it the other way round, it would mean that all those activities should be considered a part of *nayee talim*. In other words, all the work that was being done for the attainment of freedom for the country and for the reconstruction of the Indian polity should be educationally oriented.

References

Kirschenbaum, M. 1977. *Values Clarification: An advanced handbook for trainers and teachers*, La Jolla California University Associates Press.

Metcal, L.E. 1971. *Value Education: Rationale, Strategies and Procedures*, Washington, D-C, National Council for Social Studies.

Paterson, K.W.K. 1979. *Values, Education and the Adult Knowledge*, London.

Swami Ranganathanand. 1971. *Eternal Values for a Changing Society*, Bharatiya Vidya Bhavan Publications, Bombay.

Simon, S.B., Leland W. Howe and Howard. 1972. *Value Clarification: A handbook of practical strategies of teachers and students*, New York, Hart Publishing.

Wilson, J. 1972. *Practical Methods of Moral Education*, Heinemann Education Book Ltd., London.

Westermark. E. *The Origin and Development of Moral Ideas* Vol. II, Education Policies Commission, U.S.A.

3

Education for Excellence

Given the present and foreseeable advances in science and technology, and the growing importance of knowledge and other intangibles in the production of goods and services, we need to rethink the place of work and its changing status in tomorrow's society. To create tomorrow's society, imagination will have to keep ahead of technological progress in order to avoid further increases in unemployment and social exclusion or inequalities in development.

For all these reasons, it seems to us that the concept of an education pursued throughout life, with all its advantages in terms of flexibility, diversity and availability at different times and in different places, should command wide support. There is a need to rethink and broaden the notion of lifelong education. Not only must it adapt to changes in the nature of work, but it must also constitute a continuous process of forming whole human beings – their knowledge and aptitudes, as well as the critical faculty and the ability to act. It should enable people to develop awareness of themselves and their environment and encourage them to play their social role at work and in the community.

The truth is that every aspect of life, at both the individual and the social level, offers opportunities for both learning and doing. It is thus very tempting to focus too much on this side of the question, stressing the educational potential of the modern media, the world of work or cultural and leisure pursuits, even to the extent of overlooking a number of fundamental truths: although people need to take every opportunity for learning and self-improvement, they will not be able to make good use of all these potential resources unless they have received a sound basic education. Better still, a school should impart both the desire for, and pleasure in, learning, the ability to learn how to learn, and intellectual curiosity. One might even imagine a society in which each individual would be in turn both teacher and learner. For this to come about, nothing can replace the formal education system, where each individual is introduced to the many forms of knowledge. There is no substitute for the teacher–pupil relationship, which is underpinned by authority and developed through dialogue. This has been argued time and time again by the great classical thinkers who have studied the question of education. It is the responsibility of the teacher to impart to the pupil the knowledge that humankind has acquired about itself and about nature and everything of importance that it has created and invented.

The concept of learning throughout life thus emerges as one of the keys to the twenty-first century. It goes beyond the traditional distinction between initial and continuing education. It meets the challenges posed by a rapidly changing world. This is not a new insight, since previous reports on education have emphasized the need for people to return to education in order to deal with new situations arising in their personal and working lives. That need is still felt and is even becoming stronger. The only way of satisfying it is for each individual to learn how to learn. But there is a further requirement: the far-reaching changes in the traditional patterns of life require of us a better understanding of other people and the world at large; they demand mutual understanding, peaceful interchange and, indeed, harmony – the very things that are most lacking in our world today.

3.1. Principles of Education

Hence, there is greater emphasis on one of the four pillars of the foundations of education: *learning to live together*, by developing an understanding of others and their history, traditions and spiritual values and, on this basis, creating a new spirit which, guided by recognition of our growing interdependence and a common analysis of the risks and challenges of the future, would induce people to implement common projects or to manage the inevitable conflicts in an intelligent and peaceful way.

A part from this kind of education that would create and underlay this new spirit, one also needs to consider the other three pillars of education which provide, as it were, the bases for learning to live together.

The first of these is learning to know. Given the rapid changes brought about by scientific progress and the new forms of economic and social activity, the emphasis has to be on combining a sufficiently broad general education with the possibility of indepth work on a selected number of subjects. Such a general background provides, so to speak, the passport to lifelong education, in so far as it gives people a taste – but also lays the foundations – for learning throughout life.

Learning to do is another pillar. In addition to learning to do a job of work, it should, more generally, entail the acquisition of a competence that enables people to deal with a variety of situations, often unforeseeable, and to work in teams, a feature to which educational methods do not at present pay enough attention. In many cases, such competence and skills are more readily acquired if pupils and students have the opportunity to try out and develop their abilities by becoming involved in work experience schemes or social work while they are still in education, whence the increased importance that should be attached to all methods of alternating study with work.

Last, but not least, is the fourth pillar: *learning to be.* This was the dominant theme of the Edgar Faure report *Learning to Be: The World of Education Today and Tomorrow,* published by UNESCO in 1972. Its recommendations are still very relevant, for in the twenty-first century everyone will need to exercise greater independence and judgement combined with a stronger sense of personal responsibility for the attainment of common goals. The report stresses on a further imperative: none of the talents which are hidden like buried treasure in every person must be left untapped. These are, to name but a few: memory, reasoning power, imagination, physical ability, aesthetic sense, the aptitude to communicate with others and the natural charisma of the group leader, which again goes to prove the need for greater self-knowledge.

Another aspect to be studied is a learning society founded on the acquisition, renewal and use of knowledge. These are three aspects that ought to be emphasized in the educational process. As the development of the 'information society' is increasing the opportunities for access to data and facts, education should enable everyone to gather information and to select, arrange, manage and use it.

While education should, therefore, constantly adapt to changes in society, it must not fail to pass on the attainments, foundations and benefits of human experience.

3.2. Rudiments of Basic Education

By focusing on the concept of learning throughout life, it is not intended to convey the idea that by such a qualitative leap one could avoid reflecting on the different levels of education. On the contrary, some of the major principles advanced by UNESCO are issues, such as the vital need for basic education, to urge a review of the role of secondary education and to examine the issues raised by developments in higher education, particularly the phenomenon of mass higher education, which need attention.

Quite simply, learning throughout life makes it possible to organise the various stages of education to provide for passage from one stage to another and to diversify the paths through the system, while enhancing the value of each. This could be a way of avoiding the invidious choice between selection by ability, which increases the number of academic failures and the risks of exclusion, and the same education for all, which can inhibit talent.

The foregoing in no way detracts from the excellent definition of basic learning needs produced in 1990 at the World Conference on Education for All:

> These needs comprise both essential learning tools (such as literacy, oral expression, numeracy, and problem solving) and the basic learning content (such as knowledge, skills, values, and attitudes) required by human beings to be able to survive, to develop their full capacities, to live and work in dignity, to participate fully in development, to improve the quality of their lives, to make informed decisions, and to continue learning.

This is certainly an impressive catalogue, but it does not necessarily imply an overloading of curricula. The teacher–pupil relationship, the learning available in children's local environment, and an effective use of modern media (where they exist) can in conjunction contribute to the personal and intellectual development of each pupil. The 'three Rs' — reading, writing and arithmetic – are given their full due. The combination of conventional teaching and out-of-school approaches should enable children to experience the three dimensions of education —the ethical and cultural, the scientific and technological, and the economic and social.

To put it another way, education is also a social experience through which children learn about themselves, develop interpersonal skills and acquire basic knowledge and skills. This experience should begin in early childhood, in different forms depending on the situation, but always with the involvement of families and local communities.

Two observations considered important should be added at this stage.

Basic education should be extended, worldwide, to the 900 million illiterate adults, the 130 million children not enrolled in school, and the more than 100 million children who drop out prematurely from school. This vast undertaking is a priority for the technical assistance and partnership projects carried out as part of international co-operation.

Basic education is of course an issue in all countries, including the industrialised ones. From this initial stage onwards, educational contents should be designed to stimulate a love of learning and knowledge and thus develop the desire and provide the opportunities for learning throughout life.

This brings us to one of the major problem areas in any reform, that of the policies to be applied to the period of adolescence and youth, between primary education and work or higher education. To coin a phrase, *secondary schools* cut rather a sorry figure in educational thinking. They are the target of considerable criticism and they provoke a considerable amount of frustration.

3.3. Problems in Education

Among the sources of frustration are the increased and increasingly diversified requirements, leading to rapid growth in enrolments and overcrowded curricula – whence the familiar problems associated with mass education, which the less-developed countries cannot easily solve at either the financial or the organisational level. There is also the distress felt by school-leavers who face a shortage of opportunities, a distress increased by an all-or-nothing obsession with getting into higher education. Mass unemployment in many countries only adds to the malaise. There is an alarming trend that is leading, in both rural and urban areas, in both developing and industrialised countries, not only to unemployment but also to the under-utilisation of human resources.

The only way out of this difficult situation is a very broad diversification of the types of study available. One of the major concerns, of the education department is to make the most of all forms of talent so as to reduce academic failure and prevent the far-too-widespread feeling among young people that they are excluded, left with no prospects.

These various types should include both conventional education, which focuses more on abstraction and conceptualisation, and approaches that alternate school with work experience in a way that brings out additional abilities and inclinations. In any event, there should be bridges between these approaches so that errors – all too frequent – in the choice of direction can be corrected.

The prospect of being able to go back to education or training would alter the general climate by assuring young people that their fate is not sealed forever between the ages of 14 and 20. Higher education should be seen from this same angle.

A point to remember is that, side by side with universities, there are other types of higher education institutions in many countries. Some cream off the most able students while others are set up to provide specifically targeted, high-quality vocational training, lasting between two and four years. Such diversification undeniably meets the needs of society and the economy as manifested both at the national and at the regional levels.

Increasingly stringent selection in order to ease the pressures brought about by mass higher education in the wealthiest countries is neither politically nor socially acceptable. One of the main drawbacks of such an approach is that many young people are shut out from the educational process before they are able to obtain a recognised diploma; they are therefore in the desperate predicament of having obtained neither a formal qualification nor a training appropriate for the job market.

The evolution of enrolments therefore needs to be managed, but it can be kept within limits as a result of secondary education reform.

Universities would contribute to this process by diversifying what they offer:

a) as scientific establishments and centres of learning, from where students go on to theoretical or applied research or teaching;

b) as establishments offering occupational qualifications, combining high-level knowledge and skills, with courses and content continually tailored to the needs of the economy;

c) as some of the main meeting-places for learning throughout life, opening their doors to adults who wish either to resume their studies or to adapt and develop their knowledge or to satisfy their taste for learning in all areas of cultural life; and

d) as leading partners in international co-operation, facilitating exchanges of teachers and students and ensuring that the best teaching is made widely available through international professorships.

In this way, universities would transcend what is wrongly held to be the conflict between the logic of public service and the logic of the job market. They would also reclaim their intellectual and social vocation as, in a sense, guarantors of universal values and the cultural heritage. These can be seen as cogent reasons for urging greater university autonomy.

These issues take on a special significance in poor countries, where universities have a decisive role to play. In developing countries, universities must learn from their own past and analyse their countries' difficulties, engaging in research aimed at finding solutions to the most acute among them. It is also incumbent on them to propose a renewed vision of development that will enable their countries to build a genuinely better future. They must provide the vocational and technological training of the future leaders and the higher- and middle-level education required if their countries are to escape from their present treadmills of poverty and underdevelopment.

3.4. Involving Local Communities in Education

While neither underestimating the need to manage short-term constraints nor disregarding the need to adapt existing systems, it is important to emphasize the necessity of a more long-term approach if the reforms required are to succeed. By the same token, it must be stressed fact that too many reforms one after another can be the death of reform, since they do not allow the system the time needed either to absorb change or to get all the parties concerned involved in the process. Furthermore, past failures show that many reformers adopt an approach that is either too radical or too theoretical, ignoring what can be usefully learned from experience or rejecting past achievements. As a result, teachers, parents and pupils are disoriented and less than willing to accept and implement reform.

The main parties contributing to the success of educational reforms are, first of all, the local community, including parents, school heads and teachers; secondly, the public authorities; and thirdly, the international community. Many past failures have been due to insufficient involvement of one or more of these partners. Attempts to impose educational reforms from the top down, or from outside, have obviously failed. The countries where the process has been relatively successful are those that obtained a determined commitment from local communities, parents and teachers, backed up by continuing dialogue and various forms of outside financial, technical or professional assistance. It is obvious that the local community plays a paramount role in any successful reform strategy.

Local community participation in assessing needs by means of a dialogue with the public authorities and groups concerned in society is a first, essential stage in broadening access to education and improving its quality. Continuing the dialogue by way of the media, community discussions, parent education and on-the-job teacher training usually helps to create awareness, sharpen judgement and develop local capacities. When communities assume greater responsibility for their own development, they learn to appreciate the role of education both as a way of achieving societal objectives and as a desirable improvement of the quality of life.

In this respect, the stress is on the value of a cautious measure of decentralisation in helping to increase educational establishments' responsibilities and their scope for innovation. In any event, no reform can succeed without the cooperation and active participation of teachers. This is one reason why it is recommends that the social, cultural and material status of educators should be considered as a matter of priority.

The demands made on teachers are considerable, at the very time when the outside world is increasingly encroaching upon the school, particularly through the new communication and information media. Thus, the young people with whom the teacher has to deal, though receiving less parental or religious guidance, are also better informed. Teachers have to take this new situation into account if they are to be heeded and understood by young people, give them a taste for learning, and show them that information and knowledge are two different things and that knowledge requires effort, concentration, discipline and determination.

3.5. Improving Educational Standards

It is appropriate in this context to add some recommendations concerning the content of teacher training, access by teachers to continuing education, the improvement of the status of teachers responsible for basic education, and greater involvement of teachers in disadvantaged and marginalised groups, where they can help to improve the integration of children and adolescents in society.

This is also a plea for the education system to be provided not only with well-trained teachers but also with the wherewithal for delivering education of a high standard, including books, modern communication media, a suitable cultural and economic environment and so forth.

Conscious of the situation in schools today, there is great emphasis on the quantity and quality of traditional teaching materials such as books, and on new media such as information technologies, which should be used with discernment and with active pupil participation. For their part, teachers should work in teams, particularly in secondary schools, thereby helping to achieve the necessary flexibility in the courses of study on offer, thus obviating many failures, bringing out some of the pupils' natural talents, and providing better academic and career guidance with a view to learning continued throughout life.

The improvement of education, seen in this light, requires policy-makers to face up squarely to their responsibilities. They cannot leave it to market forces or to some kind of self-regulation to put things right when they go wrong.

It is on the strength of its belief in the importance of policy-makers that there is stress on the permanence of values, the challenges of future demands, and the duties of teachers and society; they alone, taking all the factors into consideration, can generate the public-interests debates that education – since it concerns everyone, since it is our future that is at stake and since education can help to improve the lot of one and all – so badly needs.

This naturally leads us to focus on the role of the public authorities. They must propose clear options and, after broad consultation with all those involved, choose policies that, regardless of whether the education system is public, private or mixed, show the way, establish the system's foundations and its main thrusts, and regulate the system through the necessary adjustments.

Naturally, all public policy decisions have financial repercussions. The Commission does not underestimate this difficulty. Without entering into the complexities of various systems, it should be understood that education is a public good that should be available to all. Once this principle is accepted, public and private funding may be combined, according to different formulae that take into account each country's traditions, stages of development, ways of life and income distribution.

All the choices to be made should, in any event, be predicated upon the fundamental principle of equality of opportunity.

As learning throughout life gradually becomes a reality, all young persons could be allocated a study-time entitlement at the start of their education, entitling them to a certain number of years of education. Their entitlement would be credited to an account at an institution that would manage a 'capital' of time available for each individual, together with the appropriate funds. Everyone could use their capital, on the basis of their previous educational experience, as they saw fit. Some of the capital could be set aside to enable people to receive continuing education during their adult lives. Each person could increase his or her capital through deposits at the 'bank' under a kind of educational savings scheme. As things stand today, a study-time entitlement could be granted at the end of compulsory schooling, so as to enable adolescents to choose a path without signing away their future.

In general, however, it would be to secondary education that we would turn our attention, given that the fate of millions of boys and girls is decided between the time they leave primary school and the time they either start work or go on to higher education. This is where the crunch comes in our education systems, either because those systems are too élitist or because they fail to come to terms with massive enrolments because of inertia and total inability to adapt.

At a time when these young people are struggling with the problems of adolescence, when they feel, in a sense, mature but are in fact still immature, when instead of being carefree they are worried about their future, the important thing is to provide them with places where they can learn and discover, to give them the wherewithal to think about their future and prepare for it, and to offer them a choice of pathways suited to their abilities. It is also important to ensure that the avenues ahead of them are not blocked and that remedial action and in-course correction of their educational careers are at all times possible.

3.6. International Cooperation in Education

There is growing tendency in the political and economic spheres, to resort to international action as a way of finding satisfactory solutions to problems that have a global dimension, if only because of the growing interdependence that has so often been emphasised. It also regretted the inadequacy of results and stressed the need for reform of international institutions to make their action more effective.

The same applies, *mutatis mutandis*, to the social and educational fields. Emphasis has been deliberately placed on the importance of the World Summit for Social Development, held in Copenhagen in March 1995. Education occupies a prominent place in the guidelines adopted there with the following recommendations:

a) a policy of strong encouragement for the education of girls and women, following directly on from the recommendations of the Fourth World Conference on Women;
b) the allocation of a minimum percentage of development aid to fund education: this slanting in the direction of education should also apply to international funding institutions, first and foremost the World Bank, which already plays an important role;
c) the development of 'debt-for-education swaps' to offset the adverse effects of adjustment policies and policies for reducing internal and external deficits upon public spending on education;
d) the widespread introduction of the new 'information society' technologies in all countries, to prevent yet another gap opening up between rich countries and poor countries; and
e) tapping into the outstanding potential offered by non-governmental organisations, and hence by grassroots initiatives, which could provide a valuable backup to international cooperation.

These few suggestions should be seen in the context of partnership rather than aid. After so many failures and so much waste, experience militates in favour of partnership, globalisation makes it inescapable.

Another justification for partnership is that it can lead to a 'win-win situation': whilst industrialised countries can assist developing countries by the input of their successful experiences, their technologies and financial and material resources, they can learn from the developing countries ways of passing on their cultural heritage, approaches to the socialisation of children and, more fundamentally, different cultures and ways of life.

UNESCO has a central role to play in developing the new information technologies in such a way that they serve the interests of quality education.

More fundamentally, however, UNESCO will serve peace and mutual understanding by emphasizing the value of education as a manifestation of the spirit of concord, stemming from the will to live together, as active members of our global village, thinking and organising for the good of future generations. It is in this way that UNESCO will contribute to a culture of peace.

3.7. Policies for Achieving Excellence in Education

At the present juncture in history, major innovations in science and technology, changes in economics and politics, and transformations in demographic and social structures are taking place throughout the world. These upheavals, which are likely to accelerate in the future, will place considerable strain on the educational community, in particular, to respond to growing needs and to meet the emerging challenges of a rapidly changing world. The exigencies of our time demand the dynamic interplay of creativity, courage and determination to make effective changes and the will to rise to the challenges before us.In response to this situation, educational reform plans on both the national and international levels need to transcend adequate planning and financial resource allocation. Educational reform policies should aim at achieving educational excellence.

In the past two decades in particular, governments and international agencies in the developing world sought to respond to developmental challenges by focusing increasingly on expanding educational opportunities. This drive by developing countries was in fulfilment of UNESCO's mission to achieve 'Education for All'. But the expansion in education was concentrated on coping with the growing demand for schooling, while the quality of education itself was not given priority. The result was overcrowded schools, outdated teaching methods based on learning by rote and teachers who have become unable to adapt to more modern approaches such as democratic participation in the classroom, cooperative learning and creative problem-solving. These are now obstacles to better education.

Significantly, the vast and rapid expansion of the education system, and its over burdening in many countries, have resulted in the inability to attend adequately to the question of educational equity, which calls for providing learning experiences appropriate to the learning needs of students with varying abilities. In the overwhelming ambition to provide education for all, the needs of students with high potential have been neglected and students with differing abilities have been treated equally.

As we move into the twenty-first century, developing countries face a multiplicity of challenges in their quest for development. Taking up those challenges requires welltrained and prepared leaders to confront socio-economic needs. The specific educational requirements of outstanding students, the 'leaders of tomorrow', must be recognised and met.

To address the situation, additional educational opportunities that provide a more advanced content and methodology must be established to cater to individual differences. Classroom teachers should be trained to accommodate the different learning needs of talented students. One of the top priorities of every school should be to develop and set challenging curricula that offer advanced comprehensive learning opportunities, in order to meet the needs of outstanding students. This is of the utmost importance for the preparation of future leaders who will spearhead the march towards sustainable development. The regular school curriculum needs to be developed to offer talented students a challenge.

3.7.1. Aiming for Academic Excellence

To strive for excellence in education means to strive for a richer curriculum, based on the varying talents and needs of all students, the realisation of each student's potential, and the development and nurturing of outstanding talent. It is also most important to ensure that teachers receive better training in how to teach high-level curricula. Otherwise, society's message to students would be to aim for academic adequacy, not academic excellence.

3.7.2. Sharing of Social Responsibilities

To identify talent and to nurture it is not the responsibility of the school alone. The role of the family and the local community in developing potential provides the basis for and complements the efforts of the school. In turn, the non-governmental organisations can play a key role in assisting communities to assume their social responsibilities. They can be very effective in developing awareness and efficiency and in promoting participation of all members of the community.

3.7.3. Importance of Educating Women

The backbone of community involvement remains the increased participation of women in the development process, an issue that has become central to human development and which will be increasingly recognised in the future. Women are currently underrepresented in almost all advanced education programmes and in most top administrative positions. The key to increasing the participation of women is education. Educating women is probably one of the most rewarding investments a nation can make. Expanding opportunities for women, and especially for women and girls of outstanding abilities, opens up avenues for the emergence of women leaders and allows them to make a valuable contribution to decision-making for the benefit of educational progress and sustainable development.

3.7.4. Schools as a Sphere of Social Action

Education has always been and is still a highly social exercise. The full development of the individual's personality is the outcome of the consolidation of personal independence and, at one and the same time, of the cultivation of a concern for others, in other words, of the process of discovering other people on the basis of a moral outlook. Humanisation, defined as the internal growth of the individual, finds its fullest expression at that fixed point where the paths of freedom and responsibility meet. Education systems are a source of human capital, cultural capital, and social capital. Instead of being 'a wolf to his fellow man' *(homo homini lupus)*, man may thus become 'a friend to man' *(homo homini amicus)* through an education that has remained faithful to its community goals.

The task, though immense, cannot be postponed, since the construction of the social order of the next century depends on it. Above all, however, only education for justice will make it possible to reconstruct a core of moral education presupposing a civic culture characterised by non-conformism and the rejection of injustice, and preparing individuals for an active citizenship in which the responsibility to participate in the life of the community replaces mere delegated citizenship.

Thus, on the principle that education is, or comes close to being, a public good, the school should be defined first and foremost as a social institution or, more precisely, as an institution belonging to civil society; in other words, it must cease to be a mere component of an economic juggernaut that crushes the tenuous links of human solidarity.

The school is defined as a sphere of public action, as an environment and locus of socialisation, which at the same time contributes to the economic and private spheres by virtue of the accumulation of the qualifications and human capital that it produces. In societies that are becoming increasingly complex and diversified in cultural terms, the emergence of the school as a part of the public sphere accentuates the indispensable role it plays in the promotion of social cohesion and mobility, and in training for community life.

In the end, nothing that happens in the school is without significance for the process of building stable societies. Schools of this kind are of crucial importance to learning throughout life. It is these schools that will provide the skills essential for lasting socialisation, that is, for the consolidation of cultures in such a way that they can resist the processes of exclusion through pro-active attitudes that can fashion novel and stimulating social roles at each stage of life. Education and socialisation go hand in hand throughout life.

3.7.5. Cohension, as a Goal of Education

As the twentieth century draws to a close, we must with some bitterness acknowledge that the hopes raised in 1900 have been disappointed and that the extraordinary technological and scientific progress which has marked the century has not led to a better balance between human beings and nature, or to more harmony in human relations. On the threshold of the next century it is important to identify the challenges and the tensions of the present, in order to point the way for education and propose educational strategies. It is from this angle that social cohesion should be seen as one of the goals of education.

Ensuring the cohesion of our societies today means, in the first place, respecting the dignity of human beings and forming social bonds in the name of solidarity. No particular philosophy or cultural tradition can claim such an approach as its own: it emerges as one of the universal aspirations which are shaping the course for education at the turn of the century. State action in various fields is directed towards social cohesion. True, the state is the emanation of a collective identity in which it finds its justification, and all its action is aimed at supporting that identity – national or civil – by basing it on the memory of a common past or the defence of common interests.

3.7.6. 'Learning to be'

The future of social integration depends also, however, on the action taken by the societies themselves, on the efforts of the non-governmental organisations, of the institutions of civil society, on the relations between capital and labour, and on human attitudes and sensibilities. This calls for lifelong education, involving not only the school, but also the home, the workplace, the trade unions or the army, which can also educate and train.

On the threshold of the twenty-first century, 'Learning to Be' reminds us of the paramount importance of respect for the individual in social and political relations, in the relationship between human beings and nature, in the confrontation of civilisations and economies. When trying to understand reality –that of humanity and that of the world – we must recognise the interdependencies which create the need for different forms of solidarity. These forms of solidarity do not come from good intentions; they result from the constraints of our time.

In the educational philosophy of the late twentieth century, social cohesion and solidarity appear as indissolubly linked aspirations and purposes, in harmony with the dignity of the individual. Respect for human rights goes hand in hand with a sense of responsibility and inclines men and women to learn to live together. Yet among the principal problems which the present-day world must face is the increasing burden of exclusion.

3.7.7. Maladies of Exclusion

Exclusion is not an invention of the end of the twentieth century. It runs through the history of humankind, which bears the mark of Cain. It is described in the mythologies and in the holy scriptures of the great religions; and exclusion, in the past and in the present, is analysed by cultural anthropology and social history. Over the last third of the twentieth century, however, since the events of the 1960s in Europe and the United States of America, it has become a current concept in the human sciences and in political language. This may be seen as a sign that it has become a social problem, or that the phenomenon has taken on unprecedented dimensions, or again that the need for social cohesion has made exclusion a more serious matter. At all events, exclusion has become one of the great challenges of the end of this century and it is for the education of the next century to address it.

3.7.8. Need for Lifelong Education

Historians of poverty have shown that modernisation processes have at different times in history led societies to regard the poor as outcasts. The phenomenon is apparent at the end of this century, first of all in the alarming character of the increasing poverty in the countries south of the Sahara, then in the unemployment that has become an enduring feature of the capitalist economies, and – last but not least – in the migration to the affluent countries of populations fleeing the poverty and lack of prospects in their countries of origin. The experience of the last decades of the century goes to show that there is no remedy for these evils except economic growth and the fundamental role of education in this connection is well known.

However, it is mainly social attitudes to poverty which are a matter for concern: instead of compassion and solidarity, we observe only indifference, fear or hatred. It is important to try to change these attitudes. Education dealing with universal history, societies and cultures all over the world, combined with a genuine education in civics, may be effective and lead to a better understanding of social otherness. To cope with the problem of unemployment we would have to rethink our present conception of education, take schooling out of its cramping context, go beyond the limits of compulsory education and, with lifelong education in view, provide for several periods of learning.

3.7.9. Improved Technologies and Acculturation

Besides, the concept of an educational society should lead us to narrow the gap between skilled labour and unskilled labour, which is one of the basic causes of inequality in the world today. The transition from technologies requiring a large workforce to technologies which are labour-saving leads inevitably to emphasis on the quality of labour, and therefore to the emphasis on education, but it also offers everyone an opportunity of devoting more time to learning. The problem of unemployment is not thereby solved, but it no longer has the same character of a stark segregation from a society based on work.

Immigration cannot be analysed solely in labour market terms, and the hostility shown towards immigrants cannot be reduced to the fear of competition. In most cases immigrants occupy jobs in the host country for which there are no local applicants because they are jobs requiring few skills or jobs that are looked down upon.

Cultural difference is another aspect of otherness. Traditional societies had at their disposal channels of acculturation which made it possible to urbanise rural populations – apprenticeship in guilds, communal life in confraternities, and domestic service. Present-day societies should develop means of acculturation which would enable immigrants to be integrated into the existing social fabric. Realisation that there is a problem here should influence present-day education systems and fit them to train adults, too, by giving them qualifications, teaching them how to learn and providing them with cultural facilities.

3.7.10. Joint Educational Efforts

If education is to play a determining role in the struggle against exclusion of all those who for socio-economic or cultural reasons find themselves marginalised in present-day societies, its role seems still more pre-eminent in the integration of minorities in society. Legal norms concerning the status of minorities have already been established and await application, but the problem is more a matter of social psychology than of legislation. To change collective attitudes to otherness, we should have to envisage a joint educational effort involving the state and civil society, the media and the religious communities, parents and associations, but also – and above all – the schools.

The teaching of history and of the social sciences in the broadest sense of the term – indeed, every form of civic education – should inculcate in the young a spirit of tolerance and dialogue, so that the legitimate aspiration to preserve traditions and retain a collective identity is never seen as incompatible with a spirit of fellowship and solidarity, and so that the maintenance of social cohesion never implies a closed, inward-looking attitude or fundamentalism. Lifelong education is, of course, a safeguard against the most painful form of exclusion – exclusion due to ignorance.

The changes occurring in the information and communication technologies – sometimes referred to as the computer revolution – increase the risk of this form of exclusion, with the result that education has a crucial role to play in the run-up to the twenty-first century. All educational reforms should therefore be undertaken in full awareness of the risks of exclusion and with an eye to the need to preserve social cohesion.

3.7.11. Education for Sustainable Human Development

Education is the cement for building sustainable human development. Comprehensive environmental education strategies and programmes need to be developed to cover both formal and informal education, with a lifelong perspective, and implemented by governmental institutions, the production sector, commerce and local communities.

Some might consider this approach too complex, yet it appears to be working in several countries in transition. The tradition of centrally planned economies often favours initial top-down approaches. The need for creating numerous opportunities soon brings in bottom-up initiatives.

As soon as we start to implement the concept of sustainable human development, the new concept of education is essential. Experience shows that the integration of knowledge and values for a more humanistic society, development of high responsibility towards the local, national and global environment, and strengthening the readiness to share an enthusiasm for living together, need special consideration and support.

3.7.12. Linking Education with the World of Work

This is another urgent task. However, bringing work situations into education is often regarded as a difficult task slope in the efforts for improving the quality of education, particularly at universities in the countries of transition. The fact that employment patterns rapidly change is used to avoid any direct connections with future employers and to declare basic knowledge as sufficient in the preparation for a changing world.

The achievements of many internationally highly recognised

universities deny such an approach. Co-operation with industry and agriculture has also proven to increase the quality of tertiary education in the countries in transition and in developing countries, particularly if supported by national authorities.

Several projects show that direct involvement of university students and teachers brings a wealth of advantages, for instance learning to work in a group; facing real problems which reach from the idea to the market; recognising that the newest information is hardly good enough for economic competition at the global level, and that international information systems have to be used; learning to acquire and organise information from different sources; looking for patterns of knowledge which could support the formation of hypotheses; designing interactions between information processing and experimental work; cooperating in pilot production; looking for market opportunities and learning about market development; recognising opportunities for the transfer of knowledge and technologies, and listing technologies which should not be transferred; including environmental standards in technological and economic considerations; developing entrepreneurial skills; and recognising self-employment opportunities, that is, replacing 'waiting for jobs' by 'creating jobs', etc.

Values are an integral part of any university agriculture project, particularly if technological and socio-economic parameters for sustainable human development are taken into account. Development of clean(er) processes and products, pollution prevention and waste management are the fields where numerous opportunities can be created.

Solving real problems by research-educational methods in tertiary education, and inquiry approaches at pre-university levels, benefits particularly the countries in transition and developing countries where urgent actions are needed for the improvement of the transfer of knowledge and technology, both nationally and internationally.

3.8. Education Empowerment and Social Healing

The educational process in the future, to the extent that we can anticipate coming events by studying present experience, will have to shoulder a contradictory burden.

On the one hand an education system is the guardian of standards: standards of academic excellence, scientific truth and technological relevance. As such the system tends to be exclusionary, concentrating energy on those students who demonstrate abilities and aptitudes that are consistent with norms of excellence. The rest will tend to be relegated to a lesser process of training for life as part of a process of exclusion from the best that society can offer.

On the other hand we live in a world which is being increasingly torn apart by intractable divisions. There is the United States in danger of entrenching a permanent dichotomy between a largely black underclass and the rest of the society, largely white. European social fabric is beginning to fray under the strains which are surfacing between native majorities and migrant worker minorities. Ethnic tensions have torn apart Bosnia and Sri Lanka, while their tribal equivalents create similar instabilities in Nigeria, Angola or Rwanda. In short, the world is crying out for inclusionary, healing, uniting influences. These cannot begin with political endeavour with much prospect of success. Often politics is driven by these very tensions. It is the education system and, in particular, the school that provides the best, perhaps the only hope of starting the healing, inclusionary social process.

The school of today and tomorrow must plant the seeds of caring so that underclasses do not become the victims of an ideology of exclusion; it must nurture the concept of an over-arching humanity in which the brilliant, the average and even the disturbed, the Muslim and the Christian, the Hausa and the Ibo, the Irish Catholic and the Protestant, all occupy an equal place in a process of permanent social inclusion.

In this sense the school, which must be the guardian of standards, must be the catalyst for human values which are as universal as the scientific truths which must be protected. Indeed, if we do not achieve a widely effective breakthrough in multicultural education, we may find that increased success in the imparting of skills can have an ultimately negative impact. It is not fanciful to anticipate a situation in which highly educated people are trained to fight each other with increasingly deadly effect.

The role which education must play in the process of empowerment can be seen in both an obvious and a more profound way. Clearly, a young person will be empowered to the extent that education imparts marketable skills. At the same time, empowerment involves social skills beginning with an understanding of how societies work; what are the systems of power and the levers to which they respond; how to influence decisionmaking and the extent to which this is affected by social dynamics. The examples can be multiplied almost indefinitely. If all of this is not facilitated by the educational process, the underclass in prosperous societies will remain permanently frozen in powerlessness; developing countries will never develop the means to advancing because they will be unable to take profitable advantage of the opportunities in the global marketplace. Furthermore, all societies, at whatever stage of development, will be increasingly subject to wrenching social tensions as the gaps between rich and poor become ever more deeply entrenched, ever more intractable.

Economic reality requires and improving technology facilitates the delivery of more and more of the substance of education by impersonal means such as video and audio tapes or even more indirectly, as in the case of distance learning. These technical advances are entirely desirable if education is to be provided in the most cost-effective way to the greatest number of people around the globe. However, there is an inherent danger against which we must guard.

Throughout history teachers have played a role more profound and subtle than that of instruction. Bringing to their vocation a passion for ideas and values together with a love of children and an understanding of the process by which you plant the seeds of motivation, the profession has inspired millions of people to become everything from community activists to loving parents; from distinguished professionals to valued leaders in every aspect of a society's life. It is imperative that we never lose sight of the teacher in this personal, interfacing sense as the critical instrument in the educational process.

References

Lulla, B.P. *Values-oriented Teacher Education*, Bombay Teachers Training College, Bombay.

Mascranahas, M. A and Justa M.R. 1989. *Value Education in schools and other essays,* Konark Publishers Private Limited,

Meyer J. Burnham B. and Choilvat. J. 1975. *Values Education. Theory, Practice, Problems and Prospects*, Waterloo, Ontario, Wilfred Lauerer University Press.

Reddy, N.Y. 1980. *Values and Attitudes of Indian Youth, Light and Life* Publication, New Delhi.

Ryan, Kelvin and McLean G.T. 1987. *Education, Character Development in Schools*, Praeger, New York.

Saraf, Som Nath. 1995. *Education in Human Values: A handbook on programme implementation* . Apeejay Education Foundation.

4

Education for Global Society

National education systems are almost invariably postulated on beliefs that flow from pre-nuclear and pre-global perceptions, and are therefore unable to provide the new paradigm of thought that human welfare and survival now requires. Outmoded orthodoxies and obsolescent orientations continue to deprive the younger generations of an adequate awareness of the essential unity of the world into which they have been born. Indeed, by fostering negative attitudes towards other groups or nations, they hinder the growth of globalism. The astounding communications technology which today encircles the globe seldom uses its tremendous potential to spread global values and foster a more caring, compassionate consciousness.

On the contrary, the media are full of violence and horror, cruelty and carnage, unbridled consumerism and unabashed promiscuity, a situation which not only distorts the awareness of the young but dulls our sensitivity to the problems of human suffering and pain. What is urgently needed, therefore, is a creative revolution in our education and communications policies. We need to develop carefully structured programmes on a global scale based unequivocally on the premise that human survival involves the growth of a creative and compassionate global consciousness. The spiritual dimension will have to be given central importance in our new educational thinking.

4.1. Need for Global Education Programme

We must have the courage to think globally, to break away from traditional paradigms and plunge boldly into the unknown. We must so mobilise our inner and outer resources that we begin consciously to build a new world based on mutually assured welfare rather than mutually assured destruction. As global citizens committed to human survival and welfare, we must use the latest array of innovative and interactive pedagogic methodologies to structure a worldwide programme of education – for children and adults alike – that would open their eyes to the reality of the dawning global age and their hearts to the cry of the oppressed and the suffering. And there is no time to be lost for, along with the emergence of the global society, the sinister forces of fundamentalism and fanaticism, of exploitation and intimidation are also active.

4.1.1. Holistic Educational Philosophy

Let us, then, with utmost speed, pioneer and propagate a holistic educational philosophy for the twenty-first century based upon the following premises:

a) that the planet we inhabit and of which we are all citizens – Planet Earth – is a single, living, pulsating entity; that the human race in the final analysis is an interlocking, extended family – *Vasudhaiva Kutumbakam* as the Veda has it; and that differences of race and religion, nationality and ideology, sex and sexual preference, economic and social status – though significant in themselves – must be viewed in the broader context of global unity;

b) that the ecology of Planet Earth has to be preserved from mindless destruction and ruthless exploitation, and enriched for the welfare of generations yet unborn; and that there should be a more equitable consumption pattern based on limits to growth, not unbridled consumerism;

c) that hatred and bigotry, fundamentalism and fanaticism, and greed and jealousy, whether among individuals, groups or nations, are corrosive emotions which must be overcome as we move into the next century; and that love and compassion, caring and charity, and friendship and cooperation are the elements that have to be encouraged as we transit into our new global awareness;

d) that the world's great religions must no longer war against each other for supremacy but co-operate for the welfare of the human race, and that through a continuing and creative interfaith dialogue, the golden thread of spiritual aspiration that binds them together must be strengthened instead of the dogma and exclusivism that divides them;

e) that a massive and concerted drive is needed to eradicate the scourge of illiteracy worldwide by the year 2010, with special emphasis on promoting female literacy, particularly in the developing countries;

f) that holistic education must acknowledge the multiple dimensions of the human personality – physical, intellectual, aesthetic, emotional and spiritual – thus moving towards the perennial dream of an integrated individual living on a harmonious planet.

4.2. Education for a Multicultual World

The challenges to education are great in a world which is increasingly multicultural. As the process of globalisation becomes a more immediate reality for the planet's population, so also comes the realisation that 'my neighbour may no longer be like me'. For many people, this may come as a shock because it challenges traditional stable visions of neighbourhood, community and nation; it questions long-established ways of relating to one's fellow human beings and it turns ethnic diversity into the stuff of everyday life.

On the one hand, economic globalisation brings the producers and the consumers of different continents and regions into functional relationship with each other. Today's global corporations are organised in such a fashion that a single product may contain parts made in dozens of factories in as many different countries. The managers and employees of these giant firms often spend more time shuttling between countries than they do at home with family and friends, rather like the soldiers of fortune of olden times. It would be disingenuous to believe that the current restructuring of the world's economic relations has no effect on the personal attitudes and values of everybody involved – from the unskilled worker in an assembly line in a poor nation to the consumer of a product which says on a tag that it was 'Made in...' a faraway country.

On the other hand, the rapid expansion of communications networks, especially the audiovisual media, has brought what used to be considered unrelated events in faraway places into the intimate space of millions of homes from metropolitan neighbourhoods to urban slums to remote villages. The exotic is no longer distant and the distant becomes ever more familiar. To the extent that the cultural industries promote the lifestyles of the Western, urbanindustrial, middle-class sectors by way of satellite dishes and video stores, the multicultural world draws closer together, and the cultural values of those lifestyles become, as it were, international standards against which local populations measure their achievements and aspirations.

4.2.1. Flexible Education System

One of the most important roles assigned to formal schooling in many countries has been to fashion good, law-abiding citizens who will share a single national identity and who will be loyal to the nation-state. Whilst this no doubt served a noble purpose, and may even have been necessary in certain historical circumstances, it also led in many instances to the marginalisation and even the destruction of numerous ethnically distinct peoples whose cultures, religions, languages, beliefs or ways of life did not conform to the so-called national ideal.

In many countries there are tensions between the purposes and requirements of a 'national' system of education, and the values, interests and aspirations of culturally distinct peoples. At the same time, in an increasingly interdependent world, conflicting tendencies pull in different directions: on the one hand, the trend toward national homogenisation and world uniformisation; on the other, the search for roots, community and distinctiveness, which for some can only be found by strengthening local and regional identities, and keeping a healthy distance from the 'others', who are sometimes perceived as threatening.

Such a complex situation represents a challenge to the education system and to state-sponsored cultural policies, as well as to the functioning of market mechanisms in the fields of communications and entertainment, those vast networks in which global cultural industries call the shots. In recent years, traditional educational policies based on the premise of a single national culture have come under increasing critical scrutiny. More and more states not only tolerate expressions of cultural diversity but now recognise that instead of being an obstacle to be overcome, multicultural and pluri-ethnic populations are the true mainstays of democratic social integration. Education in the twenty-first century must come to grips with that challenge, and education systems (in the widest possible sense) must be flexible and imaginative enough to be able to strike a creative balance between the two structural tendencies mentioned above.

4.2.2. Pluralistic Education

A truly multicultural education will be one that can address simultaneously the requirements of global and national integration, and the specific needs of particular culturally distinct communities, both in rural and urban settings. It will lead to an awareness of diversity and to respect for others, whether those others are my nextdoor neighbours, workers in the field, or my fellow human beings in a faraway country. To achieve such a truly pluralistic education it will be necessary to rethink the objectives of what it means to educate and be educated; to remodel the contents and the curricula of formal schooling institutions; to develop new teaching skills and educational methods; and to stimulate the emergence of new generations of teachers/learners. A truly pluralistic education is based on a philosophy of humanistic pluralism. This is an ethos that prizes the social realities of cultural pluralism. The values of humanistic and cultural pluralism that are necessary to inspire such educational transformation are sometimes lacking; they must be generated in the educational process itself and will in turn be strengthened by it.

4.2.3. Criticisms of Multiculturism

Many observers, however, have serious doubts about cultural pluralism and its expression in multicultural education. While paying lip service to cultural diversity, they nevertheless question the wisdom of furthering diversity through education. They fear that this may lead to the crystallisation of separate identities, the strengthening of ethnocentrism, the proliferation of ethnic animosities and, finally, to the disintegration of existing nation-states. There are certainly many current examples of exaggerated ethnic nationalisms leading to political separatism and societal breakdown, not to mention genocidal massacres and hate-filled ethnic cleansings. Yet ethnic diversity cannot be wished away and it is unrealistic to blame multiculturalist policies for the numerous conflicts that in many instances arise precisely because ethnic diversity goes unrecognised or is suppressed.

The criticism of multiculturalism (and the term means different things in different contexts) may come from ethnic nationalists who feel that the 'essence' of their nation is being undermined by foreign elements (immigrants, culturally differentiated minorities). But it may also come from concerned liberals who want to build the 'civic' nation in which every single individual has the same worth as any other, regardless of race, language, nationality, religion or culture. They feel that by emphasizing cultural or ethnic distinctions, borders and walls are erected between otherwise equal – if not always identical – human beings. It is only through education tending toward a truly civic culture to be shared by all, that differences will cease to beget inequalities and distinctiveness will no longer generate enmity. In such a world view, ethnic identities will belong to the purely private domain, and should be of no concern to public policies.

While that is surely a worthy vision, we see all around us that ethnic groups do mobilise around cultural symbols and beliefs, and that education systems are in fact at stake in today's 'cultural wars'. Whether such struggles are deeply embedded in the collective psyche (as some would hold) or are simply manipulated by opportunistic 'ethnic entrepreneurs' (as others might argue), it is not by relegating them to the backroom that democratic, humanistic values can be fostered. In the twenty-first century we should foster a democratic civic culture, based on individual human rights, and to encourage at the same time mutual respect for the culture of others, based on the recognition of the collective human rights of all peoples around the world, great or small, each as deserving as every other. This is the challenge that must be met by education in the twenty-first century.

4.2.4. Wholesome Education

Living together in harmony must be the ultimate goal of education in the twenty-first century. Unfortunately, that reality does not inform our daily life, whether at home or in school, whether at community or national level. At international level, the situation is even more difficult. Education systems tend to be nationalistic; the danger arises when they are aggressively so, to the detriment of peaceful worldwide coexistence. One of the greatest barriers to world peace is the ethnocentrism that exists everywhere in the world.

Because of the rapid advances made in science and technology, we have become a worldwide community, one 'global village'. However, most people do not realise this fact, while those who do often prefer to devote themselves to the details of their day-to-day life and notably to the attainment or preservation of personal prestige.

In the Republic of Korea, the university entrance examination constitutes the most harmful barrier to wholesome education. The examination has adverse effects on all levels of education, as well as on the cause of world peace. The Ministry of Education has tried every kind of remedial measure to minimise the negative effects of the examination, so far in vain. Any new system has immediately provoked fresh counter-tactics.

4.2.5. Educational Reforms for Change

In terms of the number of students engaged in higher education per 100,000 inhabitants, the Republic of Korea comes third, immediately after Canada and the United States of America. Qualitatively. However, there are many weaknesses and failures in producing world citizens who will live peacefully alongside others in the twenty-first century. Specifically, the ethical or moral dimension of education today in the Republic of Korea is much poorer than in ancient Korean education. While students now have more factual knowledge, their moral conduct is unacceptable to their elders. However, while the public is sharply critical of students' behaviour, it is at the same time strongly in favour of preparing young people for the entrance examination. In other words, the public does not see the contradictions inherent in today's higher education system.

Aware of the problem, the country's universities have recently been changing their curricula drastically in order to reconstruct the contents of education. Emphasis is now less on education oriented toward economic growth (that is to say, science and technology) and more on education oriented toward human or social development, drawing on age-old human values. Nowadays, people are beginning to realise that economic-growth-oriented policies in all fields have resulted in our paying a heavy moral price for having neglected the traditional values.

4.3. Education for Human Development

Both education and culture can be defined in various ways. In relation to culture, education might be referred to as a process of instilling in young people the traditionally inherited and contemporarily renewed values and beliefs which lie at the heart of cultures. Education is an agent of cultural transmission while culture provides a context of educational institutions and constitutes an essential part of education contents. Education has been placed 'at the core of the value order, and values as the sustaining force in education'. In serving the development needs of the people, both education and culture become a means to and an end of development.

The exploration into the interrelationship of education and culture will be meaningful only when it relates to development, which is a multidimensional, worldscale, evolutionary and mobilising process, and of which the human being is the origin, agent and ultimate purpose.

Many studies have been done to explore relations between education, culture and development. Taking Asia as an example, there are certain traits that have been conducive to educational and economic development.

4.3.1. Appreciation of Value of Education

The Asian stress on learning was classic. To Confucius, man is perfectible and can be led in the right path through education, especially through his own effort at self-cultivation, within himself, but also through the emulation of models outside himself. He emphasized the power of education to improve society and to teach citizenship. The Confucian political ideal was 'to rule the state by moral virtues', which had to be developed by education. He even equated the roles of education to those of sufficient food provision and a powerful army for national defence. Responding to the question 'What is to be done next after population growth?', he said, 'To make the populace wealthy', and to the consequent question, 'What next?', he simply answered, 'To educate them'.

For centuries education has formed a foundation for the entire political, social, economic and cultural life of Asian peoples. Working Asian mothers, bending low in the rice fields, had always enshrined hope in their hearts to preserve their children, by education, from the poverty that had afflicted them. The well-known Japanese image of the 'education mother', who regarded education of the children as her prime duty; the Chinese mother who travelled a long way to take evening classes for years on behalf of her disabled son and then taught the boy with her notes taken in the class; the Korean mothers who would sell their cows to pay for their children to complete schooling; the great wisdom in the sayings of India's great poet Tagore and its great politician Gandhi about the value of education – all these illustrate the value attached to education in Asia.

4.3.2. High Expectations

An ancient Chinese story tells why and how the mother of Mencius, the great Confucian scholar, moved her home three times in order that her son had good teachers, good neighbours, and good peers for a good education. Findings of many studies indicate that high expectation of parents and teachers has a positive correlation to high curriculum standards, more student hours on learning tasks, strict training drills in intellectual skills, more parent-children interaction at home, close teacher–pupil relations at school and consequently to higher learning achievement especially in such intellectually demanding courses as mathematics. Since there is no substantial difference in the intelligence quotient of most children and no children are ineducable, this cultural factor does to some extent account for the relatively high scholastic achievements of many Asian students.

4.3.3. Emphasis on the Group

By tradition, collectivism has long overwhelmed individualism in

Asian cultures. Confucianism emphasized the development of the individual as a social being, as an element of the family and of the society at large. Learning the rules of social relationships was considered an essential way to become a mature and responsible member of society. Over the centuries, Chinese intellectuals upheld the moral ideals of 'bearing the worries of the world before anyone else and enjoying the pleasures of life after all others'.

The group-oriented attitude, as displayed in the classic 'team spirit' of the Japanese, has been most conducive to both economic productivity and social cohesion. This explains partly why many Asians tend to dislike the concept of competition among individuals yet display a strong collective force of competitiveness.

4.3.4. Stress on Spiritual Dimension of Development

'Spiritual' is meant here in a cultural, moral and ethical sense. Traditional Chinese culture, based on Confucianism and Taoism, was essentially ethics-based, stressing moral cultivation of the personality. Whether the Confucian ethical principles, or the Tao's self-cultivation or the Idealist School's 'keep rationality and eliminate worldly desires', all were largely philosophies of moral humanism, by which man was examined from the point of view of ethical political relations, and the realisation of an individual's value depended on his interaction with the collective. It is widely recognised in the region that education cannot be value-free and the perception of a future is implicitly a view of the moral order of the future.

Up to the very present, in efforts to modernise, the building of both 'spiritual' and 'material' civilisations is made the twin goal of national development in many Asian countries, and education is expected as an active agent to contribute to both processes. The renewed stress on moral-values education is most recently displayed in the Kuala Lumpur Declaration by the fourth Asian–Pacific Conference of Ministers of Education and Those Responsible for Economic Planning in 1993.

4.3.5. Meritocracy Based on Performance in Examinations

Asia had the world's longest tradition of civil examination, by which state officers and civil servants were screened and selected. In theory the ultimate goal of education was the cultivation of the person in the ethical sense; in practice, it was concerned more with the preparation and selection of the ruling élite than with true education aimed at the full development of individual personality. This examination-performance-based meritocracy used to be a motivating force for learning and career achievement irrespective of class; however the over-emphasis on Confucian classics-focused examination had suppressed the creativity of many brilliant young minds and turned out to be a 'tail wagging the dog' of the education system in substantial ways.

4.3.6. Legitimisation of Authority

To Confucius, education was a forceful instrument of the ruling élite to govern the state. Through education the ruler should 'learn to care for the people' while the ruled 'learn to be obedient'. The care from the top and the obedience from the subordinate below were supposed to lead to a stable social order. The authority of the parent at home and that of the teacher at school accounted in one way for the high discipline of most Asian students. Extended to the political and economic sphere, the high authority of the state was beneficial to facilitating a co-operative, harmonious business–government relationship and to effecting government policy implementation.

Especially when the government authority develops policy environments favourable for free enterprise and fair competition, the respect of the authority will be most conducive to healthy economic growth. An authoritative modern government has been said to be one of the factors accounting for the economic miracles of East Asian economies.

4.3.7. Need for Cultural Renewal

Interwoven in the 'modernising' process, elements of cultural traditions have had both positive and negative effects on economic and social life. It is only too natural to challenge the Asian cultural tradition by asking why economies with (cultural) traditions that are so conducive to development have only recently embarked on rapid growth. Apart from the more fundamental economic-political factors impeding development, elements in traditional cultures explained in part the lag or lack of development of an industrial economy in many Asian countries.

a) *Politicisation of educational-cultural values and lack of governmental commitment to economic modernisation.* Educational institutions were made merely an instrument in political strife and an appendage to the government apparatus.

b) *Neglect of individuality.* While the collective/societal interests were overemphasised to the extreme, the individual was reduced to merely an instrument. At the same time, the rights of the individual were not made compatible with the duties.

c) *Focus on interpersonal relationships rather than on man over nature*, which for a long time resulted in underdevelopment of positive science, engineering and applied technologies.

d) *Over-emphasis on classics-oriented examination* in screening talents and potential bureaucrats.

e) *Disdain for pragmatism, utilitarianism and business.* Confucian idealism gave enormous weight to classic texts and their memorisation in schooling, neglecting sciences and technical applications. It separated brain from hand and scholarship from craftsmanship. The educated élite were entitled to rule simply by virtue of their 'moral superiority', without having to acquire practical knowledge of skills. Matters of utilitarian values were despised and business was listed as an occupation of low social status. Partly due to this cultural factor, vocational and technical education remain under-developed to this day in many developing Asian countries

f) *Gender bias.* Confucius once said that 'only the mean and women are difficult to raise'. For centuries women were reduced to an appendage at home and negligible in society. From this traditional bias in many Asian cultures a vicious cycle emerged, in which girls were not expected to play social roles in economic growth or in their families and therefore had much less schooling than boys. It also accounts much for the persistently high ratio of girls among the millions of school drop-outs in the Asian region. As elsewhere, the lower educational level of Asian women resulted in higher infant mortality, high population growth in the rural areas, worse conditions for child nutrition and health, and a stagnant economy.

'Crisis in human values', a worldwide phenomena, could also be observed in the Asian region. While education transmits cultural heritage to next generations, it has a mission to innovate traditional cultures. The negative elements in traditional cultures point to the need for their renewal in the light of the changing socio-economic contexts and education has an important role to play in effecting positive cultural value changes.

4.4. Education for Global Ethics

While striving for preservation of cultural identity and traditions, Asian nations have been increasingly aware of interregional interdependence. In response to increasing globalisation, there have been advocacy efforts made by education systems in Asian region to facilitate a desirable core of universal values, which have included the following:

a) *Awareness of human rights combined with a sense of social responsibilities.* Caution is taken that rights are not separated from duties, that the concept of human rights is not imposed from a Western ethnocentric perspective but related to cultural traditions and national/regional contexts, and that the rights of individuals are linked to those of the collectives.

b) Value of social equity and democratic participation in decision-making and government, which will be the central objective in all parts of life.

c) *Understanding and tolerance of cultural differences and pluralism,* which is a precondition of social cohesion, peaceful co-existence and conflict-resolution by negotiation instead of force, and ultimately of world peace.

d) *A spirit of caring,* a keynote value for future education, and an intrinsic quality of human compassion, which should be extended not only to the family members and colleagues, but to all the disadvantaged, the sick, the poor and the disabled, for the well-being of humankind and our planet.

e) *Co-operative spirit.* While competition can be observed in all spheres of daily life, cooperation is all the more necessary.

f) *Enterprising spirit,* a quality which is needed not only for economic productivity and competitiveness but for all life situations.

g) *Creativity,* which will always be needed for technological advances, social progress, economic dynamics and all other human endeavours.

h) *Sensitivity to gender equality,* which has been recognised as the key to development and poverty alleviation, and both a gateway to development and a measure of that development.

i) *Open-mindedness to change,* which will be the only thing which will not change, and the attitude not only to accept change but to act as an agent of positive change.

j) *Sense of obligation to environment protection and sustainable development,* so as not to create economic, social and ecological debts for future generations.

It is worth noting that most of these universal values needed for the twenty-first century have long been embedded in the age-old cultural traditions of human civilisations. They encompass the moral visions and ideals of truth, kindness, beauty, justice and liberty which were elaborated long ago by our predecessors and magnificently preserved in the treasuries of thought. The sensitivity to environmental protection was expressed in ancient China by the concern of the Taoists about the destructive consequences of technical advances to natural resources and their advocacy of 'return to Nature'. Altruism, originating in the love of one human being for another, has been respected as the highest human value in Asia for hundreds of years. Humanity in the next century might find elements of wisdom of Confucianism as relevant as it was long ago. Therefore, one way to foster universal values for future centuries is to educate the young with great books of the past and inherit the fine traditions of humanity.

Another approach to the cultivation of these universal values for global ethics is to promote, by means of education, cross-cultural learning between Eastern and Western cultures. Culturally the East and West are compatible and complementary rather than contradictory and mutually opposing. Asia's cultural learning from the West has evolved from the material dimension (modern technologies) to the institutional (political infrastructure) and the socio-psychological (values and beliefs) dimensions. It is education that has provided bridges between Eastern and Western cultures. If and when the East and West could learn and benefit from each other, integrating each other's cultural strengths – for example, the individual initiative with the collective team spirit, competitiveness with cooperativeness, the technological capacities with the moral qualities – then desirable universal values will gradually develop and a global ethic will be formed, which will be a fundamental renewal of cultures and a great contribution of education to humanity.

4.5. The Ultimate Goal of Education

Development, which aims at 'the full flowering of human potential all over the world', is the ultimate goal of both education and culture. In the Asian region, education is being emphasized as a vital force of development and culture as both an important means and an integral component of development. As in other regions, development has increasingly been seen in Asia as a complex dynamic process, embracing economic, political, social, human and environmental as well as cultural dimensions.

As the material base upon which human beings could pursue all kinds of superstructural activities for survival and growth, economic development is of primary significance to education and culture. The importance of the effect of modernisation of national economies on education and culture cannot be over-emphasized, especially for developing countries. With as many as 830 million people living in absolute poverty in the Asia–Pacific region alone, economic growth becomes an essential element of any effort in eradicating poverty and a precondition for both cultural and educational development.

Without strong national industry and agriculture, educational programmes will lack the necessary resources and even political independence will be hindered. Without material civilisation in terms of technological and infrastructure development, spiritual civilisation will have weak support and indigenous cultural identity will be eroded by new forms of cultural colonialism transmitted by powerful information technology. That is why most Asian countries have, legitimately and rightfully, regarded economic modernisation as a highest priority and made persistent efforts in striving for modernisation.

However, economic and technological advances will lose their true meaning if the humanistic and cultural dimensions are not made the central component and goal of development efforts. In the twenty-first century, when industries will be more technology-intensive and human society increasingly knowledgeintensive, human capital developed through education and training will assume increasingly crucial roles.

In the East, from Confucius to contemporary Asian thinkers, the ideal of 'a harmonious one-world' and 'a coherent human society of universal peace' has been cherished and pursued for ages. In the West, from Plato, French enlightenment, English humanism and European Renaissance to the American Declaration of Independence, the ideal of equity, justice, liberty and human dignity has been sought and fought for for centuries.

Humankind has never ceased its efforts to integrate economic with educational and cultural dimensions of development. UNDP's conception of development of the people for the people by the people corresponds to our interpretation of the dialectic interrelations of education to culture in the light of Asian traditions and contemporary contexts of globalisation.

References

Bower, William C. 1952. *Moral and Spiritual Values in Education*, Lexigton, university of Kentucky Press.

Core Group, Govt. of India . 1992. *Value Orientation Education*, New Delhi.

Gupta. N.L. *Value Education, Theory and Practice*, Krishna Brother, Ajmer. 1986.

Ruhella , S.P. *Education, Human Values and Education*, Sterling, New Delhi.

Sheshadri, C., Khader M.A. and Ddhya G.L. 1992. *Education in Values: A source book*, NCERT, New Delhi.

5

Education for Cultural Development

With more than 4,000 communities, 18 constitutionally recognised languages and hundreds of dialects, more than six major religious and hundreds of sects and more than 800 million people, India presents a very complex, plural culture which very nearly permeates every aspect of living from patterns of belief and values to hundreds of forms of creative articulation, from costumes mid foods to enormous subtleties of refinement and participation. Nothing in India can possibly escape the impact of its culture, be it politics, technology, education or development. Even the long colonial subjugation had a distinctively Indian hue while it shared many aspects with similar colonised countries.

The strong and inescapable cultural implications of education and development were recognised right from the beginning of the epic scale national reconstruction which was launched when the recently free India gave to itself, in the early fifties, a new constitution and the form of a democratic republic. In many ways India's democratic ethos and its amazing survival owes as much to the political sagacity of its people as to their innate sense of culture, their unfailing cultural literacy in spite of their depressing poverty midwidespread verbal literacy. It is the age-old resilience of Indian traditions that made them show genuine openness to new ideas while remaining firmly rooted and have, therefore, evolved their own distinctive dynamics of change and absorption. The built in resistance in Indian milieu to tyranny of any kind, whether of belief or truth or behaviour, has made it face new challenges with confidence and bring about many transmutations without tensions of rupture. The issue of education, culture and development have to be seen in this context of an enriching, if also a trifle perplexing, continuum.

Each linguistic and racial group has its own distinct cultural identity. Yet interaction has taken and continues to take place amongst regions, between different an disciplines at various levels of society, from the most affluent to the weakest sections. Culture has always been an integral part of the informal process of an Indian's education, contributing to the integrated development of his personality, sensitising him towards his environment and his natural and cultural heritage. In the present day scenario, when the world is facing numerous problems such as dissension and intolerance, destruction of the natural environment, wars and poverty, the role of culture in the developmental effort, and particularly in education, cannot be over-emphasised. It is now widely recognised that only the integration of our artistic and cultural with curriculum teaching will make the young aware of the aesthetic dimensions of life and senstitise them towards creative expression.

Education plays a very important culturising role. The converse is equally true: culture plays a very important educating role. Both the National Policy on Education, 1986 and the Approach to the National Policy on Culture (NPC) constantly emphasise the cultural consequences of education and seek to strengthen its cultural components. As stated in the NPE 1986, deculturalisation, dehumanisation and alienation must be avoided at all costs. Education must bring about a fine synthesis between change oriented technologies and the country's continuity of cultural tradition. The curricula and processes of education will be enriched by cultural content in a many manifestations as possible Children will be enabled to develop sensitivity to beauty, harmony and refinement. The Approach to the NPC also commits itself to the growth of cultural literacy along with verbal literacy and inculcation of respect and striving for creativity and excellence from the earliest levels of education.

5.1. Programme of Action

The interlinking of education and culture seeks to discover the inherent talent and potential of a child and develop his personality. With this in view, a Programme of Action has been formulaed under the NPE, right from the pre-primary stage to the highest level of formal education. Some of the salient features of this culture-education linkage are mutual participation, use of inexpensive and relevant material for cultural exposure, promotion of a concept of cultural neighborhood involving active participation of the community, curriculum reform motivation and training of teachers, and efforts to encourage the young to participate in cultural activities.

The cultural input in school education seeks to sensitise the child towards his environment and natural materials around him, and teach him to appreciate the aesthetic forms and rhythms he grows up with. The school child is also provided a basic core of facts about India's cultural heritage through folk songs, local history and archaeological artefacts. A sense of design and aesthetics is encouraged. Teacher training programmes also seek to enhance their capability for cultural instruction. Special books, educational material and audio visual facilities are also sought to be provided for schools.

Resource persons in the community, irrespective of their formal educational qualification are being invited to contribute to the cultural enrichment of education employing both the literatc and oral traditions. To sustain and carry forward the cultural tradition, the role of old masters, who trained pupils through traditional modes is being supported and recognised. India is striving to promote a symbiosis between local environment, indigenous technologies, oral traditions of literature and the demands of keeping pace with the rapid technological advances.

The languages of India have been very valuable vehicles of cultural articulation and dissemination. Development of linguistic skills and a sense of pride in mother tongues is sought to be encouraged at all levels. Learning of our classical languages and training in traditional disciplines available only in them are being seen as preservation of an important aspect of our cultural heritage and its continuing relevance.

5.2. Need for Cultural Education

The NPE as well as the approach to the NPC seek to encourage educational institutions to be in live contact with local writers artists etc. as cultural education should be seen not as an additional burden on but as an integrated component in curriculum teaching. School community interaction is sought to be institutionalised by getting local artisans, craftsmen etc. to teach/demonstrate their art to schoolchildren.

Organisation of regular visits to monuments, museums and sanctuaries is also being encouraged. Development of conservation ideas through adoption of monuments by the students and the community, taking their help to keep the monuments clean and safeguarding them will make the youth aware of their natural as well as man-made environment.

Apart from setting up small museum comers in schools, the established museums are being encouraged to reorient themselves as active centres for awareness building regarding cultural heritage. Museums have to function as more than storehouses of our ancient heritage. They have a vital role as centres of learning and education. Museum visits are sought to be systematically encouraged with each museum developing attractive programmes which would interest the young.

One of the major thrusts of the NPC would be the expansion of library facilities in the rural areas. The rural library movement is sought to be intensified through the setting up of a network of rural libraries linked with the District Library System. This would take care of the reading needs of the student community and the growing numbers of educated youth.

5.3. Role of CCRT

India started inservice training programmes two decades ago in the area of linking education with culture. The Centre for Cultural Resources and Training (CCRT) was set up at the national level to provide a cultural component in curriculum teaching and a number of teachers and teacher-educators trained in this institution are doing commendable work in schools and State Institutes of Education. CCRT training programmes are designed to enable teachers to acquire knowledge of the use of the arts and crafts in the service of education, to create an awareness of India's cultural heritage, and to inculcate a sense of appreciation of the multiple levels of cultural interaction in the country. CCRT also strives to sensitise the decision makers on the need for cultural education, especially to ap- preciate the role of the youth in the preservation of the natural and cultural heritage.

The content of the teacher training covers different aspects of India's heritage the environment and geography, the historical evolution of traditions, art and culture architecture, sculpture, music, dance forms, theatre, with emphasis on regional forms and handicrafts. In order to make teacher training adaptable for practical use in the classroom, it incorporates lesson plans integrating aspects of culture with curriculum work, preparation of innovative educational aids directly involving the child in the learning process, and demonstration of new methodologies. Practical classes in music, movement and mime, traditional crafts and technical skills are arranged to help teachers to discover the child's potential and talent and create a balance between academic studies and practical work. A cultural kit which includes slides and recorded cassettes as well as books and explanatory notes is provided to the schools from which teachers have been trained. Educational tours to places of historical and cultural interest, museums and aft galleries are organised. The first-hand experience helps teachers understand how such visits can complement classroom teaching. Since its inception, the CCRT has trained 26,710 teachers/ principals/district education officers. Besides, 33,388 students have also been directly trained by the Centre.

Each district in India is to set up a District Institute of Education and Training for training teachers at the primary level. The syllabus of this training highlights the need for an understanding of the local cultures. In some of these DIETs, resource persons trained by the CCRT are providing methodologies for a cultural input at the primary level. Colleges of teacher training are also considering a cultural input in the pre-service curriculum. Most States in India have Centres for Educational Research and Training. Each such Centre has a special wing related to cultural education. Several voluntary agencies in the rural areas are doing admirable work in the area of education, taking into account the local culture and needs.

5.4. Development of Skills and Attitudes

Popuiar basic education is becoming more and more elusive. This unattainability is reflected in its failure to encompass the mass of people, in its inability to offer a meaningful pedagogy and in its inability to offer to the people a satisfying instrument. It is amazing that not only a populous country such as India, or a less populous but perhaps poorer country as one would find in Africa, have failed in providing for education; but also the richer countries that boast of statistics of literate populace sadly lack an educated mass of people. As a result the edifice of public space, built up through literacy or informative institutions of popular education and on which the pillars of democracy were mounted, is now crumbling. Ironically, neither science nor democracy appears to be in a position to confront this fear of death.

Naturally, for some proponents of science, it is time to redefine and rechart their enterprise. It is equally so for the proponents of democracy or of the public sphere. Such a strategy may pay some dividends to those who want to save their own houses. However, it is unlikely to better the lives of the millions.

Surely our central inquiry cannot set aside the question of conducting a good life — a life that can satisfy its desires through undertaking enlightened actions. If this is our concern, how the millions can be enabled to live a good life, then surely the other concerns regarding democracy, science, theory or literacy will have to abide by this centrality or will have to be given up. Is it not legitimate to pay central attention to this question of basic education, how the people can be enabled to conduct a life which assures satisfaction?

In basic education we argue for two basic elements. The first is drilling in a productive engagement, following authoritative rules, such that the student may acquire a skill. Second is the inculcation of an attitude of aesthetics or of truth so that the student may engage with the world later in life, fearlessly, in order to know and enjoy and also in order to secure the good for which she/he has acted. We also argue that the characteristic feature of basic education is that it is non-theoretical. The goal of non-theoretical basic education is to enable the student to undertake independent action.

This summary statement regarding basic education is derived from two sources. The first is the tradition of imparting basic education in India. The second is some distinctive features of the Indian theoretical tradition that provide the ground and the content of basic education. This tradition of conducting basic education is rather old.

5.4.1. Primary Education

What is the legitimate and appropriate basis of divisions in education? A 'primary' education is normally defined as the first tier of a segmented educational system. A segmented educational system is not only the result of historical evolution in Western Europe, but also cannot be defined either on grounds of epistemology or on grounds of practical reasoning or pragmatic concerns. As a result, primary education, as existing in this segmented system of education, can neither lead the student to higher and more abstract levels of epistemic concerns nor can it lead the student to practical concerns of achieving the good in life.

There is now a likelihood of dividing the educational system in terms of its exposure to information and its ability to process information. The primary aim of this approach, it appears, is to replace skill and knowledge with an allegedly 'objective' status describable in terms of information. With the advent of new technologies of handling information, and also with the growing disintegration of society, this informational basis of education is gaining ground. As of now, the educational system cannot be divided on this ground; however, there remains a distinct trend in that direction.

Contemporary slogans around literacy are largely reducible to such a classification. Exposure to information and logical operations on that constitute the basis of divisions. Instead of going into debates, it may be briefly pointed out that a load of information is not knowledge; neither is a skill information processing capacity. Moreover, non-numeric information has to be described or literally narrated. Finally, a wish or a desire cannot be reduced to information. As a result, primary education cannot be defined on the basis of its exposure to information. Sadly, however, the latest pedagogy is being reduced to the provision of structured information. Organised money, a politics of hegemony and a group of opportunist ideologues are doing their best to enforce on the child this information-derived pedagogy, which cannot be justified on grounds of rationality and aesthetics.

This first tier of education can also not be defined by the primacy of a set of certain textbooks. Proponents of such a view define segmentation in terms of interpretive capability. In fact, the literacy view of education also proposes this iconic relevance of textual signs. Texts and textbooks assume a major significance. Connotations of civilisation, conscience and morality too are attached to this view. However, by being limited to interpretation, education here limits its capacity for inferential reasoning, its materiality and its activities on transforming the material. Moreover, such a view attaches undue importance to teleology and culture. Hence this basis of education and educational segmentation is also not acceptable.

Significantly, Indian educational practice is very different from these groups. However, in contemporary India, especially in urban areas, we have a significant presence of the institutions of these three above groups. Governmental activities are largely reducible to these practices. In contrast, the history of educational practice in India and the debates and practices on education since the middle of the nineteenth century to the middle of this one, especially the practice and thinking of Gandhi, Tagore, Bankim, Vinoba and others do provide a strikingly different alternative. In fact, in this essay, what we argue about is a summary only of this alternative Indian practice.

5.4.2. Facets of Indian Practice

Knowledge, according to Indian theorists, must have its characteristic concept and a characteristic good that is realisable. This concept must specify not only what it is but also what it is not. This unambiguity in the concept would not allow it to get mixed up with another concept. Separations are inviolable and are due to distinct epistemological depar-tures. Corresponding to four types of epistemology there are four distinct knowledge-depar-tures or systems. We are concerned here with two knowledge-departures, viz., the knowledge-system pertaining to politics, which is distinct from the know-ledge-system pertaining to wealth, economics and society. The other characteristic of any knowledge-system is the good that one may realise upon practising its concepts.

Each knowledge-departure must have its characteristic good. There are, however, pluralities of good and practices, most of which cannot be immediately recognised as belonging to the good of some particular knowledge-system. These practices therefore give rise to arts and skills. The concepts of any knowledge-system, according to the theorists, must engage in dialogues with the *vidya* practices, in order first, that the concept acquires its validating example from the common practice of *vidya*, and second, that the *vidya* in turn receives its conceptual or theoretical backing. This dialogue therefore is the first basis of the institution of acquiring knowledge and skill. The second basis of this institution is provided by the dialogues between the contending concepts of a knowledge-departure. A group of such concepts, logically coherent and cosmologically meaningful, is called a shastra.

The second type of dialogue is conducted between competing pedagogues. The third basis of the knowledge-institution is provided by a third type of dialogue, conducted between the teacher and the student. The teacher answers the queries of the student. These dialogues are held in a medium of attitude. This attitude relates to aesthetics — the state of truth. Life, queries and practices of knowledge-seeking, defending or refuting must correspond to this attitude of truth.

Knowledge is required in order to resolve doubts and thus in order to act meaningfully. Indian theorists argue for a common knowledge that is distinguishable from common sense beliefs. Such knowledge is obtained through iterated fruitful actions, through the authority of sentences. Therefore the actions in a commonly led daily life are both meaningful and knowledge-driven. We argue for four sources of validation, viz., sentence, inference, direct perception and analogy. Moreover, as argued above, knowledge is entailed not by way of justification as such, but by the realisation of good or richness of meaning and actions or iterated actions.

We summarise the arguments put forth by Indian theoreticians on the subject of the description and divisions of knowledge as follows. Knowledge cannot be described by descriptions alone. Hence an attempt to describe or limit knowledge by theories — where theories are nothing but descriptive sentences, is incomplete. The folk or common experience of doing things successfully is an equal partner of knowledge. Knowledge is also described by naming and achieved through iterated practice. Moreover, such a complete picture of knowledge is always derivable through an injunction. Such an injunction may not always be clearly visible or discernible, but it can surely be inferred. Indian theoreticians thus argue for a different scheme of knowledge division. The argued positions always refer to a source of injunction, an injunction, a theory as a description, a set of names, and an iterated practice or action orientation. Theoretical or descriptive knowledge must therefore relate itself to the examples of realised good in common life through dialogue with common people.

5.4.3. Theory and Art

These theorists argue that even an art or practice or skill may have a theory or may be theoretical. This set of four sentences or four types of knowledge describe knowledge in its entirety. An art, while being performing or iterative, would also require injunctions in order to delimit the performance and to remain correct. Similarly a theory would require, apart from the descriptive propositions, an injunction to limit the iterated performance on the nominal, through an iterated or algorithmic procedure, etc. However, while a theory pays strict attention to the descriptive propositions, an art or skill may pay stricter attention to the procedure or to the injunction or even to the characteristics that are nominal.

5.4.4. Vidya and Pedagogy

A *vidya* is defined differently. It is defined by virtue of the good that is entailed to the performer. *Vidya* is classified according to the destination. Some treatises define 64, others define 16 types of *vidya*, according to the particular good that it allows the performer to attain by way of exercising or performing through the concepts as laid out in that particular pedagogy. This classification tacitly assumes multiple forms of good, and defines a pedagogy according to the variabilities of good sought. Necessarily, concepts in this *vidya* are laid out in any of the four types of sentences described above. A pedagogy is defined in terms of a good in a such way that any performance on the pedagogic skill would necessarily involve the performer, the object of performance, the good to be attained, and above all a social milieu where the pedagogy, the concepts and the good are to be either defended or the opponent's views and performances are to be refuted, through entering into a discourse, dialogue or debate.

5.4.5. Basic Education

In this tradition of educational practice, education is divided according to whether it is theoretical or non-theoretical. Since such a division does not refer to a hierarchy, Gandhi and Tagore preferred the use of the term basic education. A non-theoretical education is basic. The goal of a basic education is to enable a student to acquire the desired fruit through his or her own actions. Basic education not only enables a person, by imparting a skill, to undertake the right action, but also provides for the meaning or the acquisition of the fruit of that action. Moreover, in case the skill fails the person's reasoning, basic education provides for the inculcation of an attitude of truth.

Non-basic or higher education is primarily theoretical. Its emphases are on inferencing, theory-defending and theory-refuting. This emphasis on theory is due to the presence of a situation of discourse. The goal of higher education is conceptualisation, defending one's own concept and refuting the opponent's concept. The instrument of these activities is theory. Basic education, in contrast, is not engaged in building, defending or refuting theories. It is therefore not in a situation of discourse.

The defining characteristic of basic education is skill formation and attitude development in a non-discourse situation. This education is aimed at the conducting of a good practical life. It is thus not primary. It can be provided to any age group or to anyone having the desire to conduct a practical and pragmatic life.

Basic education too is describable in four sentences. In basic education too we require a source of injunction (the guru), an injunction, a causal description in the form of a theory, a set of names of the terms for which the action has been undertaken, and a set of rule-based integrated practices or action orientation. Indian practice in basic education puts great emphasis on some of these four types. Basic education has the goal of imparting a *vidya*. A *vidya* offers a realisable good. It is attained and maintained in a non-discourse environment.

5.4.6. Skill in Object Transformation

The conducting of a good practical life requires skill in material transformation. Acquiring such a skill is the primary goal of basic education. It must be recognised that this formulation of our preceptors, including Gandhi and Tagore, is not only practical and meant for the good of the broadest mass of people, but is also rational. Justification of this formulation is possible on grounds of politics as well as rationality.

We may consider the *charkha* and pottery as examples of productive engagement. Such an engagement provides the student with (a) a concrete material at hand, which is the basis for later empirical investigation or action, (b) meanings associated with the following of authoritative injunctions and optative statements or even rules, (c) iterated practice that provides the skill — a cognitive and bodily endowment not reducible to information, and (d) knowledge of the particular.

In fact the objective of engaging a child in a productive engagement is not the development of a productive skill. The development of a productive skill is undertaken at an age when the child may enter the profession as a probationer. The child's encounter with the material nominal through an engagement with the productive set-up, such as in the preparation of clay or in the mastering of turning the potter's wheel, lays the foundation for a bodily and cognitive endowment. Such an endowment alone can provide the child-student with (a) those spheres of feeling that provide for the cognitive reckoning of shapes, directions, number, etc.; (b) those spheres of transformation that provide for the bodily reckoning of the transformability of material, iterated actions, etc.; (c) those spheres of reasoning that provide for inference, causal descriptions, etc.; (d) those spheres of search that look for validation, if not in inference then at least in the cosmology or in the conducts laid out in the itihasa; and (e) the relationship between desire, meaning and action, such that the child can associate action with the realisation of a good, the satisfaction of desire, providing not only a valid meaning but also the grounds of rationality in action.

In short, the child-student's productive engagement with the material nominal provides the rational basis for action. A skilled action is the next state. Basic education provides the foundation for the development of skill. Basic education in the first few years may or may not impart a specific skill. It should, however, give the student the necessary rigorous drilling — continuous and iterated action, often following rules or authoritative prescriptions. A specific productive skill may be imparted to the grown-up student either at the premises of the school or at the premises of a production set-up. The first few years of basic education provide the foundation for this skill-building. The goal of basic education is to attain a *vidya* describable in terms of a realisable good.

5.4.7. Skill Institutions and Public Spaces

Vartashastra is about those concepts that deal with wealth generation, trade and commerce, manufacturing, social exchanges — in short, much of the contemporary disciplines that are devoted to the sciences of nature and life, engineering and technology, economics and sociology. This pedagogy, as we have argued above, is after those goods which by being related to wealth, commerce, economy, etc., offer rules, algorithms, etc. for the practice of the arts and skills in such a way as to secure a validation following the performance of the *vidya*.

Therefore, the realisable good being known, the vidya would ensure a valid concept only following the undertaking of the performance. Hence the institutional features should ensure the inculcation of a theoretical or algorithmic underpinning. Second, the *vidyas*, not being in need of prior validation, would not require a generalised epistemic or 'scientific', i.e., abstract, conceptual background.

Third, these vidyas should be primarily either descriptive or algorithmic, hence value or normativeness should not be of much concern. Fourth, these *vidyas* would not require, in general, dialogues in refutation, but would mostly depend on authority and dialogue for knowledge - hence apprenticeship. Fifth, as a result and since the good of the practical life is known, these *vidyas* would not require 'specialists' and 'theoreticians' to sermonise on the normative. Sixth, these *vidyas* are designed as though to cope with the vicissitudes of uncertainty, plausibility and multiplicity of values.

It has been conjectured, for example by Bankim, that social and pedagogic institutions in India of the pre-British period were harmonious, and therefore even in its lived worlds the theme of that harmony could be accepted institutionally, at least insofar as the authority of the sovereign was willing to achieve that. Therefore *pathshalas* were not just 'elementary' schools but primarily instructional institutions in the practice of the *vidyas* of the *vartashastra*. Such instructional schools were in close cooperation with the apprenticeship of the students in parts of the lived-in world, such as forging shops or agriculture or trade. Colonisation brought an end to this state of affairs, and by about the 1830s *pathshalas* were reduced to only elementary schools. By the middle of the nineteenth century the rural population had lost the knowledge of rules and algorithms. What remained at the turn of the century were a greatly impoverished rural people with no public space left for the attaining of good in practical life or for conducting a knowledgeable dialogue. Daily life in villages had become vicious. Many sensitive minds wrote about the deplorable state of rural Bengal.

Public spaces impregnated with knowledge used to be the norm. The practical life led by the vidyas of the vartashastra, as it was limited to the descriptive, could find cosmological and thematised expression through the rather regular narratives of the narrators (*kathak*), delivered as aesthetically as possible. By about the 1850s, slowly the narrators too were to leave the scene. Bankim Chandra lamented this in his essay on public education, and surely could see that newspapers were not an alternative. The other mode of public space, that had become largely restricted by the eighteenth century, and was to vanish by the third quarter of the nineteenth century, was the institution of public dialogue in refutation on the concepts and resolutions of the pedagogues. Quite importantly, it was not only the esoteric and the abstract reasoning of the contending pedagogues that used to draw the attention of learned minds; often such dialogues were conducted on important social and ethical problems. In fact the extent to which Rammohun Roy, Dayananda Saraswati or Vidyasagar could draw the attention of both English learned minds and traditional scholars in debates on the relevance of monism or of the Veda or regarding widow remarriage, etc., was possible only because of the remaining impressions of the earlier institutions of a knowledgeable public sphere. With the demise of there dialogues, this institution too first lost its importance and then ceased to exist.

5.5. Reconstruction of Education System

Rabindranath was one to understand early the limits of the 'nationalistic' approach to education. Aurobindo defined the nation as *dharma*; Tilak defined it through the space of action; Swami Vivekananda and Swami Dayananda defined the national awakening through disenchanted actions and through action-performance (*yajna*) for the achievement of a real; Bankim Chandra defined it through devotional practice and Bepin Chandra too through such devotional practice.

Rabindranath rejected the Western notion of the nation and declared categorically the meaninglessness of a 'national' approach to the reconstruction of India. To each of them, importance was to be attached to the power of the self acquired through practice. Rabindranath, in a series of essays, dwelt on the power of the self and that of the collective, and rejected any emphasis on the latter. The collective, he argued, was to be attained through the attainment of the good of the self. The good of the self is in knowledge, as much of it is in the seeking of the universal so much of it is in the reality of life — in its particularities and in its movement towards a better and enlightened life.

This was the period when Rabindranath went to the villages in order to examine the extent and causes of poverty, paucity of drinking water, ignorance and ill health. He came closest to the traditional understanding and realised the necessity of the institutions that would bridge, through knowledge and practice, the existing gap between pure and common knowledge. The former he conceptualised as the Vishvabharati and the latter as the Sriniketan. In this experiment, life in the dwelling is in tune with the quest for the knowledge beyond, and the knowledge of the beyond gets its form in the practical performances of the dwelling. Sriniketan was thus for the common villagers. It was to bring advanced agricultural engineering and practices, irrigation and potable water, craft skills and healthy practical life, and above all education to them. Vishvabharati was virtually in the same village. It was the centre of higher learning. It was not to follow, logically, curricula and contoured content as laid down by a discipline. The dialogue in knowledge, as its motto, was to be conducted in the open, not barred from the public. The other dialogue, with the common and the practical life, was to be necessarily in the open — in the public space, through such congregations as a mela.

Rabindranath was not alone. Many, young and old, gathered around him. More important was the spread of the idea. Schools or centres came up, or existing institutions were transformed, in Assam, Bihar, Punjab, Gujarat, Maharashtra, Tamil Nadu. The sources of the idea were many and the nature of experiments too was varied. Kaka Kalelkar and Satish Dasgupta were surely to be considered exemplary.

For many practitioners the other profound fountainhead was Mahatma Gandhi. Gandhi's insistence was on the conducting of a healthy practical life as the first and abiding minimum of any education.

Skilled living is the language of life. Gandhi therefore brought to skilled living and the employment of the mother tongue an eminence in the entire scheme of learning.

It is thus important to understand that each *vidya*, for Gandhi and for a very large number of other Indians, was to be defined by the characteristic good and also by characteristic concepts. Gandhi had said quite categorically:

> I am not opposed to education even of the highest type attainable in the world. The state must pay for it wherever it has definite use for it. I am opposed to all Higher Education being paid for from the general revenue. It is my firm conviction that the vast amount of the so-called education in arts given in our colleges is sheer waste. The medium of a foreign language through which Higher Education has been imparted in India has caused incalculable intellectual and moral injury to the nation.

He and others such as Vinoba Bhave argued that education had to be self-sustaining. The crucial point meant by this is that education has to be for a realisable good alone. He said:

There is no insurmountable barrier between what is called intellectual education and the crafts.... Training in arts and crafts offers full scope for the development of the intellect. And I venture to claim that without it the development of intellect is impossible.

The famed Wardha Educational Conference of 1937 had the following among other resolutions:

> Higher Education should be left to private enterprise and for meeting national requirements whether in the various industries, technical arts, belles-lettres or fine arts. The State Universities should be purely examining bodies, self-supporting.... Universities will look after the whole of the field of education and will prepare and approve courses of studies in the various departments of education.... University charters should be given liberally to any body of persons of proved worth and integrity....

The signatories to the Wardha Declaration included Zakir Hussain, Aryanayakam, Vinoba Bhave, Kakasaheb Kalelkar and K.T. Shah.

This was a remarkable scheme. It was very close to what the Indian epistemic or validational approach to divisions of pedagogies, development of vidyas and their institutionalisation would have called for in a contemporary setting. The modernity of this approach was in its deliberate attempt at creating a public space for dialogue in knowledge. Quite remarkably, such a space was not to be institutionalised around the university. It was meant to be popular and to be outside arbitration by the state.

Equally important it was that the pedagogies were considered in such a way as to obtain their evidential base from common, contemporary practical life and also, inter alia, to sustain the transformation of the art of the practical life into a vidya by way of enriched feedback from an evidentially enriched pedagogy.

This was therefore the second dimension of public space sustained through the interactions between the pedagogies and the vidyas. Pedagogies, for their finer enrichment, were to be primarily supported privately, and only in cases of national requirement would the state's endorsement be considered necessary. Hence a 'disciplinisation' through the enforcement of disciplines was entirely rejected. Finally, as his comments about economics show, he was convinced that each *vidya* and pedagogy was meant to secure a good of its own. This good, if it was to be part of the *vartashastra*, was surely to respond to the contemporary state of affairs in the world. Perhaps the only aspect that he did not specifically speak upon was the validational and epistemic departures of pedagogies.

There were others, however, especially from among scholars in Sanskrit, who categorically emphasised this point. In Bengal alone three great scholars responded. Mm. Phanibhusan Tarkavagis brought out in Bengali a detailed commentary along with the commentaries of Vatsyayana or the Nyaya aphorisms. Mm. Yogendranath Bagchi brought out several texts, often along with commentaries on the validational-epistemological basis of knowledge, as well as the necessary conditionality on the knowledge to have its own good. Pt. Panchanan Tarkaratna brought out annotated *Puranas* and other commentaries on such texts as would relate to good-pleasure, norms and ought, etc.

The emphasis they brought was both far-sighted and of contemporary concern, because they wanted the debate to take place around the pedagogical division of knowledge and its relation of sustenance to various vidyas, the relation of vidyas to practical life and good, the crucial importance of dialogues of various types, etc. Similar efforts were noticeable also at other places in India, notably at Banaras. Some other scholars and political leaders too joined this debate notably, Krishnachandra Bhattacharya; Radhakrishnan, Radhakamal Mukherjee, Benoy Kumar Sarkar, Bepin Pal, Aurobindo Ghosh etc..

This was a debate of importance. What is noteworthy is that the debate was reconstructed variously by the state machineries, the media and political parties in such a way as to disregard the theoretical dialogues of the Sanskrit scholars. The obvious result was that Gandhi could be reduced to allegedly non-modern positions, and the debate could be shifted to a wrongly posed question about modernity *vis-a-vis* its antinomy. The constructors of this false reading of the debate finally reaped the advantage by pushing away not only the aspirations of Sanskrit scholars but also those of Gandhi and Rabindranath. The advantages were reflected in the further spread of universities and colleges, strict enforcement of 'disciplines' and discipline-based professionalisation, through urbanisation and deepening of the dependency on English in especially higher education, decimation of the knowledgeable public and pedagogical dialogues, especially from small towns and villages, conversion of dialogues into media popularisation of 'issues', near-total dependency on Anglo-American universities for higher learning, etc. They were reduced to this virtual antinomian position to Gandhi who had spoken, in contrast, about a broader base of higher education and research in such areas as sciences, engineering, economics, other social and cultural studies.

The names of Benoy Sarkar and Srinivasa Sastri are worth mentioning in this regard. Sarkar had a creative engagement with education: since 1907 he was one of the architects of national education. Early in his life he established about a dozen national schools in the districts of Malda and Dacca, joined the N.C.E. of Calcutta as a professor, wrote on the science of education and on economics, sociology, history. He was perhaps one of the most able organisers and a gifted writer. In 1940 he published one of his public lectures in the *Calcutta Review* under the title 'Sociology of creative disequilibrium in education'.

Sarkar's thesis was thus in clear opposition to the views of both Gandhi and even partially of Rabindranath. Sarkar also had argued, in the same essay, not to look to state aid in the first instance or in the second instance, but to energise independently and strive individually as often and as long as possible without support from the governmental authorities. Presumably, to Sarkar Gandhi's Wardha scheme was pedagogically unsound as based on an incomplete and inadequate recognition of the diverse demands of the individual personality and the full-blooded 'creativity' of human beings.

Sarkar's opposition to Gandhi was thus based on creative disequilibriation in each individual; swaraj or autonomy of the literary, scientific, and aesthetic; no vidya or kala is so singularly fundamental that other vidyas can be sustained by that alone. It is important to recognise that these differences are based on arguments that are deep indeed; many contemporary European critics are also trying to reformulate the scheme of knowledge-division similarly. Sarkar at the same time knew and agreed with Gandhi's pragmatism. He argued that for educating the overwhelming majority of the Indian population the Wardha scheme could be trusted.

5.6. Redefining the Goals of Education

The above provides the rational basis of action to the student as an individual. Does the same education also generate a sense of social obligation? In fact, this basic education on productive and skilling engagement provides twin bases of social cooperation.

The first base is owing to the teacher-student relationship. This is a relation of initiator-initiated or instructor-instructed. The statements of an initiator are action sentences. Such sentences should not be vitiated by any self-interest on the part of the instructor. Understandably a basic instructor is more likely to qualify for such an attitude compared with an instructor meant for on-the-job training to grown-up students. The instructional utterances of a basic instructor initiate the child student. The child student clearly recognises the importance of this authoritative source, which can issue injunctional or optative utterances preferably not vitiated by self-interest. This gives rise to the recognition of an authority.

It is perhaps even more important that the student is taught the importance of the consent of others to the action being undertaken by him. Any action, with its goal, must be declared by the undertaker, and consent to this undertaking be sought beforehand. Such consent, it may be argued, is better than that based on such principles as the principle of no-harm. This is also non-normative. Consent-seeking, being clearly non-moral, seeks to arrive at a judgement on the future. This is a superior principle of social action. However, it does not provide the bases for collaborative action. Action-orientation is one of the primary goals of a basic education. This orientation, according to Tagore, Gandhi or the other preceptors, is individualistic. The objective of basic education is to orient the individual student to undertake one's own action. In order to undertake and prior to commencing one's own action, the student must fulfil his or her debt obligation and seek consent.

Skilled practice and the transformation of objects are but little known theoretically. Basic education need not theories on this transformational practice; neither does it need to defended against an alternative practice. In fact value-pluralities and rule-pluralities are welcomed in basic education. The good of a *vidya* is unique, while action peculiarities are non-unique or plural. Basic education nurtures a respect and a dignity for the plural. However, what basic education requires is an attitude towards useful action in an unknown domain. Such an attitude, needing imagination and memory, is provided by the fabulous narratives.

One source of knowledge about one's obligations is the conduct of the preceptors. In its absence, cosmological or historical narrations on conduct appear significant. Therefore basic education does not put an emphasis on moral teaching or on the 'conscientisation' of the pupil. In contrast, it offers a pragmatic ground, through the lived life of the preceptors, to the attitude towards obligation.

5.7. Aesthetic Values in Education

Most important, perhaps, is the significance of *abhinaya* and *nataka* in basic education. The aesthetic elements here are derived from a taste of the performances that one has undertaken. This aesthetic is not derived from the goal of the action; on the contrary it is derived from the taste of the performance. Interestingly the student learns that life, roles in life and conduct in life are not damningly serious. The consternation that one faces in a contemporary school, where the children are shown a life of deadening commitment, is indeed to be laughed at.

Indian basic education is based on playfulness and an aesthetic of tasting the performances. Knowledge, according to Indian theory, is not based on the intersubjective world. The intersubjective world is either for a discourse or for *abhinaya*. Such a world has to be lived in aesthetically, i.e., with an attitude and through playing. Since basic education provides a non-discourse environment, it puts great emphasis on the aesthetic and the playfulness of *abhinaya* and *nataka*. Rabindranath designed basic education on this line. Bankim theoretically argued for it, and Gandhi thought that it was inseparable from basic education.

Cooperative work is based on cooperation between a few role-performances. A minimum of four roles are conceived. The first role is to issue authoritative instruction, based primarily on rules of performance. The second role is to describe or delineate the causal connectives, to infer, etc. The third role is to make use of narratives and to imagine. The fourth role is to put together these three and act.

The descriptive parts of the narration trains the student to understand causal relations. Such training gives the mind a capacity to investigate and enquire, to infer and to lay bare causal associations. Much of this is known as science in contemporary jargon.

Recalling the student's engagement with the charkha, from whence he acquires the bodily-cognitive skill, we may now understand that the causal description and the fabulous history enable him to undertake independent action. This is the goal of non-theoretical basic education. The goal is to enable the student to acquire skill and to undertake action independently that is perhaps partly known to him descriptively and partly known to him as narration from memory or tradition. This unknowable, or the unknown, can be acted upon by the student only if he/she has an attitude of truth and the consent of others. Such a consensual situation does not allow the student to initiate action that could be harmful to living organisms and to the tradition.

This provides us with a pedagogy and the goal of basic education, which form the summary of experience in conducting a variety of experimental basic schools by our preceptors. These schools have followed the ideas of Gandhi and Tagore and of tradition. Our attempt is to re-emphasise the importance of productive engagement and of attitude in non-theoretical basic education.

5.8. Education for an Enlightened Society

We may note a few distinctive features in the history of Indian education. Primary education was widespread even as late as the early nineteenth century. Often nearly every village would have a school, to which children would come from nearly all the population groups proportionately. Second, the curricula were the result of long practice as well as of its engagement with productive activities. There was neither any state financial support nor any control over curricula. Third, the public space of popular life and institutions was often constituted around (a) dialogue with theoretical education through varieties of institutions and fabulous historical narrations; (b) dialogue with productive activities; and (c) an attitude that was non-normative but one of forbearance, aesthetic and truth.

These unique features did not provide for a segmentation of education. The British colonial attempt was to replace this with segmented educational institutions and segmented educational content. Such attempts were resisted. Contemporary Indian education bespeaks this confrontation.

In this institution there are therefore two basic elements. First is a drilling in a productive engagement such that the student may acquire skill. Second is the inculcation of an attitude of aesthetic, of truth, so that the student can engage with the world later in life, fearlessly, in order to know and enjoy the realised good.

It is important also to recognise the institutional aspects of this approach. The distinctive features of the institution are that (a) it does not segment education in a hierarchy but divides knowledge and discourse epistemologically and therefore non-hierarchically; (b) it is not based on a divide between theory and practice and does not reduce science to a set of information - it brings knowledge to the common people; (c) science no longer remains in isolation but is created anew skilfully while the discourse with abstract theories of science continues through narration, description and an attitude of truth.

As a result, skilled practice receives its nourishment from advances in science. The student trainee becomes responsible to others in society. In short, this approach leads to an enlightened society. What is relevant socially and politically is that education becomes widespread, nourished by the material availability in its locale; it is maintained and nurtured by the local people, trained by local skill masters. It must be mentioned that this is most environment friendly as well. Such a basic education skills the population, nurtures aesthetic and an attitude of truth and of cooperative work.

5.9. Education for Good Citizenship

The debate about the aims of education, particularly in relation to the values which schools should try to inculcate in students, has, in recent times, been used by politicians as a means of justifying educational policies which support particular conservative ideological commitments. In Australia, for example, conservative politicians, committed to economic rationalism and the introduction of the market into education, have asserted that private schools provide a much better education in values than government schools. These latter schools, it is said, are generally controlled by teachers hostile to the prevailing educational philosophy of the government, which is concerned with the maintenance of educational standards and a curriculum which emphasises the basics of literacy and numeracy. Moreover, some of these schools are accused of being hotbeds of political correctness spreading dangerous, un-Australian views and worse still, undermining solid Australian values. Successive conservative governments in England allowed the 'market' to be the key mechanism for distributing educational resources and making market forces the levers of social and cultural change. In the process the conservatives successfully appropriated an educational vocabulary which could be used to lambast those schools that did not conform to their particular conception of excellence. In taking control of educational discourse, the conservatives moved the debate about educational aims away from a serious consideration of the role of education in politics and culture to a debate about how their particular vision of the good society could best be implemented and the role of education in that implementation.

There are interesting parallels to drawn here with the Australian government, which has used similar tactics in Australia, turning terms such as political correctness into pejoratives. Notwithstanding these populist tactics, there is a serious question to be asked about the nature of the values which education should be concerned to impart, since it is something of truism that there can be no neutral stance on values. Since children are the citizens of the future and the State has a stake in the kinds of adults that schools produce, a vital consideration is the kind of education that is needed for good citizenship.

References

Budhanda Swami. 1983. *How to Build Character A Primer* : Ramakrishna Mission, New Delhi.

Downey, M and Kelly, A.V. 1978. *Moral Education: Theory and Practice*, Harper and Row, London.

Power, F.C. . Higgins A. and Kolnberg L. 1989. *Approach to Moral Education,* Columbia University Press, New York.

Reddy V.N.K. 1979. *Man Education and Values*, B.R. Publishing, Delhi.

Rama Rao, K. 1986. *Moral Education: A practical approach*, Ramakrishna Institute of Moral and Spiritual Education, Mysore.

6

Education for Sustainable Development

Education is an essential tool for achieving sustainability. People around the world recognise that current economic development trends are not sustainable and that public awareness, education, and training are key to moving society toward sustainability. Beyond that, there is little agreement. People argue about the meaning of sustainable development and whether or not it is attainable. They have different visions of what sustainable societies will look like and how they will function. These same people wonder why educators have not moved more quickly to develop education for sustainability (EfS) programmes. The lack of agreement and definition have stymied efforts to move education for sustainable development (ESD) forward.

It is curious to note that while we have difficulty envisioning a sustainable world, we have no difficulty identifying what is unsustainable in our societies. We can rapidly create a laundry list of problems: inefficient use of energy, lack of water conservation, increased pollution, abuses of human rights, overuse of personal transportation, consumerism, etc. But we should not chide ourselves because we lack a clear definition of sustainability. Indeed, many truly great concepts of the human world — among them democracy and justice — are hard to define and have multiple expressions in cultures around the world. Three terms can be used synonymously and interchangeably: education for sustainable development (ESD), education for sustainability (EfS), and sustainability education (SE). We use ESD most often, because it is the terminology used frequently at the international level and within UN documents. Locally or nationally, the ESD effort may be named or described in many ways because of language and cultural differences. As with all work related to sustainable development, the name and the content must be locally relevant and culturally appropriate.

An important distinction is the difference between education *about* sustainable development and education *for* sustainable development. The first is an awareness lesson or theoretical discussion. The second is the use of education as a tool to achieve sustainability. In our opinion, more than a theoretical discussion is needed at this critical juncture in time. While some people argue that "for" indicates indoctrination, we think "for" indicates a purpose. All education serves a purpose or society would not invest in it. Driver education, for example, seeks to make our roads safer for travelers. Fire-safety education seeks to prevent fires and tragic loss of lives and property. ESD promises to make the world more livable for this and future generations. Of course, a few will abuse or distort ESD and turn it into indoctrination. This would be antithetical to the nature of ESD, which, in fact, calls for giving people knowledge and skills for lifelong learning to help them find new solutions to their environmental, economic, and social issues.

6.1. Concept of Sustainable Development

Sustainable development is a difficult concept to define; it is also continually evolving, which makes it doubly difficult to define. One of the original descriptions of sustainable development is credited to the Brundtland Commission: "Sustainable development is development that meets the needs of the present without compromising the ability of future generations to meet their own needs."

Sustainable development is generally thought to have three components: environment, society, and economy. The well-being of these three areas is intertwined, not separate. For example, a healthy, prosperous society relies on a healthy environment to provide food and resources, safe drinking water, and clean air for its citizens. The sustainability paradigm rejects the contention that casualties in the environmental and social realms are inevitable and acceptable consequences of economic development. Thus, sustainability can be consider to be a paradigm for thinking about a future in which environmental, societal, and economic considerations are balanced in the pursuit of development and improved quality of life.

6.2. Education and Sustainability

From the time sustainable development was first endorsed at the UN General Assembly in 1987, the parallel concept of education to support sustainable development has also been explored. From 1987 to 1992, the concept of sustainable development matured as committees discussed, negotiated, and wrote the 40 chapters of *Agenda 21*. Initial thoughts concerning ESD were captured in Chapter 36 of *Agenda 21*, "Promoting Education, Public Awareness, and Training."

Unlike most education movements, ESD was initiated by people outside of the education community. In fact, one major push for ESD came from international political and economic forums (e.g., United Nations Organisation for Economic Cooperation and Development, Organisation of American States). As the concept of sustainable development was discussed and formulated, it became apparent that education is key to sustainability. In many countries, ESD is still being shaped by those outside the education community. The concepts and content of ESD in these cases are developed by ministries, such as those of environment and health, and then given to educators to deliver. Conceptual development independent of educator input is a problem recognised by international bodies as well as educators.

6.2.1. Population and Resource Consumption

Two of the major issues in the international dialogue on sustainability are population and resource consumption. Increases in population and resource use are thought to jeopardise a sustainable future, and education is linked both to fertility rate and resource consumption. Educating females reduces fertility rates and therefore population growth. By reducing fertility rates and the threat of overpopulation a country also facilitates progress toward sustainability. The opposite is true for the relationship between education and resource use. Generally, more highly educated people, who have higher incomes, consume more resources than poorly educated people, who tend to have lower incomes. In this case, more education increases the threat to sustainability.

Unfortunately, the most educated nations leave the deepest ecological footprints, meaning they have the highest per-capita rates of consumption. This consumption drives resource extraction and manufacturing around the world. The figures from the United Nations Educational, Scientific and Cultural Organisation (UNESCO) *Statistical Yearbook and World Education Report*, for example, show that in the United States more than 80 per cent of the population has some post-secondary education, and about 25 per cent of the population has a four-year degree from a university. Statistics also show that per-capita energy use and waste generation in the United States are nearly the highest in the world. In the case of the United States, more education has not led to sustainability. Clearly, simply educating citizenry to higher levels is not sufficient for creating sustainable societies. The challenge is to raise the education levels without creating an ever-growing demand for resources and consumer goods and the accompanying production of pollutants. Meeting this challenge depends on reorienting curriculums to address the need for more sustainable production and consumption patterns.

Every nation will need to re-examine curriculum at all levels (i.e., pre-school to professional education). While it is evident that it is difficult to teach environmental literacy, economics literacy, or civics without basic literacy, it is also evident that simply increasing basic literacy, as it is currently taught in most countries, will not support a sustainable society.

Consider, for instance, that when education levels are low, economies are often limited to resource extraction and agriculture. In many countries, the current level of basic education is so low that it severely hinders development options and plans for a sustainable future. A higher education level is necessary to create jobs and industries that are "greener" and more sustainable.

The relationship between education and sustainable development is complex. Generally, research shows that basic education is key to a nation's ability to develop and achieve sustainability targets. Research has shown that education can improve agricultural productivity, enhance the status of women, reduce population growth rates, enhance environmental protection, and generally raise the standard of living. But the relationship is not linear. For example, four to six years of education is the minimum threshold for increasing agricultural productivity. Literacy and numeracy allow farmers to adapt to new agricultural methods, cope with risk, and respond to market signals. Literacy also helps farmers mix and apply chemicals according to manufacturers' directions, thereby reducing the risks to the environment and human health. A basic education also helps farmers gain title to their land and apply for credit at banks and other lending institutions. Effects of education on agriculture are greatest when the proportion of females educated to threshold level equals that of males.

6.2.2. Education of Women

Education benefits a woman in life-altering ways. An educated woman gains higher status and an enhanced sense of efficacy. She tends to marry later and have greater bargaining power and success in the "marriage market." She also has greater bargaining power in the household after marriage. An educated woman tends to desire a smaller family size and seek the health care necessary to do so. She has fewer and healthier children. An educated woman has high educational and career expectations of her children, both boys and girls. For females, education profoundly changes their lives, how they interact with society, and their economic status. Educating women creates more equitable lives for women and their families and increases their ability to participate in community decision making and work toward achieving local sustainability goals.

Another educational threshold is primary education for women. At least a primary education is required before birthrate drops and infant health and children's education improve. Nine to 12 years of education are required for increased industrial productivity. This level of education also increases the probability of employment in a changing economy. Few studies have been carried out on how education affects environmental stewardship, but one study suggests that a lower-secondary education is necessary to intensify use of existing land and to provide alternative off-farm employment and migration from rural areas. Finally, a subtle combination of higher education, research, and lifelong learning is necessary for a nation to shift to an information or knowledge-based economy, which is fuelled less by imported technology and more by local innovation and creativity.

6.3. Direct Impact of Education on Sustainability

Education directly affects sustainability plans in the following three areas:

6.3.1. Implementation

An educated citizenry is vital to implementing informed and sustainable development. In fact, a national sustainability plan can be enhanced or limited by the level of education attained by the nation's citizens. Nations with high illiteracy rates and unskilled workforces have fewer development options. For the most part, these nations are forced to buy energy and manufactured goods on the international market with hard currency. To acquire hard currency, these countries need international trade; usually this leads to exploitation of natural resources or conversion of lands from self-sufficient family-based farming to cash-crop agriculture. An educated workforce is key to moving beyond an extractive and agricultural economy.

6.3.2. Decision making

Good community-based decisions — which will affect social, economic, and environmental well-being — also depend on educated citizens. Development options, especially "greener" development options, expand as education increases. For example, a community with an abundance of skilled labor and technically trained people can persuade a corporation to locate a new information-technology and software-development facility nearby. Citizens can also act to protect their communities by analysing reports and data that address community issues and helping shape a community response. For example, citizens who were concerned about water pollution reported in a nearby watershed started monitoring the water quality of local streams. Based on their data and information found on the World Wide Web, they fought against the development of a new golf-course, which would have used large amounts of fertiliser and herbicide in maintenance of the grounds.

6.3.3. Quality of Life

Education is also central to improving quality of life. Education raises the economic status of families; it improves life conditions, lowers infant mortality, and improves the educational attainment of the next generation, thereby raising the next generation's chances for economic and social well-being. Improved education holds both individual and national implications.

6.3.4. Component of ESD

Education is held to be central to sustainability. Indeed, education and sustainability are inextricably linked, but the distinction between education as we know it and education for sustainability is enigmatic for many. The following section describes the components of education for sustainability.

ESD carries with it the inherent idea of implementing programmes that are locally relevant and culturally appropriate. All sustainable development programs including ESD must take into consideration the local environmental, economic, and societal conditions. As a result, ESD will take many forms around the world.

ESD was first described by Chapter 36 of *Agenda 21*. This chapter identified four major thrusts to begin the work of ESD: (1) improve basic education, (2) reorient existing education to address sustainable development, (3) develop public understanding, awareness, and (4) training.

6.3.5. Improving Basic Education

The first priority of ESD as outlined in Chapter 36 is the promotion of basic education. The content and years of basic education differ greatly around the world. In some countries, for instance, primary school is considered basic education. In others eight or 12 years is mandatory. In many countries, basic education focuses on reading, writing, and ciphering. Pupils learn to read the newspaper, write letters, figure accounts and develop skills necessary to fulfil their expected roles in their households and community. Girls, for example, may learn about nutrition and nursing. Pupils also learn how their government functions and about the world beyond their community.

Simply increasing basic literacy, as it is currently taught in most countries, will not advance sustainable societies. Indeed, if communities and nations hope to identify sustainability goals and work toward them, they must focus on skills, values, and perspectives that encourage and support public participation and community decision making. To achieve this, basic education must be reoriented to address sustainability and expanded to include critical-thinking skills, skills to organise and interpret data and information, skills to formulate questions, and the ability to analyse issues that confront communities.

In many countries, the current level of basic education is too low, severely hindering national plans for a sustainable future. In Latin America and the Caribbean, many countries have six to eight years of compulsory education with approximately five to 15 per cent of the students repeating one or more years. In parts of Asia, especially Bangladesh, Pakistan and India, many children only attend school for an average of five years. A complicating factor in this region is that many girls receive fewer years of schooling to create that average. In parts of Africa, where life is disturbed by drought or war, the average attendance in public education is measured in months, not years. Unfortunately, the lowest quality of education is often found in the poorest regions or communities. The impact of little and/or poor-quality education severely limits the options available to a nation for developing its short- and long-term sustainability plans.

As nations turned their attention to education in the 1990s and the new millennium, they have made much progress in basic education. In fact, enrolment rates in primary education are rising in most regions of the world. Also, enrolment of girls has increased faster than that of boys, which is helping to close the gender gap evident in so many countries. At the global level, the gender gap in both primary and secondary school is narrowing. Despite all of this progress, too many female children remain out of school, and the gender gap has not closed prior to the "Education For All" target date of 2005. The recognition of the need for quality basic education sets ESD apart from other educational efforts, such as environmental education or population education.

6.3.6. Reorienting Existing Education

The term "reorienting education" has become a powerful descriptor that helps administrators and educators at every level to understand the changes required for ESD. An appropriately reoriented basic education includes more principles, skills, perspectives, and values related to sustainability than are currently included in most education systems. Hence, it is not only a question of quantity of education, but also one of appropriateness and relevance. ESD encompasses a vision that integrates environment, economy and society. Reorienting education also requires teaching and learning knowledge, skills, perspectives, and values that will guide and motivate people to pursue sustainable livelihoods, to participate in a democratic society and to live in a sustainable manner.

The need to reorient basic and secondary education to address sustainability has grabbed international attention, but the need at the university level is just as great. Society's future leaders and decision makers are educated there. If these young people are expected to lead all sectors of society in a world striving toward sustainability, then the current administration and faculty members must reorient university curriculums to include the many and complex facets of sustainability.

In reorienting education to address sustainability, program developers need to balance looking forward to a more sustainable society with looking back to traditional ecological knowledge. Indigenous traditions often carry with them the values and practices that embody sustainable resource use. While returning to indigenous lifestyles is not an option for the millions of urban dwellers, the values and major tenets of indigenous traditions can be adapted to life in the 21st century.

Reorienting education to address sustainability is something that should occur throughout the formal education system; that includes universities, professional schools, and technical schools in addition to primary and secondary education.

6.3.7. Public Understanding and Awareness

Sustainability requires a population that is aware of the goals of a sustainable society and has the knowledge and skills to contribute to those goals. The need for an informed voting citizenry becomes ever more important with the increase in the number of democratic governments. An informed voting citizenry, which lends support to enlightened policies and government initiatives, can help governments enact sustainable measures. Citizens also need to be knowledgeable consumers who can see beyond the "green wash". In today's world, people are surrounded by media and advertisements. As a result, people must become media literate and able to analyze the messages of corporate advertisers.

Years of resource management has shown that a public that is aware of and informed about resource-management decisions and programmes can help achieve program goals. In contrast, an uninformed public can undermine resource-management programmes. Education has also been essential in many other types of programmes, such as public-health efforts to stop the spread of specific diseases.

6.3.8. Training

The world needs a literate and environmentally aware citizenry and work force to help guide nations in implementing their sustainability plans. All sectors — including business, industry, higher education, governments, nongovernmental organisations (NGOs) and community organisation — are encouraged to train their leaders in environmental management and to provide training to their workers.

Training is distinct from education in that training is often specific to a particular job or class of jobs. Training teaches workers how to use equipment safely, be more efficient, and comply with regulations. For instance, a training programme might teach workers to avoid changing the waste stream without notifying their supervisor. Further, if an employee is involved in a nonroutine activity, such as cleaning a new piece of equipment, she or he is instructed not to dispose of the cleaning solvent by pouring it down a storm sewer drain that leads to the river. Some training, such as training women to use solar cookers rather than cooking on open, wood-fuelled fires, involves tremendous change in social dynamics and practices. In this case, women must not only learn the mechanics of solar cookers, but they must also change daily routines of meal preparation to cook while the sun is high in the sky, rather than in the evening. Training informs people of accepted practices and procedures and gives them skills to perform specific tasks. In contrast, education is a socially transforming process that gives people knowledge, skills, perspectives, and values through which they can participate in and contribute to their own well-being and that of their community and nation.

6.3.9. Formal, Non-formal and Informal Education

For a community or a nation, implementing ESD is a huge task. Fortunately, formal education does not carry this educational responsibility alone. The nonformal educational sector and the informal educational sector of the educational community must work cooperatively with the formal educational sector for the education of people in all generations and walks of life. Because ESD is a lifelong process, the formal, non-formal, and informal educational sectors should work together to accomplish local sustainability goals. In an ideal world, the three sectors would divide the enormous task of ESD for the entire population by identifying target audiences from the general public as well as themes of sustainability. They would then work within their mutually agreed upon realms. This division of effort would reach a broader spectrum of people and prevent redundant efforts.

6.4. Reorienting Education for Sustainability

ESD is more than a knowledge base related to environment, economy and society. It also addresses learning skills, perspectives and values that guide and motivate people to seek sustainable livelihoods, participate in a democratic society, and live in a sustainable manner. ESD also involves studying local and, when appropriate, global issues. Therefore, these five must all be addressed in a formal curriculum that has been reoriented to address sustainability. Simply adding more to the curriculum will not be feasible in most schools; they already have a full curriculum. Deciding what to leave out — what does not contribute to sustainability or is obsolete — is an integral part of the reorienting process. Let's look more closely at these five components of an education reoriented to address sustainability.

6.4.1. Knowledge

Sustainable development encompasses environment, economics, and society. Therefore, people need basic knowledge from the natural sciences, social sciences, and humanities to understand the principles of sustainable development, how they can be implemented, the values involved, and ramifications of their implementation. Knowledge based on traditional disciplines supports ESD.

The challenge for communities in the process of creating ESD curriculums will be to select knowledge that will support their sustainability goals. An accompanying challenge will be to let go of those topics that have been successfully taught for years but are no longer relevant. In the event that your community has not defined sustainability goals, you can substitute principles and guidelines for sustainability.

6.4.2. Issues

ESD focuses largely on the major social, economic, and environmental issues that threaten the sustainability of the planet. Many of these key issues were identified at the Earth Summit in Rio de Janeiro and are found in *Agenda 21*. Understanding and addressing these issues are the heart of ESD, and locally relevant issues should be included in any programme related to educating for sustainability. While *Agenda 21* clearly identifies many of the critical issues that governments around the world agreed to address, additional issues were discussed for which no formal international agreement or plan of action could be reached. In addition, issues that are important to enhancing the understanding of sustainability have continued to emerge since the Rio de Janeiro conference. These additional issues, not included in Agenda 21, are part of international discussions of sustainability and include, but are not limited to, topic such as war and militarism, governance, discrimination and nationalism, renewable energy sources, multinational corporations, refugees, nuclear disarmament, human rights, and media influencing rapid change of worldviews. These issues are pertinent to reorienting education to address sustainability and should be included when relevant. Including local issues will foster innovative solutions and develop the political will to resolve them.

The last major content area in educating for sustainability stems from the major UN conferences in the 1990s and new millenium that expanded our understanding of sustainable development. Each conference advanced understanding of issues that cause much suffering and threaten global sustainability. Each conference also developed a series of requests for public awareness and understanding and identified the individual responsibilities and behaviour changes that would ameliorate each issue.

Communities creating ESD curriculums cannot teach all of the issues associated with *Agenda 21*, the statements of principles and conventions, and these major UN conferences. The quantity of study would be overwhelming. Communities should, however, select a few issues in each of the three realms: environment, economics and society. The issues selected should be locally relevant. For example, a landlocked country could study sustainable mountain development and either ignore or lightly cover protecting and managing the oceans. Some topics, such as women in sustainable development or combating poverty, have relevance to every country.

6.4.3. Skills

To be successful, ESD must go beyond teaching about these global issues. ESD must give people practical skills that will enable them to continue learning after they leave school, to have a sustainable livelihood, and to live sustainable lives. These skills will differ with community conditions. The following list demonstrates the types of skills pupils will need as adults. Note that skills fall into one or more of the three realms of sustainable development: environmental, economic, and social.

a) The ability to communicate effectively (both orally and in writing).
b) The ability to think about systems (both natural and social sciences).
c) The ability to think in time — to forecast, to think ahead, and to plan.
d) The ability to think critically about value issues.
e) The ability to separate number, quantity, quality, and value.
f) The capacity to move from awareness to knowledge to action.

g) The ability to work cooperatively with other people.

h) The capacity to use these processes: knowing, inquiring, acting, judging, imagining, connecting, valuing and choosing.

i) The capacity to develop an aesthetic response to the environment.

In addition, pupils will need to learn skills that will help them manage and interact with the local environment. Such locally relevant skills may include learning to:

a) Prepare materials for recycling.

b) Harvest wild plants without jeopardising future natural regeneration and production.

c) Grow low-water-need cotton.

d) Draw water from unpolluted sources.

6.4.4. Perspectives

ESD carries with it perspectives that are important for understanding global issues as well as local issues in a global context. Every issue has a history and a future. Looking at the roots of an issue and forecasting possible futures based on different scenarios are part of ESD, as is understanding that many global issues are linked. For example, overconsumption of such consumer goods as paper leads to deforestation, which is thought to be related to global climate change.

The ability to consider an issue from the view of different stakeholders is essential to ESD. Considering an issue from another viewpoint besides your own leads to intra-national and international understanding. This understanding is essential for creating the mood of cooperation that will underpin sustainable development. The following is a partial list of perspectives associated with ESD. Students understand that:

a) Social and environmental problems change through time and have a history and a future.

b) Contemporary global environmental issues are linked and interrelated between and among themselves.

c) Humans have universal attributes (e.g., they love their children).

d) Looking at their community as well as looking beyond the confines of local and national boundaries is necessary to understand local issues in a global context.

e) Considering differing views before reaching a decision or judgement is necessary.

f) Economic values, religious values, and societal values compete for importance as people of different interests and backgrounds interact.

g) Technology and science alone cannot solve all of our problems.

h) Individuals are global citizens in addition to citizens of the local community.

i) Individual consumer decisions and other actions effect resource extraction and manufacturing in distant places.

j) Employing the precautionary principle by taking action to avoid the possibility of serious or irreversible environmental or social harm even when scientific knowledge is incomplete or inconclusive is necessary for the long-term well-being of their community and planet.

When taught to a generation of pupils, such perspectives will become infused into local worldviews.

6.4.5. Values and Social Justice

Values are also an integral part of ESD. In some cultures, values are taught overtly in the schools. In other cultures, however, even if values are not taught overtly, they are modeled, explained, analysed, or discussed. In both situations, understanding values is an essential part of understanding your own worldview and other people's viewpoints. Understanding your own values, the values of the society you live in, and the values of others around the world is a central part of educating for a sustainable future. Two common techniques — values clarification and values analysis — are useful to the values component of ESD.

In ESD, values have different roles in the curriculum. In some ESD efforts, pupils adopt certain values as a direct result of instruction or modeling of accepted values. In other cultures, studying the relationship between society and the environment leads pupils to adopt values derived from their studies. In cultures where inquisitiveness is encouraged, pupils come to value curiosity and questioning. In democratic societies, pupils also develop shared values around concepts of democratic process, community participation in decision making, volunteerism, and social justice. Each of these approaches contributes to the overall goal of sustainability.

Social justice is another realm of study that involves values. Social justice, which is considered a central part of ESD in most countries, includes meeting basic human needs and concern for the rights, dignity and welfare of all people. It includes respect for the traditions and religions of other societies and cultures, and it fosters empathy for the life conditions of other peoples. Ecological sustainability and resource conservation are considered part of social justice. Preserving and conserving the resource base of others prevents people from living in disadvantaged circumstances. Social justice concerns related to preservation of resources (e.g., fossil fuels, old-growth forests, and species diversity) extends to future generations; this is called inter generational equity. Values taught in school need to reflect the larger values of the society that surrounds the school. Where appropriate, the opinions of community members can be solicited. Then, a full range of values influenced by local traditions, aboriginal groups, ethnic populations, immigrants, religions, media and pop culture will be revealed, inventoried and considered for relation to and inclusion in ESD. In addition, curriculum decisionmakers will decide if new values, which will help communities reach their goals of sustainability, need to be included in the curriculum.

6.4.6. Strengths Model

The cost of reorienting education to address sustainability is so great that nations cannot afford to rely on a remediation model to retrain the world's 59,000,000 teachers. Rather than primarily retraining inservice teachers to teach sustainability, we need to design new approaches to pre-service and inservice teacher education to address sustainability. One such innovative approach is the "strengths model." In this approach, every discipline and every teacher can contribute to sustainability education. Many topics inherent in ESD are already part of the formal education curriculum, but these topics are not identified or seen to contribute to the larger concept of sustainability. Identifying and recognising components of ESD is key to moving forward. Fortunately this step is easy and affordable.

To implement the strengths model, begin by ensuring that educators and administrators understand the concept of sustainability and are familiar with its principles. Once they understand the concept of sustainability, educators from each discipline can examine the curriculum and school activities for existing contributions to ESD. Next, educators can identify potential areas of the existing curriculum in which to insert examples that illustrate sustainability or additional knowledge, issues, perspective, skills or values related to sustainability.

After identifying existing and potential contributions, leaders can create awareness among the educational community of these contributions to the larger ESD picture. Then, these contributions can be woven together to create ESD programmes that are taught overtly to pupils and students. In this approach, the synergistic strengths of combined educational disciplines can convey the knowledge, issues, skills, perceptions and values associated with ESD.

No one discipline can or should claim ownership of ESD. In fact, ESD poses such broad and encompassing challenges that it requires contributions from many disciplines. For example, consider these disciplinary contributions to ESD:

a) Mathematics helps students understand extremely small numbers (e.g., parts per hundred, thousand, or million), which allows them to interpret pollution data.

b) Language Arts, especially media literacy, creates knowledgeable consumers who can analyse the messages of corporate advertisers and see beyond "green wash."

c) History teaches the concept of global change, while helping students to recognise that change has occurred for centuries.

d) Reading develops the ability to distinguish between fact and opinion and helps students become critical readers of political campaign literature.

e) Social Studies helps students to understand ethnocentrism, racism, and gender inequity as well as to recognise how these are expressed in the surrounding community and nations worldwide.

Each discipline also has associated pedagogical techniques. The combined pedagogical techniques and strategies of each discipline contribute to an expanded vision of how to teach for creativity, critical thinking, and a desire for life-long learning — all mental habits that support sustainable societies.

The contributions of the environmental education and science education communities to the environmental strand of ESD have been well-documented in the literature; however, equal attention has not been focused on the social and economic strands. Yet, the efforts of schools to create more just, peaceable, and equitable societies suggest that the social strand appears to be well-developed in many countries. In fact, schools that have programmes in multicultural education, anti-racist education, gender equity, anti-bullying, and peace education contribute substantially to the social strand of ESD.

Use of this strengths model requires that a cadre of educators and administrators, who are sufficiently well-versed in the transdisciplinary concepts inherent in ESD, pull together the disciplinary and pedagogical pieces to form a comprehensive ESD programme. The integration process will prevent omissions and duplication. In order to create a generation of educators and administrators who understand the strengths model, it must be employed by institutions of teacher education and overtly taught to pre-service professionals.

6.5. Evolving Nature of ESD

In reorienting education to address sustainability, it is important for educators not to lock the definition, content, scope, and methodology of ESD into a static timeframe. The temptation exists to use *Agenda 21* to define ESD curriculums; however, the global discussion and understanding of sustainability has grown greatly since the 1992 Earth Summit. Educational efforts must reflect this broader understanding and its evolving nature.

While *Agenda 21* clearly identifies critical issues that governments around the world need to address, the concept of sustainability continues to evolve as societies change and as our awareness and perceptions of Earth, humanity and human-environmental interactions correspondingly change. Subtle changes, such as a shift in focus or emphasis, will of course be regional in nature and reflect the conditions of local ecosystems and cultures. As a result of the maturing nature of sustainability issues, those educating for sustainability should continually adapt the content, scope and methodology within geographic and temporal contexts. This constant adaptation will require flexibility on the part of educators as they work together on local and international projects. Definitions and practices that are admirably effective in one part of the world can be ineffective or inappropriate in another.

6.5.1. Challenges and Impediments to ESD

While many nations around the world have embraced the need for education to achieve sustainability, only limited progress has been made on any level. This lack of progress stems from many sources. In some cases, a lack of vision or awareness has impeded progress. In others, it is a lack of policy or funding. According to Charles Hopkins, who has spoken with people at many levels of involvement in education, twelve major issues stymied the advance of ESD during the 1990s and new millennium. By addressing these critical impediments in the planning stage, governments can prevent or reduce delays or derailment of ESD efforts and, ultimately, the attainment of sustainability. In addition to these generic issues, governments at all levels will need to address issues that are specific to local conditions.

6.5.2. Building Awareness

The initial step in launching an ESD programme is to develop awareness within the educational community and the public that reorienting education to achieve sustainability is essential. If government officials or school district administrators are unaware of the critical linkages between education and sustainable development, reorienting education to address sustainable development will not occur. When people realise that education can improve the likelihood of implementing national policies, regional land and resource management programmes, and local programmes, then education is in a position to be reoriented to help achieve sustainability. This awareness forms the essential first step in the reorienting process.

Fortunately, at the international level, ESD is recognised as important and central to the success of sustainable development around the world. At the sixth meeting of the UN Commission on Sustainable Development, delegations from countries worldwide repeatedly mentioned the importance of ESD in achieving goals of sustainability. It was apparent that they were ready to move forward with the next steps; however, the importance of ESD must reach beyond the delegations and permeate the educational community and the general public.

Inherent in building awareness are efforts to outline important linkages between education and more sustainable societies. In large part, perceiving a need brings about a corresponding change in educational systems. Unfortunately, the need to achieve sustainable development is not perceived today as sufficiently important to spark a large response in the educational community. If leaders at all levels of governance are to make progress, the recognition and active involvement of the education sector is imperative.

6.5.3. Inclusion of ESD in the Curriculum

Each country faces a fundamental decision in addressing an ESD strategy. Each country must decide on a method of implementation—whether to create another "add on" subject, or to reorient entire education programmes and practices to address sustainable development. Nations also need to clarify whether their educators are being asked to teach about sustainable development or to change the goals and methods of education to achieve sustainable development. The answer to this question will profoundly affect each nation's course of action.

In reality, education related to sustainable development will be implemented in a wide range, in both depth and breadth. In some communities, ESD will be ignored; in others it will be barely addressed. In some, a new class dedicated to ESD will be created, and in others the entire curriculum will be reoriented to address sustainability. Communities must be aware of the limitations of educating about sustainable development. Teaching about sustainable development is like teaching the theory behind an abstract concept or teaching the principles of sustainability by rote memorisation. ESD in its real and effective forms gives students the skills, perspectives, values, and knowledge to live sustainably in their communities. At the same time, true education is not indoctrination or inculcation.

Experimentation will determine what level of ESD will be appropriate and successful for communities to meet their sustainability goals. For example, a community may weave a few themes of sustainability into the curriculum, only to find the additions will not achieve sustainability for their community. In cases where schools carry total responsibility for ESD, complete curricular reorientation of education at all levels will probably be necessary. In communities where informal, non-formal, and formal education unite to create an integrated ESD programme for citizens of all ages, a less intense approach in the formal education system might be effective. As programmes are developed and implemented, problems will occur. Flaws and questionable practices will need to be addressed as ESD continues to develop and mature.

6.6. Educational Reform and Economic Viability

The effectiveness of the world's educational systems is already critically debated in light of the changing needs of society. The current widespread acknowledgment of the need for educational reform may help advance ESD. If it can be linked to one or more priorities of educational reform, ESD could have a good chance for success. However, if promoters try to add another issue to an already over-burdened system, the chances of success are slim.

One current global concern that has the potential to drive educational reform in many countries is economic security. Around the world, ministries of education and commerce are asking: What changes will prepare a workforce that will make my country economically viable in the changing economy of the new millennium? One, educational effort that can boost the economic potential of entire nations is educating females. During the last decade, some national leaders have recognised that educating the entire workforce, both males and females, is important for economic viability. In addition, Lawrence Summer of the World Bank says, "Once all the benefits are recognised, investments in the education of girls may well be the highest-return investment available in the developing world."

Accordingly, some nations are removing barriers to girls attending school and have campaigns to actively enroll girls in school.

Further, aligning education with future economic conditions is difficult, because economic and technological forecasting is an art based on imprecise science. Answers are elusive.

To be successful, ESD will need to catch the wave of educational reform. ESD proponents need to identify and illustrate the linkages between the principles of sustainability and the long-term economic well-being of each nation. If ESD can be linked to the current global educational reform movement, educating for sustainability will be swept along with the energy of the reform effort. If, however, the wave is missed, proponents of ESD will be looking for a foothold in the curriculum and trying to convince teachers to wedge sustainability principles, knowledge, issues, skills, values and perspectives wherever possible. Linking to the reform movement can guarantee ESD to every child in school, while inserting ESD into the curriculum will be left to the whim of individual teachers. In the case of the latter, ESD will be characterised by huge gaps or possible redundancies.

The International Commission on Education for the Twenty-First Century, which was chaired by Jacques Delors, released its report, *Learning: The Treasure Within*, to UNESCO. The report strongly recommends that all reform be conducted in the spirit and essence of sustainable development and calls for the full-fledged pursuit of reorienting education to attain sustainability. Accordingly, ESD and goals for sustainability have a legitimate place in whatever changes emerge from national or regional educational reform efforts.

Sustainable development is a complex and evolving concept. Many scholars and practitioners have invested years in trying to define sustainable development and envisioning how to achieve it on national and local levels. Because sustainable development is hard to define and implement, it is also difficult to teach. Even more challenging is the task of totally reorienting an entire education system to achieve sustainability.

When we examine successful national education campaigns, we find they often have simple messages. For example, messages that encourage us to vaccinate our children and boil our water, or discourage us from driving drunk and taking drugs, are simple concepts compared to the complex range of environmental, economic, and social issues that sustainable development encompasses. Success in ESD will take much longer and be more costly than single-message public-education campaigns. Rather than being clear, simple and unambiguous, the concepts involved in ESD are complex. Their complexity stems from the intricate and complicated interactions of natural and human systems. The challenge to educators is to derive messages that illustrate such complexity, without overwhelming or confusing the learner.

6.7. Community Participation in ESD Programme

Perhaps the greatest obstacle to reorienting the world's educational systems is the lack of clarity regarding goals. Education for sustainable development remains an enigma to many governments and schools. Governments, ministries of education, school districts, and educators have expressed a willingness to adopt ESD programs; however, no successful working models currently exist. Without models to adapt and adopt, governments and schools must create a process to define what education for sustainability is with respect to the local context. Such a process is challenging. It calls for a public participation process in which all of the stakeholders in a community carefully examine what they want their children to know, do and value when they leave the formal education system. This means that the community must try to predict the environmental, economic and social conditions of the near and distant future.

Public participation processes whereby stakeholders examine the needs and desires of a community and identify essential elements of basic and secondary education can be adapted and implemented in many types of communities. Seeking the opinions of parents and workers to shape the education of their children will be a totally new idea in some cultures. Although community consultation and other forms of public participation can be effective tools, they should be introduced slowly and in accordance with local traditions and cultures where they have not been used previously. However valuable, the community consultation process is not without pitfalls. For example, an organised, educated, and articulate few might dominate the process; people who have received little formal education may not feel they have the expertise to take part in or contribute to the process; and the worldviews and life experiences of some people might prevent them from perceiving or accommodating the changes that will come to all regions of the planet in the coming decades. In these cases, how the outcome of the process is used becomes important. A continuum of implementation exists, ranging from ruthlessly implementing the results of a skewed process to totally ignoring the outcomes of the process. The interpretative, political, and interpersonal skills of the implementation team are key in this effort.

ESD carries with it the inherent idea of implementing programmes that are locally relevant and culturally appropriate. Just as any sustainable development program must take into consideration the local environmental, economic and societal conditions, so too must ESD programs consider these same conditions. As a result, each region must create its own ESD programme. It is impossible to create an international, or even in many cases a national, curriculum that would be relevant to all communities.

It should be apparent to ministries of education and school districts that developing locally relevant ESD curriculums will be facilitated by creating public participation processes that allow communities to shape the major ideas underpinning their own curriculums. Rather than spending time searching for curricular models to adapt, it would be better to invest time and resources in developing processes by which communities of different sizes and traditions can define their own ESD programs.

6.8. Transdisciplinary Framework

ESD by nature is holistic and interdisciplinary, and depends on concepts and analytical tools from a variety of disciplines. As a result, ESD is difficult to teach in traditional school settings where studies are divided and taught in a disciplinary framework. In countries where national curriculums describe in detail the content and sequence of study in each discipline, ESD will be challenging to implement. In other countries where content is described generally, ESD will be more easily implemented, although doing so will require creative teachers who are comfortable and skilled at teaching across disciplines.

6.8.1. Sharing the Responsibility

Popular thinking promotes the myth that an informed society is solely the responsibility of the ministry of education. In reality, however, the ministries of environment, commerce, state, and health also have a stake in ESD, just as they have a stake in sustainable development. By combining expertise, resources, and funding from many ministries, the possibility of building a high-quality, successful education programme increases. Every sector of the government that is touched by sustainable development can play a role in ESD and the reorienting process. At the UN meeting of the Commission on Sustainable Development, ministries of the environment have taken the lead in stating that education, awareness, and training are essential tools in bringing about sustainable development. Ministries of the environment need to work with both formal and nonformal sectors of the education community to implement ESD. In addition, it is absolutely essential for teachers to be involved in the process of building consensus concerning ESD.

6.8.2. In-service and Pre-service Training

The successful implementation of a new educational trend will require responsible, accountable leadership and expertise in both systemic educational change and sustainable development. We must develop realistic strategies to quickly create knowledgeable and capable leadership. It is unrealistic to expect nations to retrain 59,000,000 teachers and thousands of administrators in either - or both - ESD and educational change. We must find ways, such as employing the strengths model, to use existing skills. Two models of human resource development currently exist: inservice training and pre-service training. In the first, experienced professionals are provided with additional training. Then, they reshape existing programs by drawing on their new knowledge, previous expertise, understanding of national and local systems, and network of contacts. In pre-service training, concepts, principles, and methodologies are provided during initial training. The new professionals then step into their jobs with ESD as part of their expertise. Pre-service training is more cost effective than retraining educators and administrators later in their careers. For initial success in ESD, both inservice and pre-service training are necessary.

Many resources currently exist in the educational and administrative labor pools. Talented educators, especially in the fields of environment, population, and development, already teach strands of ESD and could easily expand their focus to include other concepts of sustainable development. Fortunately, every educator in every discipline has some existing strength to contribute to ESD via the strengths model. In this approach, the synergistic strengths of combined educational disciplines can convey the knowledge, issues, skills, perceptions and values associated with ESD. However, use of this strengths model requires that someone be sufficiently well-versed in ESD to pull together the pieces and to form a complete picture of the role that individuals, communities and nations must play in a sustainable world.

While the effort can begin with the current teaching professionals around the globe, it is clear that teacher education institutions need to reorient pre-service teacher education to include ESD. Teacher education programmes need to produce professionals who not only teach sustainability themes but also can "pull together" the various disciplinary strands that will give their students a holistic understanding of a sustainable future and the role of individuals, communities and nations in a sustainable world. The development of this cadre of expertise will profoundly affect how rapidly nations will begin the move toward sustainability.

Institutions of teacher education are ideally situated to play central roles in educational reform and teacher educators are the key change agents. Teacher educators train new teachers, provide professional development for practicing teachers, consult with local schools, and provide expert opinion to regional and national ministries of education. Teacher educators write not only pre-service teacher-education curriculum, but also contribute to committees that create teacher-education standards and officially mandated curriculum for primary and secondary education. Because of this broad influence in curriculum design, implementation, and policy setting, faculty members of teachereducation institutions can bring about far-reaching educational reform — even beyond training the teachers in the world. The question is, who will work with the teacher educators to develop their expertise?

To support global implementation of ESD, we need international cooperative programs for administrators, curriculum developers, teacher educators and lead teachers. These programmes should maximise and leverage the knowledge base and strengths already existing in the labor pool.

6.9. Financial and Material Resources for ESD

Perhaps one of the greatest expenses of implementing ESD will come with providing appropriate basic education. Basic goals, which were established at Jontiem and reaffirmed at Dakar, include educating more children and increasing the universal average minimum of schooling to six years. Meeting these goals will require hiring many more teachers. These new teachers must be trained, and current teachers must be retrained, to reorient their curriculums to address sustainability.

The good news is that many countries are spending a larger percentage of their gross national product (GNP) on education. Two-thirds of the 123 countries listed in the UNESCO World Education Report 2000 that reported public expenditures on education as a percentage of GNP in both 1990 and 1996, reported spending more in 1996 than in 1990. Although governments are prioritising education in terms of funding, how much of this funding is going to reorient education to address sustainability? Simply providing more education does not reduce the threat high resource consumption poses to sustainability.

One of the reasons why many experts perceive that little progress has been made regarding ESD since the Earth Summit in 1992 is that few financial resources have been dedicated to reorienting education to address sustainability. In fact, national and local governments have spent little on ESD beyond improving basic education. Yet, effective ESD will depend on funding at both national and local levels. At the national level, financial resources must fund curriculum, administration and teacher education. At the local level, resources must finance curriculum development and accompanying materials, as well as teacher training.

Reorienting education to address sustainability will require new financial resources.

One of the major problems with ESD is that current education must continue while the new curriculum is being designed and developed. The reality is that educators are so busy with the task at hand — planning, daily teaching, evaluating progress, writing reports — that they have little time or energy to research and create new curriculum. Teachers cannot be expected to do two jobs — design curriculum and teach — during the transition phase. Of course, current teachers should play an advisory role, but core design tasks should not fall exclusively on their already burdened shoulders. New funding and resources need to be provided during the start-up phase; governments cannot expect local administrations and educators to donate in-kind services to accomplish this important task.

Locally relevant and culturally appropriate curriculums and other educational materials often vary intranationally. For example, Chile extends several thousand kilometres from north to south. In the Atacama Desert of the north, environmental concerns involve the ocean and marine life; in the humid-temperate south, concerns involve the forests. As a result of these great distances and geographic diversity, a series of regional curriculums based around a common model would be more appropriate than one national curriculum. This same intranational diversity exists in many nations. Accordingly, regional and local curriculum could benefit many nations with internal diversity.

In addition, many countries are evaluating new educational technologies and strategies to implement them. ESD is already woven into many of these technologies. For example, many free sources of environmental data are available on the World Wide Web as are other teaching resources such as lesson plans. Governments and school districts investing in these technologies will offset expenditures with access to free ESD information and materials.

6.10. Development Policy

To succeed, ESD must have an authoritative impetus from national or regional governments that will drive policy development. The omission of such an impetus proved to be the downfall of the 1970s global effort to infuse environmental education into the elementary and secondary curriculums. This same fate could befall the ESD effort.

The reality of any educational reform is that success depends on both "top down" and "bottom up" efforts. Administrators at the top echelons of ministries are in a position to create the policies that will make reform occur. Together, administrators, teachers and community leaders at the local level must interpret what the policy should "look like" locally.

In order to bring about the major changes required by ESD, we need to nurture a climate of safety. Policymakers, administrators, and teachers will need to make changes, experiment, and take risks to accomplish new educational and sustainability goals. They need to have the authority and support of the educational community to change the *status quo*. Teachers must feel that the administration will support their efforts if parents or vested interest groups in the community question or criticise their initiatives. We need to develop and implement policy to ensure administrators and educators at all levels have the right to introduce new or controversial topics and pedagogical methods. Of course, an overzealous few could abuse these rights; therefore, a system of checks and balances within professional guidelines and cultural context should also be in place.

Perhaps the most difficult obstacle to address in implementing ESD is that of popularity. While many countries agreed that ESD is important, the themes of sustainability are not prevalent in popular cultures or governmental policies. For example, one principle of sustainable development is that the rates of use of renewable resources should not exceed their rates of regeneration. Yet, many societies have developed or are developing a "disposable culture." Disposable beverage containers, food wrappers, plates, and eating utensils pass through our lives daily. We use them once and then discard them to be buried, burned, or dumped in the water. This disposable culture is using such resources as trees and fossil fuels more rapidly than they can be replaced. Because principles of sustainable development are not currently woven into daily life and governmental policy, the emergence of ESD could become an important "bottom-up" driver of community-based sustainable development. ESD could shape and encourage behaviours and ethics that support an informed, knowledgeable citizenry that has the political will to achieve a sustainable future.

References

Department for Education and Skills (DfES). 1999 *A better quality of life: a strategy for sustainable development for the UK.* HMSO, London .

De Souza, G. and Gebremedhin, T. 1998 *Sustainability in agricultural and rural development.* Ashgate, Aldershot .

Elliott, J.A. 1999 *An introduction to sustainable development.* Routledge, London .

Martin Purvis and Alan Grainger (editors). 2004. *Exploring Sustainable Development: Geographical Perspectives.* Earthscan, London .

Reid, D . 2004. *Sustainable development: an introductory guide.* Earthscan, London .

Wakernagel, M. and Rees, W.E. 1996. *Our ecological footprint: reducing human impact on the Earth.* New Society Publications, Toronto.

7

Education and Social Cohesion

Historically, education systems have played an important role, not only in developing human capital, but also in promoting societal cohesion through the development of values and social and national identities. In this chapter the focus is on the review of some of the literature on the relationship between education, conflict and social cohesion through drawing together literature on education and social capital, education and conflict, and education for citizenship, peace and human rights. In part this serves to highlight the renewed importance of education and social cohesion within the new PostWashington development paradigm, but also to problematise education's non-linear and complex relationship with these issues.

7.1. Violence and Insecurity

Drawing on research carried out by the World Health Organisation, the UN *Report on the World Social Situation 2005: The Inequality Predicament* notes that in 2002 around 1.6 million people died from intentionally inflicted injuries with men more likely than women to be both victim and perpetrator. While suicide accounts for over 50 per cent of deaths, armed conflicts caused around 35 per cent and interpersonal violence 15 per cent of deaths. However, Africa and Latin America differ from the global patterns with more lives lost to violence and crime than to suicide. Furthermore, in 2004, more than 17 million people were living as refugees or internally displaced persons owing to violence or the threat of violence.

Perhaps unsurprisingly in light of the events of September 11, 2001 and subsequent military conflict in Afghanistan and Iraq, there is increasing concern over violent conflict. Both the UN report on the World Social Situation and the UNDP Human Development Report place special emphasis on the causes and effects of increased conflict. The trend in conflicts can be interpreted in a variety of ways. As the UNDP report notes, while in 1991 there were 51 conflicts taking place globally, in 2003 there were only 29. However, more people are dying in these conflicts, and more of the dead are civilians than in earlier wars. Likewise there has also been a shift both in the nature and the geography of those wars and conflict.

Their geographical location of war and conflict has changed with the vast majority now taking place in low-income countries. Between the years 1946-89, low-income countries accounted for around onethird of all conflicts; between 1990 and 2003, this increased to nearly a half. As the UNDP notes, 40 per cent of the world's conflicts are in Africa. Of the 25 countries ranked lowest in the human development index in 2004, 23 are in Africa, and 20 are currently or have recently been in conflict. Nine of the ten lowest countries on the Human Development Index have experienced some form of armed conflict since the 1990s, and seven in recent years, while five of the ten countries have the lowest life expectancy; nine out of the ten countries that have experienced conflict in recent years have the highest child mortality rates, and eight out of the ten countries with the lowest primary enrolment rates have experienced some form of conflict since 1990.

From these examples we can see that conflict and development are clearly linked in both directions – increased conflict blocks development, and failed or uneven development works as a catalyst to produce conflict. Furthermore, recent concern over failed states reflects the late realisation amongst developed nations that problems of violence and conflict in low-income countries may not end at the borders. Conflict, it seems, in the postSeptember 11 world, has become a transnational problem that cannot be avoided.

While interstate and civil wars raise widespread media attention, rises in violence and murder are often hidden from view. The UN report notes an increase in both crime and interpersonal violence, particularly in Latin America and the Caribbean, with slower increases in Africa, the Arab States, Eastern Europe and the CIS, and South-East Asia and the Pacific. Murder rates and levels of human development normally have an inverse relationship, with the highest murder rates taking place in middle or low-income countries.

While the causes of homicide and violent crime are complex, a recent comprehensive cross-country study carried out by World Bank researchers on the relationship between violent crime and inequality highlights a high positive correlation.

The UN draws a clear causal relationship between poverty and inequality and violence, crime and armed conflict. This in turn raises questions about the relationship between rising inequality and poverty in many parts of the world and the rising levels of violence.

While the literature in this area remains contradictory on the causes of violence, conflict and civil wars, there is consensus on the damaging effects it is having on development indices.

The UNDP report notes how conflict and civil war are undermining the possibility of achieved the MDGs with conflict undermining nutrition and public health, destroying education systems, devastating livelihoods and retarding any prospects for economic growth.

In synthesis what we can note is a growing 'social' crisis running alongside processes of globalisation that manifests itself in violence ranging from street crime, to civil wars to international terrorism. Whether this can be attributed directly to processes of globalisation is of course another matter, but regardless of this it is clear that since the 1990s and most visibly since 2001, concerns with social integration, social cohesion and good citizenship have risen up the international policy ladder and these have serious and important implications for education systems. While the 1980s were characterised by a clear focus on the economic function of education systems, the mid1990s onwards have seen that economic focus combined with concern for issues of social cohesion. One of the first signals for this shift that we will turn to was the emergence of the concept of social capital within the World Bank.

Education provides knowledge to pupils about social contracts between individuals and the state, providing a context to develop appropriate norms and behaviours for upholding those contracts, and a forum within which different social groupings interact and learn about each other. Education systems also explain the consequences for breaking social contracts.

The overly simplistic positive representation of the relationship between education and social cohesion that typifies the work on social capital is however challenged. At the national level there is no correlation between aggregate levels of education and social cohesion. However, there are close links between income inequality and inequality in access to education inequality is the most important causal factor in relation to social cohesion. The analytical framework deployed by social capital researchers avoids issues such as class, race and structural inequality which have provided the core material for social scientists over the last century.

The somewhat romantic view of education's socially cohesive role is also challenged by authors many who argue that, just as social capital has its dark side, so schooling does not necessarily transmit positive values and behaviours to students. On the contrary, in a myriad of ways, education systems may well be contributing to social breakdown by reproducing gender, ethnic and class inequalities. Beyond that violence in schools promotes attitudes that often run contrary to socially cohesive and tolerant societies.

The conclusion to be drawn is that it is not just more education, but a particular type of education that might promote positive social integration.

7.2. Citizenship and Human Rights Education

The urgency of the need to tackle war and violence, to foster a national identity without the counter-effects of patriotism, to promote inclusion and to recognise rights as universal have led to acceptance of citizenship education and human rights education as legitimate sites of learning. International pressures towards good governance have also been influential in countries dependent on aid. It is likely that globalisation will generate concerns about global citizenship, albeit for a number of different economic and social reasons. Citizenship and human rights education covers a wide variety of issues ranging from civics, political education, national identity, global education/global citizenship, environmental education, peace education, gender/equity critiques of citizenship, inter-culturalism and ethnic minority inclusion. It can take place in a wide range of social settings and serve a range of purposes.

Citizenship and human rights education falls under six areas:

a) formal curriculum of schools and higher education;

b) organisational structures of schools: student councils, student unions;

c) links and work with the community;

d) non-formal education or popular education;

e) training courses for public officials; and

f) public awareness campaigns, using media and road shows.

Citizenship education increasingly overlaps with human rights education, with the latter being embedded within the former in an increasingly globalised world. Citizenship refers to a citizen's particular relationship with a single state while human rights refer to more general global rights and responsibilities of a citizen of the world. The increased recognition of human rights as being universally applicable and integrated into national law reflects how processes beyond the economic have been globalised over recent years, and how these processes begin to blur the line between local, national, regional and global identity formation.

During the post1970s globalisation phase there has been renewed interest in citizenship education worldwide.

Injustices and inequalities have persisted locally, nationally and globally, a concern exemplified in the establishment of the United Nations Decade for Human Rights Education. Likewise, in the United Nations Convention on the Rights of the Child signed in 1989, there is particular emphasis on education as a conduit for developing tolerance, peace and respect for others, amongst the young. Migration and globalisation are viewed as placing pressures on nation states to address issues of social integration and develop a balance between national unity and national diversity with education being seen as a natural tool to facilitate this. A recent OECD report noted:

The issue for education is how to develop not only successful individuals with good workplace skills, but also 'democratic citizenship' – an outcome both linked to, and supportive of, social cohesion. Defining the qualities we might wish to see in citizens of democratic societies remains a political and context-dependent task. It might include qualities such as fairness, tolerance and a co-operative approach, recognition of the value of social norms, and a civic spirit. While education and informal learning, in isolation, cannot create model citizens, they can, alongside other factors, make a constructive contribution. Devising a policy response will require clear objectives, keeping a balance between the 'nation-building' role of civic education and its role in valuing and recognising social diversity.

There is growing concern in many societies that young people are disinterested and disengaged from the political system, and that citizenship education can provide a route towards stimulating a re-engagement with politics. Citizenship education has been seen as a means to influence, modify and improve the behaviour of youth groups. engaged in anti-social behaviour. The end of the Cold War led to the need, particularly in Eastern Europe, to promote democratic behaviour. Finally, particularly in Europe, citizenship education has been seen as a means to counter the rise of racist and anti-democratic movements that utilise the rise in immigration to promote fear and social dislocation.

While in any particular country interest in education and citizenship and human rights may be triggered by a particular combination of these elements, there is a growing appreciation of the role of education in promoting and strengthening social cohesion and tolerance within societies undergoing processes of rapid social change such as those associated with globalisation.

As interest has developed so too has a burgeoning literature exploring these issues in both North and South. The International Consensus Panel report *Democracy and Diversity* developed by the University of Washington identifies four key principles for teaching citizenship.

1) Students should learn about the complex relationships between unity and diversity in their local communities, the nation and the world;
2) They should study the ways in which people in their community, nation and region are increasingly interdependent with others around the world;

3) The teaching of human rights should underpin citizenship education in multicultural nation-states,
4) Students should be taught knowledge about democracy and democratic institutions.

In the literature reviewed, it is clear that citizenship and human rights education takes place in schools, either primarily as a particular subject, or integrated across the curriculum as part and parcel of many subjects. One Commonwealth report noted how citizenship and human rights education was nested inside a range of different curriculum, such as 'The Constitution' (Pakistan), 'Moral Education' (Malaysia), and 'Social Studies' (Jamaica). In the UK, citizenship education is currently taught as a specific subject. However, in many parts of the world, it was a key development for nation building after the defeat of colonialism. Central to any analysis of citizenship is its particular definition in each locality where it is used. Who determines who is and who is not a citizen? And, what might inclusion entail in terms of rights and responsibilities? Citizenship education can just as easily promote xenophobia and racism as it can promote tolerance, peace and respect for diversity.

Because citizenship is so contested, teachers are often forced into deciding whether they are there to socialise and mould children into loyal citizens or to transform them into active agents seeking to challenge unequal structures. There is a problem with the literature on citizenship and human rights in that it is much easier to research social exclusion and demonstrate the role of education in addressing these issues than it is to measure the impact of that education on the issues themselves.

Research on the Dominican Republic on the impact of USAID funding for democracy and citizenship education found that while increasing individual knowledge, efficacy and other supportive democratic values, it decreased the sense that governmental institutions are worthy of citizen trust. This type of research highlights the political and politicised nature of these types of education programmes. In respect to this, USAID needs to be clear what the objectives are for their educational programmes and perhaps tailor courses according to whether they are seeking to challenge undemocratic regimes or support newly democratic ones.

UNESCO, in a broad review of human rights and citizenship education of member states, welcomed the fact that many more countries were recognising its importance and were developing plans to integrate it across the curriculum. However, they were also concerned that this type of education was not accorded the financial resources necessary for its efficacy. They suggested that there was a gap between the rhetoric of many states and the practical and financial measures necessary for implementing a systematic programme of education for citizenship and human rights.

The UNESCO report stressed the importance of integrating citizenship and human rights education in formal education settings with the non-formal education delivered by NGOs and other civil society organisations. They also raised a number of key issues and topics for this type of education including the promotion of language teaching and mother tongue education to foster intercultural understanding. Secondly, they called for gender to be understood within the framework of the UN Conference on Women, and to be integrated both into curricula and institutional practice within education systems. Thirdly, they were concerned that insufficient effort was being directed towards racism, racial, ethnic and religious intolerance. Fourthly, they called for a broader integration of education directed at promoting environmental awareness. Fifthly, they suggested that in response to the rise of endemic diseases and increases in drug and alcohol abuse that raised awareness of these issues should be promoted. Finally, they called for the enhancement and strengthening of programmes promoting democratic values and practices, tolerance and peace.

7.3. Education and Violent Conflicts

Education is one of the building blocks of human development. It is not just a basic right, but also a foundation for progress in other areas, including health, nutrition and the development of institutions and democracy. Conflict undermines this foundation and also contributes to the conditions that perpetuate violence. Violent conflict destroys education infrastructure, reduces spending on schools and teachers and prevents children from attending classes. Schools are often a target for groups hostile to the government because of the association with state authority.

According to a DfID commissioned report, 82 per cent of the reported 113 million children out of school were from crisis and post-crisis countries. While this figure is contested, it nevertheless highlights the importance of addressing the education/conflict relationship. As we also noted above, the vast majority of post 1990s conflicts took place in low-income countries, and that there appears to be a strong relationship between poverty, inequality and violence.

The recent UNDP report observes that half of all primary schools were closed or destroyed during Mozambique's civil war between 1976 and 1992. The Oxfam Education Report too showed that twothirds of the African countries affected by conflicts at that time have enrolment rates of less than 50 per cent. Furthermore, the UNDP state that countries in conflict are likely to spend less on education, and parents are less likely to send girls to school for fear of violence. They highlight that the ratio of girls to boys enrolled in primary schools was 0.83 for 18 low-income countries that were in conflict at some point since 2000 and 0.90 for those not in conflict. Similarly, poor children are far more likely to be deprived of education and affected by conflict than wealthier children. For the reasons elaborated above, there is an increasing consensus in the literature that if we are serious about reaching the MDGs, and particularly the educational MDGs then we need to address conflict as an integral part of any comprehensive poverty reduction strategy and ensure that education systems are geared up to prevent, cope with, deal with the after effects and generally contribute to the promotion of non-violent solutions to the wide range of inequalities that have emerged out of recent processes of globalisation.

7.4. Effects of War on Education

Across recent literature reviewed on conflict and education, there is increasing recognition of the highly complex relationship between education and violent conflict that will be reviewed in this section. Conflict affects the educational chances of children in a range of different ways. There are three different levels at which violent conflict can effect education. Firstly, it affects children directly through the loss of relatives, physical violence, and rape, need to leave home etc. Secondly, the damage caused by war can have a direct affect on the possibility of attending school: danger to get there; economic situation no longer allows for children to pay for schooling. Thirdly, educational infrastructure and institutions become targets and destroyed – either accidentally or for political reasons. Schools can also be occupied and used as bases for warring factions.

There is a range of ways that violent conflict directly affects education:

a) teachers and children stop going to school out of fear of physical danger, and schools can become recruiting grounds for child soldiers;

b) schools are destroyed – in East Timor over 80 per cent of schools were destroyed in September 1999;

c) violence in schools can increase as a reflection of the violence outside;

d) increases in sexual and gender abuse in schools in areas of conflict, which leads families to keep their children at home;

e) psychological effects of conflict impact on children's ability to learn;.

f) both educational access and quality can be destroyed;

g) funding to education from the state and the family can be reduced;

h) education institutions can often become the battleground upon which wars are fought; and

i) increases educational inequalities, as richer students are more likely to be able to continue in education and escape the effects of war.

All these suggest that there is a need for an urgent response to the impact of war and conflict on the education of future generations.

Despite the appearance of education as victim of and solution to violence, recent research has noted how education often contributes to the promotion of violence. Many analysts agree that war and conflict are generally caused by exclusion. Issues such as political, cultural and economic inequalities, lack of trust in government, mistrust and suspicion between different ethic and religious groups, and lack of avenues for peaceful interaction. Recent research highlights how education has two faces, and its negative side can promote rather than reduce the chances of violent conflict.

Through social exclusion, violence and indoctrination, schools can serve as powerful weapons to produce rather than reduce violence. One example of this relationship is pointed out by the UNDP who highlight how school exclusion as a result of poverty contributed in Sierra Leone to young people joining the rebel armies:

Education provides another example of how violent conflict creates a cycle that is hard to break. One survey of ex-combatants in Sierra Leone found that an overwhelming majority of those who joined the brutal rebellions were youths who had been living in difficult conditions prior to the onset of the war. Based on interviews with 1,000 ex-combatants, the survey found that half had left school because they could not afford the fees or because the school had shut down.

There are multiple ways by which school systems reproduce social inequalities, increase tension and are a catalyst for war. However, in some countries it is the school system itself that promotes xenophobia and racism towards ethnic groups/religious minorities, and from this sows the seeds of war and conflict. Schools in South Africa during Apartheid, in Kosovo, and in Taiwan prepared children, psychologically and militarily, for conflict in explicit ways. These schools thus perpetuate the range of inequalities and prejudices that existed beyond school walls rather than challenging their legitimacy.

There are different types of violence that can take place in relation to education moving from direct, to indirect, to repressive, and finally alienating violence. Contemporary schooling structures serve to reproduce inequalities, as well as reproduce and convey powerful masculine and authoritarian environments, disseminating a highly nationalist and essentialist notion of citizenship that negates the pluralistic reality of societies. One can cite a range of examples of violence in education: the uneven distribution of education and educational opportunities; education as a weapon of cultural repression; denial of education as a weapon of war; manipulation of history for political purposes; the manipulation of textbooks; the conveying of images asserting superiority of one group over another; and, segregated education.

On a more positive note, it can be said that education is not necessarily or wholly deleterious. Each level of educational violence – direct, indirect, repressive and alienating – has its educational antidote/

counterpart: education for peace, education for all, 'education for democracy' and 'education for cultural diversity'. These types of analyses point towards the need to attend to both issues of access in low-income countries and also issues of quality, as well as to recognise the complex and doubled edged nature of education as a system of knowledge production.

7.5. Education in Emergencies

Education in emergencies is a relatively new field of action and an even newer area of inquiry and investigation. 'Emergency programmes', of which education is one area, can be defined as "all programmes for refugees and displaced or conflict-affected populations, as well as disaster victims". These programmes seek to guarantee access to education in conflict situation, to take into consideration the special psycho-social needs of youth and adults, contribute to societal reconstruction and reconciliation. Education in Emergencies can be subdivided into the following categories: education for refugees, education for internally displaced persons (IDPs), education under conditions of armed conflicts, insecurity and instability, education for reconstruction after armed conflicts and catastrophes.

Within this field, UNICEF and UNHCR are particularly active. Likewise, UNESCO has developed a range of educational interventions in this field. The Interagency Network on Education in Emergencies (INEE) was set up by UNICEF, UNCHR and UNESCO in 2000, seeking to coordinate action, research and evaluation in this area and ensure that EFA goals in conflict areas are not forgotten. Its objectives are to:

a) share knowledge and experience;

b) promote greater donor understanding of education in emergencies;

c) advocate for education to be included in emergency response;

d) make teaching and learning responses available as widely as possible;

e) ensure attention is paid to gender issues in emergency education initiatives;

f) document and disseminate best practices in the field; and to move towards consensual guidelines on education in emergencies.

The field of education in emergency and post-emergency situations is new. It is underresearched and poorly evaluated, and there is little analysis of the effectiveness of programmes. Within the field we can loosely divide the types of educational interventions in terms of the nature of conflicts.

There is a growing recognition in the programmes and research that education cannot be seen simply as an emergency measure but that it needs to be integrated into broader long-term development objectives.

The Women's Commission for Refugee Women and Children lists a series of measures used in the field:

a) structured recreational activities for children and young people;

b) development of youth centres;

c) formal education;

d) vocational training;

e) accelerated short-term education programmes;

f) bridging programmes;

g) life skills education;

h) teacher training; and

i) distance courses.

The wide variety of activities reflects the need to think beyond children and beyond formal schooling. Conflicts are highly complex phenomena and thus need highly sophisticated educational responses. A total of 14 principles that might be regarded as exemplary and comprehensive standards for "emergency education" are noted below:

1. The right of access to education, recreation and related activities must be ensured, even in crisis situations.
2. Rapid access to education, recreation and related activities should be followed by steady improvement in education quality and coverage, including access to all levels of education and recognition of studies.
3. Education programmes should be gender-sensitive, accessible to and inclusive of all groups.

4. Education should serve as a tool for child protection and prevention of harm.
5. Education programmes should use a community based participatory approach, with emphasis on capacity-building.
6. Education programmes should include a major component of training for teachers and youth/adult educators, and provide incentives to avoid teacher turnover.
7. Crisis and recovery programmes should develop and document locally appropriate targets for resourcing standards, adequate to meet their educational and psychosocial needs.
8. All crisis-affected children and young people should have access to education, recreation and related activities, helping to meet their psychosocial needs in the short and longer term.
9. Curriculum policy should support the long-term development of individual students and of the society and, for refugee populations, should be supportive of a durable solution, normally repatriation.
10. Education programmes should be enriched to include life skills for education for health, safety, and environmental awareness.
11. Education programmes should be enriched to include life skills for education for peace/conflict resolution, tolerance, human rights and citizenship.
12. Vocational training programmes should be linked to opportunities for workplace practices of the skills being learned.
13. Governments and development cooperation agencies should promote co-ordination between all agencies and stakeholders.
14. External assistance programmes should include capacity building to promote transparent, accountable and inclusive system management by local protagonists.

This broadening of the field and focus of 'emergency education' reflects the shift from seeing education in emergency situations as a problem of delivery and logistics, to recognition of the complex relationship between education and development. Education is now considered a central component of any pre-conflict, conflict, and post-conflict situation, as both a catalyst to resolve issues but also as a potential contributor to the generation of conflict.

7.6. Education for Peace

One direct pedagogical intervention that education can bring to pre-conflict, conflict and postconflict situations is that of 'peace education'. The peace education discourse and literature, as might be expected, overlaps with the citizenship and human rights education literature and many researchers, contribute to both fields. Specifically, much of the peace education work promotes a pedagogical approach that can develop pro-active conflict resolution and prevention attitudes that can transform societies.

Types of 'Peace Education' activities include:

a) breaking down a segregated and developing an integrated education system;

b) promoting mother tongues and foreign languages and the establishment of bilingual schools;

c) developing new teaching materials and revising examination contents;

d) anchoring peace-building and conflict-preventive work in the curriculum;

e) participative structure and opening of schools through peer group education;

f) recreational and integration offerings for children and young people;

g) conflict and reconciliation work in community work;

h) training of teaching staff; and

i) international exchange measures.

In some of the literature reviewed there is some concern expressed over the lack of theoretical sophistication in the area; the implication here is that there is a great deal of practical action but little theoretical and conceptual development. There is widespread disagreement as to what peace education is; there is little or no consensus on the ability of peace education to achieve its objectives and there is insufficient empirical evidence and analysis to explore what does and does not function. Yet despite the criticisms, in much of the literature there is a commitment to moving the pedagogy and practice of peace education forward.

References

Andreopoulos, George J. and Richard Pierre Claude, Eds., 1997. *Human Rights Education for the Twenty-First Century*, University of Pennsylvania Press.

Boulding, Elise, 1988. *Building a Global Civic Culture: Education for an Interdependent World*, Teachers College Press.

Fisk, Larry and John Scheilenberg, 2000. *Patterns of Conflict: Paths to Peace*, Broadview Press.

Reardon, Betty A., 1995. *Educating for Human Dignity: Learning About Rights and Responsibilities*, University of Pennylvania Press.

Ray, Douglas, Ed., 1988. *Peace Education: Canadian and International Perspectives*, London: Third Eye Publications,.

Smith, David C. and Terrance R. Carson, 1998. *Educating for a Peaceful Future*, Kagen and Woo, Ltd..

UNESCO, 1997. *UNESCO and a Culture of Peace: Promoting a global movement*, UNESCO Publishing.

8

Education for the Globalised World

From obscure origins in French and American writings in the 1960s, the concept of globalization finds expression today in all the world's major languages. All these dimensions have impact on the field of comparative education as well as on other fields of endeavour. Nevertheless, interpretations of the precise nature of dynamics depend strongly on the perspectives of the observers. In this 'borderless' economy, national governments are "relegated to little more than transmission belts for global capital or, ultimately, simple intermediate institutions sandwiched between increasingly powerful local, regional and global mechanisms of governance".

The 19th century era of the classical Gold Standard, they note, was also a period of economic integration. The sceptics consider the hyperglobalist thesis to be fundamentally flawed and politically naïve since it underestimates the enduring power of national governments to regulate international economic activity. The sceptics a recognise the economic power of regionalisation in the world economy, but assert that by comparison with the age of world empires the international economy has become considerably less global in its geographical embrace. The transformationalists, like the hyperglobalists, consider globalisation to be a central driving force behind the rapid social, political and economic changes that are reshaping societies. However, they are less certain of the direction in which trends are leading and about the kind of world order which it might prefigure. For transformationalists, the existence of a single global system is not taken as evidence of global convergence or of the arrival of a single world society. Rather, they argue, "globalization is associated with new patterns of global stratification in which some states, societies and communities are becoming increasingly enmeshed in the global order while others are becoming increasingly marginalized". The new patterns require reformulation of vocabulary from North/South and First/Third World, recognising that new hierarchics cut across and penetrate all societies and regions of the world. These remarks show that the concept of globalisation is complex. The term is viewed differently even within particular academic disciplines, and across disciplines the variation increases further.

8.1. Comparative Education

Comparative education is by nature an interdisciplinary field. This provides a valuable meeting point for disciplinary perspectives, but also increases the potential for confusion. To place in context subsequent remarks about the contemporary nature of the field and the extent to which it has become globalised, it is useful to sketch some dimensions of its history and evolution. An alternative view might be that the field had multiple origins; but it is undeniable that significant work was developed in Europe and the USA. During the 20 th century, the field gathered momentum and spread.

In 1971, UNESCO in Paris launched Prospects: Quarterly Review of Education, initially in parallel English and French versions, then from 1973 also in Spanish, and by the 1990s also in Arabic, Chinese and Russian. In 1995, the subtitle of the journal was changed to Quarterly Review of Comparative Education. The English-language International Journal of Educational Development was launched in the UK in 1981, and is also considered a major journal in the field. To these journals were added many seminal textbooks.

The WCCES was formed 1970, having evolved from an International Committee of Comparative Education Societies which had been convened by Joseph Katz, of the University of British Columbia in Canada, in 1968. Five societies came together to form the Council, namely:

— the Comparative & International Education Society (CIES) of the USA, which had been founded in 1956;

— the Comparative Education Society in Europe (CESE), which had been founded in 1961,
— the Japanese Comparative Education Society (JCES), which had been founded in 1964,
— the Comparative & International Education Society of Canada (CIESC), which had been founded in 1967, and
— the Korean Comparative Education Society (KCES), which had been founded in 1968.

Over the decades, the number of constituent societies in the Council has fluctuated, but in 2002 the WCCES had 30 societies. Of these, 23 were national or sub-national societies (Brazil, Bulgaria, Canada, China, Czech Republic, Cuba, Hong Kong, Germany, Greece, Hungary, India, Israel, Italy, Japan, Korea, Philippines, Poland, Russia, Spain, Taiwan, UK, Ukraine, and USA), five were regional societies, and two were language-based societies. While the total list of constituent societies was impressive, in some countries and regions the societies have been fragile. The organisations have depended on the enthusiasm of a few individuals, and have commonly operated on a voluntary basis with low budgets. The fragility can be illustrated by comparing the 2002 WCCES list of constituent societies with that for 1993.

In 1993, the WCCES had 31 constituent societies, but only 25 were still on the list in 2002 because six had ceased to exist. These were:

— the Asociación Argentina de Education Comparada (AAEC),
— the Asociación Colombiana de Educación Comparada (ACEC),
— the Egyptian Group for Comparative Education (EGCE),
— the London Association of Comparative Education (LACE),
— the Nigerian Comparative Education Society (NCES), and
— the Portuguese Comparative Education Society (PCES).
— the Asociación de Pedagogos de Cuba (Sección de Educación Comparada) (APC-SEC),
— the Comparative Education Society of Asia (CESA),
— the Comparative Education Society of Hong Kong (CESHK),
— the Comparative Education Society of the Philippines (CESP), and

— the Ukraine Council for Comparative Education (UCCE).

Also, a new Argentinean group had formed and had expressed intention to apply for admission to the Council; a parallel group had been formed in Venezuela; and in France a body had been created under the title Association pour le Développement des Échanges Internationales et de la Comparaison en Éducation (ADECE).

The most obvious activities of the WCCES have been the organisation of periodic World Congresses of Comparative Education. The first Congress was held in Canada in 1970, and was followed by ones in Switzerland, United Kingdom, Japan, France, Brazil, Canada, Czechoslovakia, Australia, and South Africa.

The most recent Congress was held in South Korea in 2001, and the next will be held in Cuba in 2004. Other WCCES activities include advocacy for the field. The WCCES is affiliated to UNESCO as a Non-Governmental Organisation (NGO), and makes official representations to the international community through that body. The WCCES also operates a website, which contains links to organisations and educational institutions related to the field.

Like all such global bodies, however, the WCCES has constraints in its operation. In all academic circles there are prima donnas and factions, and in a world society of members from so many traditions and contexts it is often difficult to reconcile the diversity of interests and priorities. There are also diplomatic difficulties in finding acceptable venues which are also convenient for the gathering-in of colleagues from all over the world.

The WCCES statutes do not declare any official language, but most WCCES affairs are conducted in the English language. English has gained dominance as an international language, but this is not a neutral form of globalisation. By convention, arising from the fact that the original Secretariats were located in Ottawa and then Geneva (Switzerland), French has also been a permitted language for communication for the WCCES.

During the last decade, however, French has been little more than a token vehicle for official deliberation of WCCES affairs. The WCCES Officers are very aware of the imbalances that can be associated with language, and welcome suggestions on ways to promote the field of comparative education in multiple languages.

Another bias arises from the geographic spread of WCCES member societies.

Although the WCCES has constituent societies in every continent, and has also held Congresses in every continent, several parts of the world do not have direct representation in the Council. Thus in 2002, following the demise of the Nigerian and Egyptian societies, the only African society was that serving Southern Africa. South America was represented only by Brazil; and the Arab States were not represented at all. By contrast, Europe and Asia were well represented. Nevertheless, the WCCES may certainly be considered a global body; and in many respects it is also globalising. It brings together scholars from different parts of the world for exchange of ideas, and promotes joint projects. Certainly a great deal more can be done to facilitate the development of comparative education in different regions of the world and to promote the global dimensions of the field; but the WCCES does at least provide one vehicle to do this.

The field of comparative education, at least in some parts of the world, has drawn strongly on the theoretical bases of the social sciences. To some extent, therefore, shifts in dominant paradigms within the social sciences have been reflected in shifts in the field of comparative education. This includes the rise of positivism in the 1960s and 1970s, and the popularity of post-modernism in the 1980s and 1990s. However, comparative education scholars have tended to use a fairly limited set of tools from the social sciences display many commentaries based on literature reviews, but relatively few studies based on survey research, and almost no studies based on experimental methods.

Concerning the nature of reality, comparative educators would tend to see reality as somewhat subjective and multiple, rather than objective and singular. Epistemologically, comparative educators would tend to interact with that being researched rather than acting independently and in a detached manner from the content.

Axiologically, comparative educators would tend not to see research as value free and unbiased; rather, they would accept the notion that their research is value laden and includes the biases of the researcher. During the 1960s, the dominant focus was on high-human-development countries.

By the 1980s/1990s, however, the balance had shifted significantly. It still showed bias towards these countries, but included a much greater focus on low-human-development countries. Thus, whereas in the 1960s 73.1 per cent of the articles in Comparative Education Review and Comparative Education focused on high-human-development countries, and 15.0 per cent focused on the low-human-development countries, in the 1980s/1990s these proportions were 43.1 and 23.3 per cent.However, the nature of the themes, and the methodological approaches, have been very different in different parts of the world at particular periods in history.

During the 1990s, however, these two worlds showed some signs of convergence. As China opened up, and as English became more widespread, scholars in China paid more attention to the literatures and to methodological approaches in Western countries.

Academic interchange between the two cultures increased, facilitated by translations of English-language books into Chinese and by cross-national visits by both sides. It is arguable that the flow of ideas from the opening up was unbalanced: Chinese scholars were influenced by Western traditions much more than Western scholars were influenced by Chinese traditions, and the number of books translated from Chinese to English was considerably smaller than the number translated from English to Chinese. However, some Western scholars have certainly explored Chinese academic traditions in depth, and have gained from doing so. The 1990s and initial years of the present century have also brought some broadening of geographic interest among the different scholarly communities.

In China, the volume of scholarly analysis of education in less developed countries has been much more modest. This has partly reflected priorities, insofar as policy makers have felt that less can be learned from poor countries than from prosperous ones. It has also reflected the fact that although overseas-Chinese communities exist in many parts of the world, China has had fewer political and cultural links with Africa, Western Asia and Latin America.

Nevertheless, some broadening of geographic interest has been evident in Chinese-language publications, both in the mainland and in Taiwan. Despite these observations about convergence, however, it remains the case that the topics chosen for comparative analysis, and the methodological approaches, have continued to vary considerably in different parts of the world.

Gender, for example, has been a much stronger topic for focus in Western countries than in Asian societies; and analyses of the World Bank and other international agencies have been much more common in the English-language journals than in the Chinese, Japanese or Korean journals. Similarly, not all societies have been equally interested in themes of postcolonialism, multiculturalism and civil strife. Thus, while it is increasingly possible to talk of about a global field of comparative education, it is necessary to recognise continued variations.

The forces of globalisation, they suggest, provide both an imperative and an opportunity. The imperative arises from the changed environment brought by globalisation, and the opportunity arises from the increased interest in international affairs among academics, policy-makers and practitioners. The field of comparative education, they argue, can be revitalised and can secure fresh relevance within the new environment. Various other scholars have also noted ways in which the field of comparative education can grapple with issues of globalisation. One major factor is that comparative education is naturally concerned with cross-national analyses, and by its very nature encourages its participants to be outward-looking.

Cross-national forces of change are reflected in dominant paradigms, methodological approaches, and foci of study. Time-space compression and improved access to people, places and societies have assisted the field to develop in important ways. Among the institutions which promote globalisation are the various national, regional and language-based comparative education societies and the global body which brings them together, the World Council of Comparative Education Societies (WCCES).

Most of the national, regional and language-based societies hold annual and biennial conferences which attract participants from outside the countries, regions and language groups which the societies mainly serve; and every few years the WCCES organises a World Congress of Comparative Education. These events increase the interflow and promote internationalisation. However, imbalances in access remain, and comparative education is certainly not yet (and may never become) a homogeneous field to which scholars from all countries and language groups have equal access. Within the field, globalisation has itself become an important topic for study and has affected the nature of discourse.

The majority recognise that cross-national forces exist and that in some ways they have become stronger than in the part, but who point out that cross-national forces have long been an important influence on education systems and that national governments still retain major roles in the education sector.

Since by nature comparative education is an interdisciplinary field, the potential for common conceptions seems very limited. Issues of marginalisation have been specifically highlighted by specialists in comparative education within the context of globalisation. Such work can contribute to broader, multidisciplinary analysis beyond that specifically concerned with education.

8.2. Global Education Charter

The Global Education Charter focuses on the implications of Global Education for bodies responsible for school policies in Europe. Global Education shall be made a principle in schools, in the curriculum and in teacher training courses, taking into account the fact that working in the formal sector is a very strategic and important way to influence overall educational changes. The Charter presents a series of arguments for political and educational decision makers to take up the challenges we have to face today and will have to face tomorrow. It is intended to stimulate the debate about how education should be organised, how the curriculum should be formed in order to keep up with rapid changes in a more and more interdependent society, by translating the globalisation issues into school programmes. The aim of the Charter is to attract as well as encourage policy makers and educators to support the ideas and ideals of global education in formal school programmes.

Globalisation is an obsessively recurring word in every type of discourse which tries to describe and explain social, economic and political developments in the world today. In the past few decades, processes related to globalisation induced major changes—economic, technological, cultural, demographic, environmental and political - which require a definition of responsible global citizenship.

The world we live in has evolved into a single social system as a result of many ties of interdependence among various countries. Recent history unquestionably shows that the lives of men and women of this planet may be influenced by facts, processes, organisations and networks thousands of kilometres away. While globalisation may be said to have begun hundreds of years ago with the expansion of western influence to various parts of the globe, it was not until this century—after World War II more particularly—that it became a fact.

World-wide economic relations—largely through the activity of multinationals—as well as social relations, modern communications and transport allowing a fast flow of information, persons and goods are both causes and characteristics of globalisation as a process that led and leads to an interdependent world. However, globalisation did not develop evenly: indeed, it was accompanied by inequality and conflict.

The global development of economic and social relations has been parallelled by wide disparities between North and South. The prevalence of market economy tenets, and economic and technological advances world-wide are countered by unequal world economic growth, imbalanced distribution of cognitive and material resources, the spectre of damage caused by an unwise development of resources and hazardous uses of technological progress. If the development of our planet into a planet village is accepted as a fact, the assessment of the benefits and costs of globalisation, the interpretation of the process as such is a highly controversial issue.

In different contexts, in various parts of the world and in respect of various sides of globalisation, the phenomena and processes that help building today's global/planet village are perceived ambivalently as positive or negative, good or bad, beneficial or damaging, profit-making or loss-making.

Global education may help people realise that globalisation expresses the course of the future social development and that it depends on us all whether developments benefit only a privileged part of the globe's population or humanity as a whole. Global education is an answer to globalisation processes and their chances as well as risks. Major political changes in recent years such as the opening of the

Berlin Wall and the rising tide of democratisation in Central and Eastern Europe, in the Republic of South Africa, in Central and South America, etc. seem to support an optimistic view of globalisation and its effects. However, this has also been a time when ethnic and religious conflicts deteriorated into cruel wars in various parts of the world. While there has been growing awareness of the common needs and wants of people the world over, how exactly can the different views on giving access to the Earth's resources be reconciled is still an open question.

In order to function in an adequate and respectful way in our society, young people and adults have to remember through education and constantly consider the fundamental equality in diversity of human beings, the need for respecting other cultures and races and for condemning violence, coercion and repression as social control mechanisms. Global awareness and global consciousness has been documented in more than one way in recent decades.

Firstly, it was the media that gave access to globalised information, culture and life styles. Consciousness of global change as growing interdependence and the need for international cooperation was complemented by a systematic response to change promoted mainly by international organisations such as the United Nations, UNESCO, the Council of Europe, OSCE.

More and more, individuals and organisations, supporters of global education realise that people and their leaders clearly need developing attitudes and behaviours conducive to the acceptance and promotion of interdependencies and cooperation among nations. Many international covenants and declarations prepared and enacted by these institutions over time contain suggestions, recommendations and lines of action for both the design and the implementation of professional global education programmes, seen as relevant educational responses to the challenges of the contemporary world.

Such covenants and declarations, conveying the firm belief in the educational potential of school, include outstanding statements for global citizenship that sum up values and principles seen as a foundation for a world where cooperation among persons equal in rights and dignity may eventually be a fact. Educators should be aware that such values and principles must constantly be reinvented, changed and asserted through learning processes.

Decision makers and educators should also be highly sensitive to the fact that these values and principles cannot be taken for granted to be universal: this is a major challenge. Empathising and valuing different cultural perspectives in the context of other values system is a demanding requirement of global education. Such international documentation reveals intellectual and political perspective changes across the world in recent decades, and illustrates the fact that various phrases advanced by the specific action of international organisations convey in different ways a common awareness of educational priorities which are in line with changes in the world we live in.

Global education as a movement of ideas and an educational trend is seen as an attitude and a response to the increasing globalisation in every realm of modern life. The scope of global education has grown steadily for the past twenty years. The American and Canadian experience provided the impetus. Although different from development education, human rights and peace education, inter- and multicultural education, global education gives a broader perspective to what has traditionally been referred to by these special education areas, and stresses the strong interdependencies and links between the economic, technological, socio-political, demographic and cultural aspects of social life.

8.3. Global Education Strategies

Global education, as a style of learning and way of thinking, encourages people to identify links between the local, the regional and the world-wide level and to address inequality. Global education stresses their interrelationship for humanity as a whole and the close link with international contexts. It addresses issues according to an interdisciplinary approach and gives central importance to all aspects of interdependency, based on active and participative educational methods.

As a special educational action, global education is characterised first of all by interdisciplinarity and by its interculturally-oriented approach, by the above-said theme focus and by the learning objectives which pursue to develop the competencies required of global citizenship. Advancing new opportunities for education, global education is promoted as giving an insight into globalisation phenomena, allowing the acquisition and development of skills and competencies required by individuals to adjust to the challenges of a changing society.

Global education, more than just a strategy of enabling people to understand the world we live in, is also a specific way of action for reshaping the world, for helping human beings to achieve personal and community empowerment. Global education is centred on global learning which develops the abilities to understand, to feel and to act against the background of multiple interdependencies, and which is future-oriented.

While global learning cannot be achieved without specialist knowledge, knowledge acquisition is not its foremost aim. Global learning mainly aims to develop the abilities to make decisions on one's own life, competently to take part in social practice and express solidarity with those whose fundamental rights are violated.

Global learning is defined as comprehensive, anticipatory, participative, person-centred, situational, based on the stimulation of thinking apt to cope with interdependencies. It is a kind of learning focussed on issues, based on self-motivation and independent effort.

As a learning process, global education facilitates development of the abilities to feel, to think, to judge and to act so that young people may cope with the intellectual and emotional challenges of a global existence. Global learning aims to master tensions, particularly those occurring, subject to context, between:

— globalisation and local potential for action ocomplexity and inevitable oversimplifications olife experience universalisation and individualisation

— uncertainty and the need for certainty

— future orientation and the confrontation with historically determined events and processes

— knowledge acquisition and development of social competencies

Global education, as a perspective of thinking, judging, feeling and acting incorporates the dimensions of learning, life style and action, stressing the relationship of values and standards for humanity as a whole, emphasising international contexts, and enabling children to actively participate in the construction of their future.

Global education is aiming at providing orientation in the present and future world. To develop the skills for understanding the world we live in and for competent and moral action therein, global education must facilitate:

- knowledge of others and acceptance of life in a pluralistic world;
- awareness of the fact that global relations are complex and that we have to understand globalisation from different perspectives;
- an analysis of how global relations affect us through the cause-effect and purpose-means relationship;
- admission and acceptance of interdependencies and interferences that shape our local, regional and national identities in a global context;
- development of concern for justice, for sharing rights and responsibilities in the perspective of global citizenship;
- opening/diversifying the forms of learning, including critical media literacy;
- evidence that people can influence life through participation against injustice, exploitation and repression;
- readiness for personal and group action;
- awareness of implications of present choices/decisions and actions;

8.4. Areas of Global Education

Global education to comprise four major areas on the art and knowledge of living together on Planet Earth:

a. Empathetic education (to learn to understand the others, to learn to put ourselves in the place of others , to see problems with the eyes of others, to be empathetic to others)

b. Solidarity education (to develop a sense of community that transcends group, state, or race limits, to work/campaign for an end to inequality and social injustice)

c. Mutual respect and understanding education (to open up to other cultural areas/worlds, to invite others to participate in/join one's own culture)

d. Education against nationalism (to open up to other nations, to communicate, to avoid attitudes/expressions/behaviours rooted in prejudice and stereotypes).

Global eaucation broadens the horizons of knowledge and allows a critical reflection on one's own and others' identities and life styles, and by so doing it helps avoiding misinterpretations and stereotypes. The learning processes specific of global education aim at developing a permanent global-local relationship in an attempt to meet the need to build our lives by acting.

Knowledge and awareness of global processes are no aims in themselves. They make no sense unless they are aimed at developing attitudes and competences apt to foster sensitivity and social participation in young people. Through a specific body of knowledge students must be introduced to the language and issues of global education.

Global education should stress structural interdependencies between North and South, and between development trends in the North and in the South. Learning processes, rather than providing knowledge as such, should pursue to integrate attitudes, skills and knowledge, also taking into account the relationship between knowledge and context.

The body of knowledge should be so conceived as to allow students to explore and use the interdisciplinary and cross-curricular links provided by the school programme. Political and educational decision makers and educators have to understand the need for and potential of global education.

School programmes clearly need to promote attitudes and behaviours conducive to the acceptance and development of interdependencies and cooperation between nations. The spiritual, emotional and physical capabilities needed today to master the reality and complexity of our lives are intellectual and socio-emotional instruments that must be oriented to a globalising perspective of the art and knowledge to live together.

The development of attitudes and skills that global education is supposed to support and stimulate pursues to make children able to avoid indifference and the lack of concern. It avoids a simplistic and one-sided thinking which maintains cliches, bias and stereotypes, allowing their negative social effect to persist.

The aim of global education is to bridge the gap between knowledge (and even understanding) and responsible action, helping young people develop political skills and confidence to use them. Comprehensive global education efforts which emphasise the relationship between global and local issues should enable students to develop and express their concern for equity, social justice and personal and environmental well being.

The intellectual skills developed through global education are to give students competent access to the complex and interdependent fields/aspects of human rights, sustainable development, peace, citizenship and the environment. They should enable students to grasp the multi- and intercultural dimensions of our identities and the complex interdependencies of contemporary life in their positive or negative instances designed and assessed in context.

Critical thinking and critical approaches essentially mean comparing local and global phenomena and processes, and analysing their causes and reasons thereof. Students should use as much as possible approaches involving contrast, comparison, assessment by their recourse to criticism. Students should also learn to deal with new information technologies, which are linking us daily with the world.

Students would have to develop their social communication, decision-making and conflict-solving skills. They have to learn to share responsibilities, to accept different perspectives as a source of mutual enrichment and empowerment. Such skills are the basis for access to and use of strategies for participation and involvement in local, national and international affairs. These skills should develop awareness of the interrelationship between human action and decision-making.

The introduction and promotion of global education in schools, as a new dimension of learning, can and should entail important curriculum changes perceived as good innovative or reform actions. Global education is identifiable in pedagogical practice as a cross-curricular approach, as a disciplinary approach with special emphasis on globalising aspects, or as special extra curricular projects or programmes.

By developing the emotional value of learning in addition to its cognitive one, global education relies heavily on interactive techniques which help adjust the content and form of learning to the aims of global education.

Global education has proved its reforming potential and that inasmuch as education is concerned, there is not one pedagogy, but different pedagogies adjusted to specific contexts. In this way, cultural and political pluralism as a global education principle shows in school practice as pedagogical pluralism.

It is this pedagogical pluralism that must give students, too, a voice in the definition of programmes and specific activities. Global education as a wide-ranging tool of intervention has to be promoted in a special learning environment, which facilitates the gradual development of the sense of curiosity and pleasure of discovery, and allows the acquired knowledge to be put to practice .

Global education is seen by its proponents and practitioners not only as a valuable source of social learning and socialisation, but also as a reservoir of institutional change and improvement of school in order that what happens within be less academic and better adjusted and integrated to real-life changes.

Global education is emerging as a challenge and chance to the institutional development of schools, which means the need for a more open and flexible curriculum, as well as for the development of a democratic climate in school and a learning environment. Educational policy makers will have to reconsider the role of school which, rather than being seen as an instrument of perpetuating nationalistic goals, should open children to a world perspective and enable them to live together in a world facing chances but also threats never known before.

Policy makers and school authorities are called upon to give institutional support to global education in school by:

— introducing/stimulating global education projects and programmes through the formal curriculum;

— facilitating the establishment and cooperation of Centres for global education;

— facilitating partnership networks between North and South institutions and persons, school links with global education-oriented national or international Centres;

— providing pre- and in-service teacher training in order to stimulate teachers to take an interest in access to professional global education culture.

Many global education projects have proved that different aspects, like fund-raising or partnership, can turn palpable, particularly if there is cooperation with public authorities, and with national and international centres specialising in global education.

8.5. Education in Knowledge Society

Education is the center of the knowledge society, and the school its key institution. These will of necessity become central concerns of the knowledge society, and central political issues. In fact, the acquisition and distribution of formal knowledge may come to occupy the place in the politics of the knowledge society which the acquisition and distribution of property and income have occupied in our politics over the two or three centuries that we have come to call the Age of Capitalism. In the knowledge society, clearly, more and more knowledge, and especially advanced knowledge, will be acquired well past the age of formal schooling and increasingly, perhaps, through educational processes that do not center on the traditional school. But at the same time, the performance of the schools and the basic values of the schools will be of increasing concern to society as a whole, rather than being considered professional matters that can safely be left to "educators."

In the knowledge society, for the first time in history, the possibility of leadership will be open to all. Also, the possibility of acquiring knowledge will no longer depend on obtaining a prescribed education at a given age. Learning will become the tool of the individual available to him or her at any age if only because so much skill and knowledge can be acquired by means of the new learning technologies. In fact, developed societies have already become infinitely more competitive for individuals than were the societies of the beginning of this century, let alone earlier ones. Within the worldview of the Knowledge Society, constructivism, complexity, and new views of knowledge that stress its implicit and social nature are major "drivers" for the creation of new knowledge use paradigms.

The concept of Development seems to have disappeared from our vocabulary. Dissemination has become the generic term for all knowledge transfer or communication activities. But we need knowledge use (KU) models that will discriminate among vastly different models of research-based knowledge use as well as an understanding of how these models differ from other KU models that are not particularly research-based in terms of the source of knowledge.

At the most fundamental level, there seems to be a tension between two vastly different, almost diametrically opposed, conceptions of knowledge acquisition. One extreme seems to be a conception of filling an "empty vessel" with facts or information. Information is "objective," easily communicated, and easily apprehended. Facts speak for themselves.

Products and programs can be adopted and implemented. At the other extreme images of engaging or supporting "communities of learners," of individual learning as a complex reconstruction of cognitive frames and meanings/values, or of organizations that must "restructure" and become "learning organizations."

A related tension is between attending to/defining, simple, universal "needs" of knowledge users versus attending to the "voice of the customer" through a protracted "conversation" that results in continuous feedback that effectively couples with the knowledge production process. The distinction between two paradigms:

a) *The Dissemination Paradigm,* in which some form of knowledge, produced someplace, is broadly disseminated to many users, often at some distance, physically and sometimes culturally, from the point of knowledge production. Thus the knowledge is "external" to the user system. From the knowledge producer's standpoint, the challenge is to communicate with and achieve producer-intended forms of use of this knowledge among many potential users. Dissemination, marketing, mass media, on-line information systems, and telephone 800 numbers for information services become some of the vehicles for communication between producer and user.

b) *The Systemic Change Process Paradigm,* in which the main focus of knowledge use and production is in one location .whether that is a person's head or a large organization. The knowledge use process is local, complex and dynamic. And most of the knowledge production is "local." Externally produced knowledge (ideas, products, programs, technologies) may be stimulative or facilitative, but this use of external knowledge is often incidental or subordinate to achieving synergistic changes in group or organizational structures, policies, operating procedures, and perhaps even the working environment of the organization and in the attitudes, skills, motives, values, and shared visions of those involved in this form of systemic change process.

"Research-based" knowledge may be represented more by processes of local disciplined inquiry and reflection than by the products of externally produced research. But this is rarely an either-or situation, rather it is a melding of knowledge in many forms from many sources.

Many current conceptions of KU involve some mixture of these two paradigms. Thus, we have extension agents and linking agents, technical assistance providers, trainers, consultants, and other forms of "external assistance" that may support the local systemic change process.

It would be monumental hubris to believe that education R&D could by itself accomplish such a transformation that will be, as Drucker says, a concern for our entire society. However, education R&D could be a powerful catalyst. Yet that is likely to happen only if there are equally profound transformations in the practice of education R&D.

Clearly, one place to start would be to focus on the production, transfer, and promotion of use of "reliable" knowledge by all those concerned with improving education in a Knowledge Society. "Knowledge utilization" seems an apt term to define this area of challenge to the education R&D community.

Over the past half-century there has been a significant change in what information scientists have been concerned with. We have seen a massive expansion in the scope of information science from concerns focused primarily on physical science content to concerns with content that includes the physical, social and behavioral sciences along with content in a multitude of applied fields.

We have moved from preoccupation with archives and collections to concerns with dissemination, marketing and distribution, and then to concerns with implementation, utilization and impact. We have moved from preoccupations with tangible, formal formats and channels to inclusion of less tangible, informal formats and channels.

And especially during the last decade, we have contended with the implications of digitalization, hyper-media, the Internet and computer-augmented learning and information processing. We have dealt with needs of users in fields beyond the scientific disciplines (e.g., business, industry, health, education, public policy) we have discovered that scientific and technical information alone is rarely sufficient to meet users' needs.

Craft knowledge usually must be melded with scientific knowledge. All these changes have had a profound effect on our conceptions of the design and operation of effective information systems, and more fundamentally on our conceptions of knowledge and the processes of knowledge utilization.

In the Knowledge Society, constructivism, complexity, and new views of knowledge that stress its implicit and social nature are major "drivers" for the creation of new knowledge use paradigms. To make this assertion clearer let us explore what may be some useful dimensions for conceptualizing or "mapping" the current domain of thinking about knowledge utilization.

Four dimensions are particularly useful to consider. At the most fundamental level, there seems to be a tension between two vastly different, almost diametrically opposed, conceptions of knowledge acquisition. One extreme seems to be a conception of filling an "empty vessel" with facts or information. Information is "objective," easily communicated, and easily apprehended. Facts speak for themselves.

Products and programs can be adopted and implemented. At the other extreme images of engaging or supporting "communities of learners," of individual learning as a complex reconstruction of cognitive frames and meanings/values, or of organizations that must "restructure" and become "learning organizations."

At mid-century, American psychology, under the influence of a prevailing behaviorism, accepted the assumptions of an objectivist epistemology. In this view, knowledge is seen as the accumulation of discrete pieces of evidence.

George Kelly termed it accumulative fragmentalism. Emphasis is placed on logical thinking rather than understanding. However, by the mid-1960s, social science moved away from the behaviorist value neutrality and detachment back to an earlier problem-oriented tradition to confront a problem-fraught national agenda.

In education, findings in cognitive psychology and a new interest in constructivism supported this emphasis. Constructivism offers a different view that focuses attention on the processes of interpretation that lead to understanding. According to constructivist theory, knowledge is developmental, internally constructed, and socially and culturally mediated.

Learners actively construct their knowledge in their attempts to make sense of their world. This philosophy also shifts attention from teaching to focus more directly on learning and student knowledge formation. A particular version of constructivism places an emphasis on situated learning and on communities of practice. In the field of the psychology of learning, Lev Vygotsky has exercised great influence through his model of social constructivism.

Vygotsky emphasizes the influences of cultural and social contexts in learning and supports an active discovery model of learning. Vygotsky distinguishes three levels of knowledge: "manifest content" (facts, data), "instrumental knowledge" (methods, skills, procedures), and "structural knowledge" (knowledge structures and underlying modes of thinking). He asserts that learning and human development is a social and collaborative activity that cannot be taught to anyone.

The learner must construct his or her own understanding. However, the teacher or others can act as facilitator. According to Vygotsky's concept of the zone of proximal development, problem solving skills can be placed in three categories: those performed independently, those that cannot be performed even with help, and those that fall between these extremes, the tasks that can be performed with help from others. It is in this last category, the zone of proximal development, that optimal learning should be supported.

This learning should take place within meaningful contexts that are close to the contexts in which knowledge is to be applied. Although when we consider these ideas we may typically think of a child in a school room setting, they apply to all forms of human learning including that of educational researchers, policymakers or educational practitioners. A particular version of constructivism places an emphasis on situated learning and on communities of practice. Situated learning is a general theory of knowledge acquisition. Lave argues that learning is situated, that is, as it normally occurs learning is a function of the activity, context, and culture in which it occurs.

Social interaction is a critical component of situated learning. Learners become involved in a "community of practice" which shares specific beliefs and behaviors. As newcomers move from the periphery of the community to its center, they become active and engaged within the micro-culture of the community. Thus, learning outside and inside schools advances through collaborative social interaction and social construction of knowledge.

People tend to treat information as self-contained and objective. It is something that you can write down or capture in some other form, accumulate, possess, store on a shelf or put in a database, compile, quantify, lose, find, retrieve, process, or distribute. In contrast to information, knowledge is associated with a "knower." Knowledge is hard to access or transfer to another. Knowledge is something that we digest or assimilate. It involves the knower's understanding. Thus, as we shift to conceptions of more complex knowledge we must place more emphasis on people and less emphasis on tangible objects or inanimate information systems.

One of the main characteristics of complex knowledge is that to master it requires mastery of several different component pieces of knowledge organized in the form of a system. Another characteristic is that use of complex knowledge depends on methods that are not mere algorithms. The complexity of such knowledge also comes from the fact that corresponding conceptions the cognitive constructs . of one person can be very different from those of another person. Moreover, these complex cognitive constructs are difficult to understand, to model, and to communicate. Thus current research on students' learning, understanding, and knowledge acquisition is substantially different from that of just a few decades ago. Explicit (codified) knowledge is formal in character. It can be expressed in words, numbers, symbols and graphics. It can be easily communicated through print and digital media and shared in the form of data, formulas, pictures, drawings, codified procedures or general principles.

Tacit knowledge is personal and context-specific. It involves cognitive aspects such as mental models, scripts, and schemata. It also includes subjective, intangible factors such as beliefs, perspectives and values, as well as hunches, intuitions, and insights. It may be tied to the senses, related to skills in body movement, or embedded in personal perceptions or physical experiences.

Tacit knowledge is thus often very difficult to describe to others. However, beyond this distinction between explicit and tacit knowledge are knowledge production. Beginning with the individual but then moving on to groups and organizations, these models conceptualize a "knowledge spiral" among four interactive methods of knowledge conversion: socialization, externalization, combination, and internalization.

Through socialization, tacit knowledge is shared through participation in joint activities that may produce shared mental models, routines, expectations, metaphors or even micro-cultures that are employed as frameworks for social or work interaction. Successful socialization requires that participants empathize enough to relate to each other's feelings and incorporate each other's beliefs, feeling, emotions, perceptions and sense-making. These kinds of exchanges usually require protracted shared experiences.

Externalization labels the process by which tacit knowledge is converted to explicit knowledge. Through this process, intuitions, images, sense-making schema, and the like may be transformed into explicit statements, metaphors, diagrams, concept maps, hypotheses, plans, models or other tangible forms. Combination describes the more familiar area of public knowledge and academic knowledge.

This is the explicit form of knowledge that is commonly produced and communicated through books, journals, and other publications and depicted in other tangible media forms. Through the process of internalization, explicit knowledge is converted to tacit knowledge, usually through learning by doing and through application or implementation.

The concept of the "spiral of knowledge" as conceived by Nonaka and Takeuchi involves at least two important propositions. First, knowledge creation is amplified in greater than a linear fashion when all four forms of knowledge conversion are deliberately pursued and reflected against each other. Second, the spiral emerges when the interaction between tacit and explicit knowledge is elevated from a lower level, the individual, to higher levels, e.g. the work group, a community of learners, or an entire organization.

When we refer to the "gap" between educational researchers and practitioners, the analysis is typically centered on failures in formal communication, that is, transfer of explicit knowledge. However, on further reflection, it becomes apparent that the "gap" is rooted in failures in knowledge transfer involving all four areas in this "knowledge spiral."

This model of knowledge posits that the basis of all knowledge creation is the mobilization of tacit knowledge. However, the majority of our educational research journals are concerned with combination, the explicit to explicit knowledge conversion which is least directly associated with tacit knowledge.

Moreover, this model makes obvious that unless successful socialization between researchers and practitioners occurs on a close and frequent basis, with participants truly understanding and empathizing with each other, efforts to transfer knowledge are likely to fail. In the absence of effective socialization the concept of "two cultures" that fail to communicate with each other will be perpetuated.

There has also been a major shift from thinking about knowledge as residing with individuals to thinking of knowledge as embedded in a group or community. Perhaps, it is our experiences in school that have reinforced the conception of learning as an individual activity. However, studies of knowledge use in organizations reveal that adults encounter very different experiences in which knowledge is developed and actively shared within work teams. Moreover, the social structures extend well beyond work teams or communities of learners.

Libraries, technical information centers, and the like constitute the formal information system. In most fields of science, the formal information system is actually a marketplace of competing information systems. Each finds its unique function and audience.

The individual's cognitive system is a system of motivation, intelligence, and creativity, of cognitive structures, of perceived relevance of information inputs and uses of information out-puts. Ultimately, all other systems support this one. If nothing happens in this system, then nothing happens. Thus, sense-making, evaluation of knowledge claims and warrants, and the construction of knowledge models and relation-ships are markedly different. Indeed the personal and professional goals they seek, the social systems in which they live, and even the time frames they confront in addressing problems differ.

Researchers and practitioners live in different communities of practice with markedly different values, beliefs, and ideologies. However, there is a different body of literature that points to the benefits of researcher-practitioner communication and collaboration.

Within the field of education these findings about the advantages of collaboration between researchers and practitioners have been noted. Such forms of collaboration are among the basic design concepts undergirding the Strategic Education Research Plan (SERP).

The SERP would promote new, long-term collaborations among the research, practice, and policy communities; give educators a voice in defining the problems to be studied; and spur the development of institutions that further the demand for research. The SERP in particular pays attention to "critical mass" with "requisite variety" working in school-based settings over substantial periods of time.

In US, the National Academy of Education (NAE) "Recommendations Regarding Research Priorities", echoes a similar theme, and again with a concern that these types of education R&D programs should be conducted in field- and practice-based contexts: A general theme of the findings and recommendations is that progress toward high achievement for all students has been impeded by the belief that research, students' learning, and teachers' learning can be studied in isolation from important matters of context.

Both the SERP and the NAE "Recommendations" embrace the conception of supporting R&D that is conducted in "Pasteur's Quadrant." However, they go beyond Donald Stokes' image of a lone Pasteur to call for collaboration among groups of highly qualified researchers and practitioners who could collectively engage in disciplined inquiry and reflection as they proceed to engage in long-term programs of R&D situated in school-based contexts.This recent interest in conducting much more research in Pasteur's Quadrant, as envisioned in the SERP, directly addresses the need to create conditions and contexts long-term, field-based, collaborative work, focused on significant educational problems, with critical mass and requisite variety among both researchers and practitioners that might engender much more productive research outcomes.

Among those outcomes there would likely be a much deeper understanding (and appreciation) of the complexities of creating and transferring usable scientific knowledge bearing on real educational and social problems. Perhaps only after we have gained more experience in conducting these kinds of efforts will a sufficient number of education researchers and policy makers really begin to comprehend and appreciate the complex nature of the research-to-practice challenge.

Moreover, we find that appropriate literature and job aids (e.g., case studies, handbooks, failure analysis findings, codes, protocols, software) as well as intensive preparation and continuing education programs support all these engineering professions.

Education has at best a very primitive, disorganized, and relatively ineffective engineering counterpart. Hence, the applied aspects of education research knowledge transfer are very weak.No matter how rigorous our disciplinary knowledge (sociology, psychology, anthropology, economics, neurology, etc.) may become, it must be complemented with engineering (development) knowledge regarding applications, scaling-up, institutionalization, and the like.

We must create appropriate "engineering" professions in the field of education. If these professions are not developed, then most practical R&D applications problems (such as going to scale) are likely to remain unsolved.

And most education R&D, no matter how high its quality, will likely remain justly accused of being impractical, irrelevant, or grossly ineffective in addressing BIG education problems in satisfactory ways. If utility is seen as important, then perhaps some of the analysis should start from the use end of the education research application problem. For exampie, back-map from outstanding examples of educational improvement to try to identify the "plausible" causes, and where and how (if at all) did the results of research play a part. One might consider applying a "contingency" theory of user contexts.

In most fields where there are effective research-to-practice connections, the "order of magnitude" rule generally applies, that is, for every one research dollar, there may be ten development dollars, 100 dissemination dollars, and 1,000 implementation dollars.

In the field of education we rarely get much beyond low multiples, e.g., increases of two or three times, for the progressive stages. As education becomes more critical in terms of national priorities, there may be some greater concern about addressing this research utilization problem. The literature related to knowledge utilization in the field of education is immense. However, only a modest fraction of this literature is based in research or evaluation studies.

The need for improved educational development activity, but cautions that research and development should be viewed as a collective concept and enterprise. The role of knowledge produceer and also stresses the importance of relevant evaluation techniques to both development and diffusion activities. The roles needed to retrieve basic or applied knowledge, derive practical implications from it, and distribute to people who can use it.

There were four aspects of the public education system which distinguish education from other systems:

— vulnerability to the social environment;
— professional self-image and values of educational personnel;
— diffuseness of education goals; and
— need for coordination and control of the primary clients as well as of employees.

8.6. Technological Assistance

New technology is needed for transforming behavioral science knowledge into effective practice. Teaching is seen from this perspective as a technique that can be analyzed by subdividing it into components and improved by developing better teaching forms and diffusing them to schools and teachers who adopt them and put them into practice. The political perspective rejects this mechanistic view. Interests of various groups come into play in any significant educational change effort. Conflict, bargaining, and the application of political, economic, and bureaucratic power exert influences on the dynamics of a major change effort, often modifying the outcomes in ways that are hard to anticipate or control.

More fundamentally, the cultural perspective looks to basic differences in values and beliefs. The cultural perspective emphasizes the need to affect changes in meanings and values of those within the organization. And it also explains why resistance can be so intractable and changes so slow when an innovation runs counter to deeply held values and beliefs or when change activity forces different micro-communities within an adopting system to confront differences in values and beliefs that had heretofore remained unexamined.

Technical assistance provided to educational decision makers, administrators, and practitioners. Educational practices and, in particular, educational regulations became increasingly complex in the aftermath of "Great Society" legislation.

Educators needed information and skills that were adapted to local settings, local problems, and local resources. Dissemination systems were not adapted in this way. Even the educational extension agents, who might be familiar with local factors, could not provide adapted information that was missing from the dissemination system in the first place.

Technical assistance specialist constituted a different kind of professional. Drawing upon their own experience as well as the dissemination system, technical assistance specialists could provide adapted information and advice to educators. Under many authorizations from the 1960s to the 1980s, technical assistance specialists have worked with local personnel on problems of needs assessment, program development, evaluation, staff training, and so forth.

8.6.1. Networking in Support of Knowledge Utilization

Networking in support of knowledge utilization assumes that expertise is shared by educators in a peer network; they are each other's technical assistance specialists. Many complex topics are, and will probably continue to be, associated with specialists' expertise. However, many "how-to" topics in education are associated with peer expertise. At the local level, teachers' centers have been established to facilitate the sharing of peer expertise. At the regional and national levels, networks of educators with common concerns have arisen in some cases spontane-ously, and in others as components of change programs.

Moreover, perspectives about the KU process have shifted to highlight the complexities and dynamic transactional aspects of KU. Knowledge is no longer viewed as an inert object to be sent and received, but a fluid set of understandings shaped both by those who originate it and by those who use it.

Knowledge use is thus seen as a learning process. Dissemination is a process requiring a match among originated knowledge, the needs, contexts, prior experiences, values and beliefs of intended users, and the content, media, formats, and language used in getting the outcomes into the hands, minds, and activities of users. The goal of dissemination is utilization the critical element is that the research outcome must be understood and the individual or organization must incorporate the new information within prior understandings and experiences.

8.7. Education and Human Development

Development was taken-for a long period of time-to mean rising income. A common view used to equate development with growth in average income, though since the 1970s there was a shift in emphasis on income distribution and poverty reduction. Although, the role of social services -particularly basic health and education-also received greater emphasis in the 1980s, these services have been viewed mainly as instruments for raising the incomes of the poor. It is only since the inception of the Human Development Reports (HDRs), that the view has been that human development-defined as enlarging people's choices-is the overriding purpose of income growth and economic development. This approach towards improving human well being covers all aspects of human life for all people, both now and in the future. It goes far beyond the narrowly defined concept of economic development to cover the full development of all human potential. It emphasizes the need to put people-their needs, their aspirations, and their capabilities-at the center of the development effort. The human development perspective has now moved into the mainstream of the development debate.

It is now widely accepted that it provides an alternative and more comprehensive view of development to that equated exclusively with economic growth. As emphasized by Nobel Laureate Amartya Sen, what is valued are people's achievements—their "beings" and "doings" or their "capabilities". This contrast between the income-centered approach to development and the human development capability approach is instrumental in distinguishing the ends and means of development.

The 1997/98 Egypt Human Development Report (EHDR) cited the example of how the income-centered approach assesses investment in "human capital" entirely in terms of the extra income the investment generates. By contrast, the human development approach emphasizes that people's ability to read and write, be knowledgeable, capable and healthy should be considered ends in themselves, with positive effects on labour productivity, physical environment and reduced poverty as a welcome consequence.

The human development approach also treats the meaning of poverty differently. Capability and human poverty, the concepts introduced in the UNDP Human Development Reports, see impoverishment as multidimensional. It is more than a lack of material well being; it can also mean the denial of opportunities and choices to lead a long, healthy, creative life and a decent standard of living, enjoying dignity, and the respect of others.

The Egypt Human Development Report initiative has been identified as one of the most successful from among more than 100 such national Human Development Reports across the developing world. The essential bridge between concepts of human development and their practice was built and a common language consequently evolved between researchers and policymakers. This allowed for four essential links to be made so as to reach the ultimate beneficiaries of the new human development paradigm:

— Links between concepts.

— Policy and program formulation

— Implementation, and

— Institutionalization

Each bridge was strengthened by focusing on the production of accurate and meaningful information, generating awareness and consensus among thinkers and practitioners and on building a constituency that would ensure national ownership of the Human Development Report that combines autonomy with legitimacy.

The human development concept was given a strong impetus by the construction of the Human Development Index (HDI) to measure both the level and evolution of progress. The HDI has been successful in serving as an alternative measure of development, replacing GNP per capita. It is based on several distinctive components; indicators of longevity, educational attainment and income.

Within the limits of these three components, the HDI has served to broaden substantially the empirical attention that the assessment of the development process receives. As a composite index HDI not only avoids some of the inadequacies of other indexes, such as GNP, but measures the distance between the best and worst performers and avoids a ranking by income averages.

It can be disaggregated by gender, region, and socio-economic groups. The index, which is constructed every year, measures average achievements in basic human development in one simple composite index and thus enables ranking a country among other countries of the world.

In other words, the HDI value for a country shows the distance that it has to travel to reach the maximum value of 1, or its shortfall, and also allows for inter-country comparisons. These and other related issues have been the subject of a series of UNDP HDRs as well as national HDRs, such as the (EHDR). Egypt is in the medium human development category, with an HDI value in 1998 equal to 0.623.

Thus Egypt has to make up a shortfall in human development of about 38 percentage points, for example, while Canada, at the top of the HDI, has to make up for only 7 percent, and Sierra Leone, at the bottom, has to make up 75 percent. As unsatisfactory as it might be, the HDI indicator of a faltering human development status raises the question of whether it is the income level or the inadequate provision of social services are constraining human development in Egypt.

It is now widely recognized that the link between economic prosperity and human development is neither automatic nor obvious. However, the comparison between the ranking of a country on the HDI and by its level of income per capita, may reveal the links between economic growth and human development.

According to the UNDP Human Development Report, Egypt is placed at the 119th position out of 174 countries. However, this rank is eleven places lower than its GDP per capita rank. This can be interpreted to indicate a considerable scope for reallocating the available resources to the improvement of people's lives.

In other words, effective policies are required to translate the benefits of economic growth into the well being of all the Egyptians. Thus a combination of both factors, income growth and sound policies, determines human development and its enhancement.

Examining the trends in human development, the Report shows that Egypt was the second fastest country in achieving progress in human development. Starting from low human development with an HDI value of 0.430 in 1975 Egypt improved its HDI to 0.623 in 1998. The links between human development and economic growth can be mutually reinforcing.

But these links can also be unbalanced as a result of rapid human development with little growth, or of fast growth with slow human development. Generally, the index of GDP per capita has been higher than the HDI. With 3.5 percent annual growth in real GDP per capita in 1975-98 Egypt achieved a near 34 percent reduction in the shortfall of the non-income components of the human development index.

However, it is indicative that while the Egyptian economy was growing at slow rates during the 1985-1995 period, human development was also improving at a slow pace. Just as human development encompasses aspects of people's lives that are much broader than income, so poverty should be seen as having many dimensions. Poverty from a human development perspective focuses on a denial of choices and opportunities for living a tolerable life.

Therefore, the human-or capability-poverty does not just consider income, but rather the indicators of the most basic dimensions of deprivation: a short and unhealthy life, and lack of basic education and a lack of access to public and private services and resources. The

Egypt HDR 1996 has estimated the measurements for both income and capability poverty. These estimates suggested that capability poverty is generally higher than income poverty in Egypt.

While 23 percent of the total population live below the national poverty line, more than one-third falls in the category of human deprivation. Thus, while 15 million Egyptians are income poor, more than 23 million are capability poor. The Report found that population in rural Upper Egypt is the largest deprived group.

Obviously great efforts are needed to provide wide and improved education, health, and public work programs to the rural areas, especially in Upper Egypt. A thorough analysis shows that Egypt experienced relatively high-income growth in most years between the 1960s and the 1970s, with below average human development. It was however, unable to fully translate its growth into better education and health, and by the 1980s, the lack of broadly based human capital acted as an important break on rapid growth.

It is clear that if a better link is to be created between income and human development, it is mandatory to adopt policies that distribute economic and social assets and opportunities more equitably. Various human development indicators can be helpful to examine inequalitics between poor and rich, between genders, and between rural and urban areas.

Disaggregation of these indicators not only reflects disparities between groups but also reveals who are the most deprived and the extent to which they have shared the benefits of progress. In urban Egypt, for example, the combined enrolment ratio is around 60 percent for the poor and 80 percent for the rich. Thus, the low human development level of the "poor" is not only because they are below the poverty line, but also because they have lower literacy rates. Similarly, the poor have less access to infrastructure. It is widely recognized that the national average of different indicators fails to reflect the advances made by all groups in the country. Better understanding of the process of development should measure the gains and losses of various social groups and regions.

While the average for Egypt is 82 percent, the average for females is about 76 percent, and the female enrolment ratio is as low as 52 percent in Fayoum, whilst the highest ratio for girls is achieved in

Suez. Egypt is facing an overriding challenge of eradicating illiteracy. Some progress has been achieved in this respect.

In 1992 almost half of the adult Egyptians were literate. By 1999 the literacy rate had risen to 56 percent. Despite the fact that the urban-rural gap had narrowed, rural Upper Egypt made slower progress in literacy achievement. The gap is wide between the bottom and the top. The usefulness of the HDI goes beyond its absolute level, and beyond changes in this level in the long run.

The HDI measures the average achievements in a country in three basic dimensions of human development-a long and healthy life, knowledge and educational attainment, and a decent standard of living. Countries are ranked in the global HDRs on the basis of HDI values. A challenge for every country is to proceed towards the highest level of achievement on each of the human development components. Hence, from a policy perspective both the value of the HDI and its component and the relative position of a country on the human development ladder can advance our understanding of development achievements as well as challenges ahead. Since Egypt began producing its national Human Development Reports it has become clear to all those concerned with the well being of the Egyptian people that Egypt's ranking is unsatisfactory and indicative of an equivocal human development status.

An examination of the three key indexes of human development (life expectancy, educational attainment and per capita income) helps identify areas of success and the shortfalls. In fact, the way HDI is constructed presents the relative share which can be attributed to each of its components. In other words if countries are ranked according to life expectancy alone, Egypt would have been ranked in the 104th position instead of the 119th. Many developing countries with similar or even lower levels of per capita income enjoy higher literacy rates than Egypt. The literacy rate would increase to the levels achieved in China or Jordan, Egypt's HDI would significantly increase, reflecting an improvement in human development. The educated are always apt to make reasonable choices within a well-designed human development strategy. Moreover, they are the most likely to translate the human development policies into effective and sustainable actions, creating upward achievements in all areas of human life.

Well-educated people are more productive, healthier, more creative, and ultimately richer in all dimensions of the word. Indeed, education stands at the top of those factors determining the human development level. As such, education is both an input and an output of the human development process. As input, education is indispensable for progress in all spheres of human development. As output, education is the axiom for building-up human capabilities, a focal interest of human development, given its primary role in enabling people to fully participate in socioeconomic and political development. Present and future perspectives of human development in Egypt depend largely on how far it will succeed in implementing a future oriented reform in its education system.

Moreover, such a reform is indispensable for maximizing Egypt's potential to benefit from the ongoing globalization process, while avoiding, or at least minimizing, the negative impacts of this process on the country's human development. The reform and development of education are necessarily linked with the needs, ambitions, pressures and challenges to be faced by Egypt in the future and in the light of the continuous and ever accelerating forces of change in this century. Indeed, the core objective of effective education is to promote those capabilities that are the driving force of progress, and equally, to benefit from the development of various resources of the society in a continuous and complementary way. When exploring education for the future it is necessary to refer, even briefly, to the changes occurring in today's world and which impact on life in a way that is unprecedented in the history of humankind.

The most important change, of course, has been the phenomenon of globalization including the impact of the scientific, technological, and information revolutions accompanying it, both as cause and effect. Though globalization's initial trend appears, at first glance, to be mainly concerned with economic change, its implications will certainly be felt across wider areas in the lives of societies and individuals, to span increasingly to political, social and cultural spheres.

Globalization is no longer limited to geography, but affects cultural and intellectual space, and the accumulation of knowledge. With its new horizons, mechanisms and achievements, it presents immense opportunities for progress, prosperity and welfare, but also numerous perils, making it necessary to re-think and re-arrange many of the policies, plans and responsibilities involved in the administration of society and the conduct of human life.

Many of these challenges are the product of dangers inherent in the free-market system and its speedy economic transfers without duc safeguards to control its activities and operations, and its impact on human development and people's needs in the long run. Also ignored are the effects of its advanced technologies which widen the gap between the rich who control resources and the poor who are keen on consuming these goods.

This form of globalization with its scientific and technological revolutions stands currently as the major concern of the international community in general, and of the developing South in particular. This is largely due to its negative impact on issues such as equity, cultural values and identity, environmental protection, preservation of natural resources, and on the very air we breathe and the water we drink.

One of the main features of globalization and its links with the market economy lies in the sudden shift from production relying heavily on human labor and capital to one relying on knowledge and intellectual creativity and their technological applications including the invention of technological instruments themselves.

Scientific discovery no longer necessarily precedes application; it is industrial need which generates the scientific agenda as new materials are created according to required specifications. This new intellectual power has led the accumulation of knowledge to become the most important component in the process of production, while decreasing the relative importance of traditional factors, i.e. land, raw materials, labor and financial capital.

The preponderant factor in relative and competitive advantage and added value lies now in possessing intellectual capital with its capacity for accumulation and ever-increasing effectiveness. This turning point in the production process has abundantly shown the economic futility of employing cheap labor with limited educational level in the production of goods and services, as it cannot meet the quality standards required for competing in the free world market.

In the light of these developments the need becomes imperative for higher standards of education designed to produce a vanguard of scholars, and eventually create a knowledge-oriented society which provides high value and marketable learning and teaching opportunities for its citizens.

Such an environment would produce inventive leadership and highly trained human capital capable of creating wealth as well as sustainable conditions for prosperity and welfare, contrary to the claims of the first Club of Rome in its report on the "Limits of Growth" with its dismal Malthusian predictions.

In this new world of soft, rather than hard power, and given the relative failures of economic models of development planning followed by most countries of the South, the concept of "human development" has emerged as a sine-qua-non for real overall sustainable development. This approach has since become the chief concern of development policies, priorities, and allocation of resources.

Human knowledge has therefore loomed larger to the forefront of educational and training institutions as a vital contributor to development goals at world, regional and national levels. In brief, there are no limits to the horizons of balanced progress as long as the development of the human factor remains its moving engine for which education is highly responsible. Among international investigations on the role of education in human development, which aim at enhancing the capacity to respond positively to the challenges of globalization, are reports prepared by two UNESCO committees recruited from different regions and in different fields, to review the role of education and culture in the framework of globalization.

Education is a deeper and more congenial way to serve human development: it will help combat poverty, exclusion, ignorance, repression and wars. The principle of "education throughout life" is emphasized in both the Delore and Dequillar reports, as well as the need to re-think the different stages of education and the link between them and the world of work.

This principle makes allowances for different stages of education, diversification of educational courses, and the continuing nature of acquiring knowledge and skills and enhancing the value of each. The Dequillar Report, "Our Cultural Diversity", deals mainly with different aspects of culture and its components, including values and heritage, the darker side of globalization in relation to development, and the problem of inter-relations between the values of globalization and national and cultural identities.

These global trends have led nations to assert the value of their own cultural wealth and varied traditions which cannot be measured by dollars or centimeters, and also to try, at the same time, to contribute to the establishment of values for a global ethical system.

On the Arab regional level, in 1990 the Arab Thought Forum (Amman) prepared a document titled "Education of the Arab Nation in the 21st Century" to which was added a "Amman Educational Declaration". The focus was the challenge of the future, which would depend on well-educated citizens with the knowledge, skills and problem-solving abilities required for coping with the modern world. This cannot be achieved unless societies work towards change, by developing and revising the educational system, its goals, structure, method, and practices, in appropriate ways to suit and respond to those changes provoked by the international, scientific, technological, and democratic revolutions as well as by regional economic blocks.

The "Amman Educational Declaration" calls on the Arab world to recognize the necessity of joint action, and the value of an Arab regional grouping as requisites for economic, social, educational and technological progress, referring to studies and lessons gained by other regional blocks. The outcome of joint action would be more than the total sum of its individual components.

In the Arab world the crucial ingredients necessary for progress are potentially present: a vast geographical space, a large population, a viable market that would encourage investments, and the required labor force. Specialists estimate the minimum limit needed for a population size capable of survival and competition in the 21st Century should not be less than one hundred million literate people, half of them, at least, with a secondary education, and at least a quarter with university and postgraduate education.

In addition, the Arab Organization for Education, Culture and Science (ALESCO) has prepared a document entitled "Towards a Future Vision of the Education of the Arab Nation",. The document reviews a vast range of issues concerning the future of Arab education, and warns against holding on to the present system with its inadequate content and practices. It warns in strong terms that a new Arab educational system will be of no use if we content ourselves with ad-hoc reform here and there, or with just patching up aspects of the system.

The whole educational structure including content and methods should be rethought. Such overall renewal should start by creating an organic and cohesive link between education and the new social, economic and cultural structures needed to build a new society. Moving from international and regional levels to the national level in Egypt, the issue of education in the 2lth Century has been discussed in a large number of conferences and seminars.

These have covered trends in planning for the education of the future with a view to overcome present problems. Some have dealt with the educational system from an overall perspective, while others with specific stages, curricula or components of the educational structure.

In higher education, a mention must be made to the national conference held by Cairo University on the "University of the Future". One important document dealing with the future of education in Egypt was prepared by the Ministry of Education in 1992, with the title "Mubarak and Education—A Look At the Future". It draws a detailed picture of the educational system on the grounds that education is, for Egypt, a national security concern, which makes reform imperative at all levels, including teacher training, the upgrade of buildings and facilities, curricula, and improved finances, as well as the introduction of modern educational technology.

These comprise, in their interactions, consistency and integration, a set of human development priorities that are at the heart of comprehensive and normative societal objectives, which the education of the future should help achieve. This aim can be achieved by reaffirming the prerequisites of social integration that is characterized by solidarity, cohesion, and a common culture based on shared values but also providing the necessary space for variations and for a dialogue guaranteeing the balance of interests.

This will materialize through the provision of educational opportunities and the right of access to all educational institutions, thus basing social mobility on ability rather than family, wealth or influence. What is needed at this stage, where poverty hits a significant number of people, is to provide disadvantaged students with material aid to help them continue their studies.

The principle of equal opportunity in education, together with the right to work, represent an effective instrument for generating leadership from all social levels. Such diversified leadership with its broad interests and concerns is likely to push the process of development towards a future in the interest of all citizens.

It will also contribute to the prerequisites of political stability and social peace. This target relates to the need to provide individuals with the knowledge, skills, problem-solving abilities needed to act effectively and efficiently, and to upgrade the level of national production, making use of appropriate technology in the work place. It is imperative that labor skills should not only serve the requirements of large business projects and export competition.

Attention should also be extended to the various agricultural activities of small holdings and industries, and to all other activities that help the national economy fulfil Egypt's overall needs and satisfy those of its citizens. Development of a Democratic Way of Life should extend to the various aspects of democracy, whether in terms of thought, organization or action.

It involves participation in decision making, shouldering the responsibilities of implementation, follow up and evaluation of action in the different spheres of national activity. This will enhance the rights of the Egyptian citizen, as well as create a deep sense of belonging and involvement in the process of development with all its rewards and sacrifices.

For Egypt to continue in this role it will require an understanding of the necessary prerequisites, the ways and means of successful interaction and effective negotiation skills. It also comprises the promotion of Arab cultural and scientific creativity, integration and cooperation in common scientific research, in different fields of educational investment, and the establishment of a comprehensive Arab Common Market to face the high competitiveness of other world economic blocks.

The creation of a common consciousness, aware of the need to preserve a healthy, clean and unsullied environment, as well as the rational use of its resources, has become imperative. Special attention must be given to priority problems such as the scarcity of water, the depletion of traditional energy sources, and the misuse of agricultural land. These are the key elements in the set of general objectives through which the education system is expected to participate, in the achievement of overall development. Again, it is a set or group of objectives each of which is fundamental yet not sufficient in itself to reach society's developmental target. The balance of these elements over time must be made between society's demand on education and its functions, on the one hand, and the private demand of the individual family and other interest groups on the other hand. To achieve this balance it is absolutely necessary not to let one category of demands or interests to be met at the expense of others. In sum, the general objective of education is to expand society's access to new and renewable knowledge by acquisition, assimilation, dissemination, and utilization. Knowledge should also be availed to the largest number of scientists, scholars, innovators and teachers, and reach a critical mass of the labor force to guarantee its continued growth and utilization. By so doing a crucial condition for competing in the world market would be achieved.

The cultural equation would also be changed, with innovation replacing the prevailing current traditional mode. These disparities should be carefully examined to ensure understanding and diagnosis of the realities in their historical, social and technical context. It is essential to avoid superficial, misleading diagnosis and vagueness which may lead to the adoption of a limited policy of reform, to formal rather than real changes, or to the inability to discern the complexity of considerations in the process of real change. It may also lead to a gap between the official position with regards renewal and development and what can be actually achieved on the ground. The result may well be old oil in new bottles, that is, old measures or institutions carrying new names and labels. Below are some of the critical issues prevailing in the current imbalances in education, namely:

— Between the values of human development and those of the economic sectors as regards priorities, investments and long term returns. Developmental efforts and modernization programs have remained captive to economic concepts of economic growth. The goal now is to pay human development more attention than was paid since the beginning of the seventies with the understanding that education is a vital national enterprise.

— Between the role of different social, cultural and elite segments of the population in formulating the objectives, policies and strategies of education, on the one hand, and the executive state machinery's monopoly on educational reform, on the other hand. In recent years a measure of broader national participation in the development of curricula and some educational policies has been observed. This trend, however, needs more broadening and elaboration, with continued debate and consultation, supporting this development.

— Between societal demand for education and the needs of self-development vis-à-vis the family and individuals looking for social mobility, personal profit and higher incomes through institutional certification.

— Between utilizing education to increase overall production and productivity in different spheres, such as goods and services, or science and culture, and education's role in generating, consumption, status symbols, and influence peddling.

— Between decentralized administration, with its attendant freedom, and flexibility in school administration, teacher, and educational methods, combined with parental participation in school activities, and centralized administrative control governing the process, operations and activities of the educational system, and the inflexibility of its bureaucratic regulations and measures.

— Between the educational curricula with their fixed syllabi, text book principles and reliance on rote learning as opposed to curricula for the development of thinking, innovation and inventiveness or self-education, including the use of technological and information systems and library use.

— Between support for equal opportunities in education and for the principle of education for all on the basis of ability and talent. Also, between the sifting and exclusion of students depriving them of their right to continue their studies, on one hand, and private fee-charging schools and universities in which education depends on financial power and social status of students.

— Between the role of education in promoting a common national character with enriching variations, thereon leading to the consolidation of national unity, and the variety of sectoral and foreign educational institutions that serve the interests of their founders. Experience has shown the difficulty of efficiently supervising the curricula of these private institutions and their influence on the formation of basic requirements of citizenship.

— Between the commitment to the physical, mental, social and spiritual capacity of students, on one hand, and a concentration on the intellectual and informational aspects on the other.

— Between basing education on the principle of teamwork and the value of group effort and basing it on individual effort and inventiveness in the age of institutional production and innovation.

— Between increasing concentration on a scientific and technological orientation, change and regard for the future, vis-a-vis concentration on heritage solutions of the past, linear, non-relational or absolute facts and judgements.

— Between the values of globalization and the market with their requirements and their technological, media and cultural effects, and the exigencies of nationalism, patriotism, development of an Arab culture, renewal of its institutions and dynamics, and a positive and critical interaction with the Third Wave and its scientific, technological and information achievements.

In light of the present quantitative and qualitative assessment of the educational structure, education's progress towards the future can be delineated in five major dimensions. These should be considered in the planning of the seventh development plan until the year 2017.

The dimensions are horizontal, vertical, in-depth, related to policies, and concerned with democracy and culture. The following discussion will elaborate on the first three aspects. It is envisaged that the system will allow for educational opportunities for all, young or illiterate adults, with no consideration to family, social or economic status, whether in urban or rural regions, boys or girls, or adults in different fields of work. This is to decrease, to the utmost possible degree, regional and gender discrepancies.

The vertical dimension refers to opportunities provided for extending the number of years of education following the primary and preparatory levels; that is, educational opportunities at the secondary and university levels, as well as postgraduate studies. It is hoped that the number of years for basic education would reach twelve, with the secondary level included by the end of the seventh development plan.

This extension of schooling will constitute an adequate base for university education and will help level the educational pyramid. An attempt will be made here to identify ways towards estimating the quantitative indices of the future growth of education in both the horizontal and vertical dimensions.

Material, human and organizational resources can be known, the volume of achievement or inadequacies in performance can be measured, and the related reasons and factors can be diagnosed. It is to be noted that both the horizontal and vertical dimensions will benefit from educational technology and distance learning.

These new mediums will increase the opportunities for education and learning, and help disseminate programs for adult education and eradicating illiteracy. In sum, emphasis is set here on the need for defining quantitative targets and good planning of educational activities.

In the in-depth dimension includes the targeted qualitative development with its five interlaced factors: comprehensive knowledge, awareness of basic concepts of knowledge systems, development of thinking, learning through the technology of education, and, lastly, the practice of scientific research. These aspects deserve further thought as they form the crux of the goal for improving the quality of education. Comprehensive and integrated knowledge has been organized into the following disciplines: religious education, language, humanities, social sciences, physics, mathematics, technologies and aesthetics.

It is supposed that all curricula should include selected topics from these disciplines at all levels of education and should be revised with the renewal and growth of knowledge therein. Each of these disciplines has its own basic concepts that help understand nature, life, society, human relationships, and the percepts of religion. All help promote understanding, analysis and interpretation of knowledge and could, if interrelated, provide a comprehensive and integrated perception of reality. This is exactly what is meant by the concept of interdisciplinarity where a subject is understood within a total perspective. It is therefore necessary to formulate curricula and select subjects so that the student should recognize the basic concepts of each of these disciplines, as regards their rationale, methodology and interrelationships with other disciplines. This depth-dimension factor lies in what can be achieved through good curricula, which take into consideration physical, mental, social, spiritual and aesthetic maturation as well as that of skills. It means the development of "the total person" and his/her capacities. This integrated growth is the sum of curricular activities, student-teacher relationships and relationships between the students themselves.

In today's cultural, scientific, and technological context, an educational philosophy that is predicated on the immutability of human abilities, has become completely discredited. The true function of teaching and learning activities is to provide the means, circumstances and motives to help students improve and ripen their abilities in a continuous way. Abilities and talents are not immutable. They are dynamic, progressing or receding according to circumstances which help them grow and develop, or wither and die. Furthermore, the concept that defined intelligence as one attribute, frequently related to academic skills or acquisition of knowledge has been recently discredited. Educational, psychological and biological studies indicate variations in human intelligence, speaking of intelligence in the plural not in the singular. There are many kinds of intelligence: social, motor, verbal, abstract, mathematical, musical, plastic and inspirational intelligence.

The new concept of "excellence for all" in education is based on this understanding. It demands new strategies to help develop the different kinds of intelligence students possess, and guarantee their utilization in those spheres of work suitable to each individual. Scientific thought comprises well-known skills in learning, understanding and interpretation, starting from the collection of sufficient data, definition of objective, sorting out, analysis, comparison, contemplation, experimentation, and cause/effect relations. Such a scientific orientation also calls for more learning throughout life, especially in self-education. It is clear that today's world requires this type of mind set, given the speed of scientific discovery and the information and communication revolutions. There is also the increasing awareness of the limitations of verbal, oratorical and past-oriented cultures facing the competitive challenges of continuously new knowledge in our globalization age.

References

Banks, James A. 1997.*Educating Citizens in a Multicultural Society.* New York: Teachers College Press.

Diaz, Carlos, Byron G. Massialas, and John A. Xanthopoulos. 1999.*Global Perspectives for Educators.* Boston: Allyn and Bacon.

Lynch, James. 1989.*Multicultural Education in a Global Society.* London and New York: Falmer.

O'Riordan, Tim, ed. 200. *Globalism, Localism, and Identity: Fresh Perspectives on the Transition to Sustainability.* Sterling, Va.: Earthscan.

Parker, Walter C., ed. 1996. *Educating the Democratic Mind.* Albany: State University of New York Press.

Tye, Barbara Benham, and Kenneth A. Tye. 1992. *Global Education: A Study of School Change.* Albany: State University of New York Press.

9

Holistic Education

All over the world educationists are grappled with one central and all-encompassing question: what kind of education is needed for what kind of society of tomorrow? They are conscious of the new role of education and the new demands made on educational systems in a world of accelerating economic, environmental and social change and tension. They have come up with some of the underlying principles which are universal and common to the aims of educators, citizens, policymakers, and other partners and participants in the process of education at all levels.

According to them education, formal and non-formal, must serve society as an instrument for fostering the creation of good citizens. All approaches to redesign the educational processes must take into account the basic and agreed-upon values and concerns of the international community and of the United Nations system such as human rights, tolerance, and understanding, democracy, responsibility, universality, cultural identity, the search for peace, the preservation of the environment and the sharing of knowledge.

There is no denial that the purpose, the aim and drive of the educational institutes must be to equip the students with the most excellent technological proficiency so that the students may function with clarity and efficiency in the modern world. But a far more important purpose than this is to create the right climate and environment so that the students may develop fully as total human beings. Total human being means not only a human being with inward understanding, with a capacity to explore, to examine his or her inward state and the capacity of going beyond it, but also someone who is good in what he or she does outwardly. The two must go together. That is the real issue in education: to see that when the students leave the school, they are well established in goodness, both outwardly and inwardly.

In order to achieve this, educational process must awaken the intelligence of the student so that he or she may 'flower in goodness'. The cultivation of a global outlook, a love of nature and a concern for fellow human beings and environment should be part of the scheme of education. In order to achieve this, education has to cover the four distinct dimensions of the human personality beginning with the physical body, the development of intellectual and aesthetic sensibilities, the development of socially desirable moral values and finally, the inner dimension of spiritual growth.

9.1. Meaning of Holistic Education

Throughout the history a widely scattered group of experts all over the world have pointed out that the education of young human beings should involve much more than simply molding them into future workers or citizens. The Swiss humanitarian Johann Pestalozzi, the American transcendentalists, Upanishadic thinkers of India and many stalwarts of the "progressive" education movement insisted that education should be understood as the art of cultivating the moral, emotional, physical, psychological, artistic, and spiritual—as well as intellectual—dimensions of the developing child.

An emerging body of literature in science, philosophy, and cultural history provides an overarching concept to describe the holistic education. As expressed in these works holistic education facilitates the students to identity, meaning, and purpose in life through connections to the community, to the natural world, and to spiritual values such as compassion and peace. Besides, holistic education also aims to call forth from students an intrinsic reverence for life and a passionate love of learning. This is done not through an academic "curriculum" that condenses the world into instructional packages, but through direct engagement with the environment.

Holistic education can be described as: "At its most general level, what distinguishes holistic education from other forms of education are its goals, its attention to experiential learning, and the significance that it places on relationships and primary human values within the learning environment." The general philosophy of holistic education may be discussed under two categories: the idea of *Ultimacy* and the notion of *Sagacious Competence.*

9.1.1. Ultimacy

1. Religious, as in becoming "enlightened". Spirituality is an important component in holistic education as it emphasizes the connectedness of all living things and stresses the "harmony between the inner life and outer life".
2. Psychological, as in Maslow's "self-actualisation". Holistic education believes that each person should strive to be all that they can be in life. There are no deficits in learners, just differences.
3. Undefined, as in a person developing to the ultimate extent a human could reach and, thus, moving towards the highest aspirations of the human spirit

9.1.2. Sagacious Competence

1. Freedom (in a psychological sense).
2. Good judgement (self-governance).
3. Meta learning (each student learns in his "own way").
4. Social ability (more than just learning social skills).
5. Refining values (development of character).
6. Selfknowledge (emotional development).

In holistic education, the teacher is seen less as person of authority who leads and controls but rather is seen as "a friend, a mentor, a facilitator, or an experienced travelling companion". Open and honest communication is expected and differences between people are respected and appreciated. Cooperation is the norm here, rather than competition. The reward of helping one another and growing together is emphasized rather than being placed above one another. Teachers help young people feel connected by fostering collaboration rather than competition in classrooms. They encourage reflection and questioning rather than passive memorisation of "facts".

9.2. Purpose of Ancient Indian Education

The direct aim of ancient Indian education was to make the student fit to become a useful and pious member of society. Inculcating the civic and social duties among the students was also a part of ancient Indian educational system. The students were not to lead a self-centred life. They were constantly reminded of their obligations to the society. Convocation address to the students as found in the *Upanishads* show how they were inspired to be useful members of the society.

The most important idea governing the ancient system of education was that of perfection, for developing the mind and soul of man. Ancient Indian education aimed at helping the individual to grow in the power and force of certain large universal qualities which in their harmony build a higher type of manhood.

The ancient Indian educational system focused on building a disciplined and values-based culture. Human values such as trust, respect, honesty, dignity, and courtesy are the building blocks of any free, advanced society. The convocation address found in *Taittiriya Upanishad* throws significant light on the qualities required to be developed in the students which are not very different from the qualities that modern educational systems are trying to impart and hence we quote a few lines from it here:

> Speak the truth. Practise righteousness. Make no mistake about study. There should be no inadvertence about truth. There should be no deviation from righteous activity. There should be no error about protection of yourself. Do not neglect propitious activities. Do not be careless about learning and teaching. There should be no error in the duties towards the gods and manes. Let your mother be a goddess unto you. Let your father be a god unto you. Let your teacher be a god unto you. Let your guest be a god unto you. The works that are not blameworthy are to be resorted to, but not the others. The offering should be with honour; the offering should be in plenty. The offering should be with modesty. The offering should be with sympathy. Then, should you have any doubt with regard to duties or customs, you should behave in those matters just as the wise men do, who may happen to be there and who are able deliberators, who are adepts in those duties and customs, who are not directed by others, who are not cruel, and who are desirous of merit. This is the injunction. This is the instruction. This is the secret of the scriptures.

This convocation address outlines some of the domestic and social duties of students in very clear terms. Accordingly students are: to honour father, mother, teacher, and guest as gods; to honour superiors; to give in proper manner and spirit, in joy and humility, in fear and compassion. Lastly, the pupil is also asked not to neglect his health and possessions. This convocation address is very important in understanding the role of ancient Indian education in building a values-based culture.

Discipline like character is an essential quality for personal as well as social life. It consists in obedience to laws, rules and decisions. In this regard we must admit that ancient Indian system of education played a major role in making students realise their duties and responsibilities and emphasized on the necessity of discipline for an orderly social life. Character and discipline cannot be imparted to an individual by preaching or through speeches. While students can be imparted with the knowledge of what is moral and what is immoral, what is discipline and what is indiscipline what is character and what is characterless, they can be made to act in conformity with the required standard of behaviour, only through personal example. These qualities are acquired by emulation in addition to education.

It is only by generating these qualities in individuals the ancient Indian educational system prompted the students to utilise their educational attainments and capacities for the benefit of society restricting their own selfish desires and prevented them from acting in a manner harmful and detrimental to the common good. Mere knowledge of what is virtue and what is not does not enable an individual to be virtuous.

Just as an ordinary stone requires a beautiful design and long and continued effort of an expert sculptor in chiseling and engraving in order to make it a beautiful idol, a proper blueprint or scheme and a constant and vigilant and untiring efforts of all those concerned are necessary, to make a child into a worthy individual. A very useful observation has been made by Swami Vivekananda in this context:

The character of any man is but the aggregate of his tendencies, the sum total of the bent of his mind. We are what our thoughts have made us. Thoughts live: they travel far. Every work that we do, every movement of the body, every thought that we think, leaves an impression on the mind stuff. What we are every moment is determined by the sum total of these impressions on the mind. Every man's character is determined by the sum total of these impressions. If good impressions prevail, the character becomes good, if bad, it becomes bad. When a large number of these impressions are left on the mind they coalesce and become a habit. The only remedy for bad habit is counter habits; all the bad habits that have left their impressions are to be controlled by good habits.

The ancient education system aimed at character formation through proper development of moral feelings to make the students really learned, pure in their life, thoughts and habits. Teaching of values, ideal life led by teachers, and examples of extraordinary personalities cited from the epics, poetry, literature and history-all these helped to mould the character of students. The ancient Indian educational system also aimed at the development of personality by eulogisinig the feeling of self-respect, by encouraging the sense of self-confidence, by inculcating the virtue of self-restraint and fostering the powers of discrimination and judgement.

The ancient Indian thinkers fixed for education certain life-long objectives that require lifelong effort to achieve and realise. These objectives were summarised in triple formula which gave a wide and lofty framework to the ancient system of education.

> *asato ma sadgamaya*
> *tamaso ma jyotirgamaya*
> *mrityorma amritam gamaya*
>
> (Lead me from falsehood to truth
> Lead me from darkness to light
> Lead me from death to immortality)
> (*Brihadaranyaka Upanishad*, I.3.28)

To them the ideals of truth, light and immortality constituted a triune unity, each subsisting in the other. The students were not allowed to forget that they had within them a higher self beyond their little personal ego, and that numerous ways and disciplines were provided by which they could realise the higher self.

The holistic education of ancient India involves a harmonious blending of the knowledge of the outer world (*avidya*) and that of the inner-world (*vidya*). The former, as it were, enables a man to keep his body and soul together and the later, i.e., *vidya*, the wisdom, leads him to immortality, freedom from all sufferings of the world of change.

It may be noted here that the Lord Buddha preached the middle path which lies between the two extremes, viz., gross sensualism or vile pleasure-seeking on the one hand and extreme asceticism or the severest self-mortification on the other hand. He laid stress on purity of conduct, truthfulness, love and benevolence, obedience to parents and respect for the elders, non-drinking, charity and kindness and mercy to all living beings. *Ahimsa* (non-violence) towards life is recognised as an integral principle of his practical morality. The spirit of Buddhism was very liberal and accommodating. These values have become very essential for survival of human race in the present day situation.

The ancient Indian thinkers felt that a healthy society was not possible without educated individuals. They framed the educational setup carefully and wisely aiming at the harmonious development of the multiple dimensions of the human personality. This is an essentially a universally applicable educational framework highlighting the purpose of human life and interconnectedness at all levels of existence as a basis of human values. In this system understanding oneself is as important as understanding the world. According to them without a deep understanding of one's relationship with nature, with ideas, with fellow human beings, with society, and a deep respect for all life, one is not really educated.

Another unique feature of this educational system is that it aims at creating a mind that is both scientific and spiritual at the same timeone that is enquiring, precise—rational and sceptical but at the same time has sense of beauty, wonder, aesthetics, sensitivity, humility, and an awareness of the limitations of the intellect. It also aims at developing a mind, which is rational, flexible and not dogmatic, open to change and not irrationally attached to an opinion or belief should.

In this system of education both scientific and spiritual quests are the complementary quests, one for the discovery of the order that manifests itself in the outer world of matter, energy, space and time and the other for discovering order in the inner world of human consciousness. Actually they are both quests for truth into two complementary aspects of a single reality which is composed of both matter and consciousness.

For an ordered, gradual and holistic development of human personality and to secure a progressive balance and harmony of growth, the ancient educational thinkers developed another unique concept viz., the *Purushartahs*. *Purushartha* is translated to mean a human goal, an object of desire, consciously pursued. This significant concept of development upholds the legitimacy of man's desire for economic security (*artha*) and sensuous aesthetic satisfaction (*kama*) and spiritual welfare (*moksha*). This scheme is further elaborated in the following diagramme:

Human Needs/Pursuits

Material well-being	*Spiritual well-being*
—Bodily needs (*kama*) —Needs of material well-being (*artha*) —Need for social and moral order (*dharma*)	—Need to overcome overcome suffering and realise oneself (*moksha*)

But it does not support the insatiable greed which could destroy the possibility of realising them. Both wealth and pleasure are goals only pursuable in society, but they can be successfully pursued only if society has at least some amount of stability and harmony.

Dharma is claimed to be an important factor in the maintenance of social stability and harmony. Therefore, the observance of dharma, in virtue of its being a necessary condition of social stability and harmony, is insisted upon as an indispensable ethic for the pursuit of wealth and pleasure. *Dharma* is an ethical law which prevents human beings from falling into crooked ways of the ordinary and unbridled demands of impulses, desires, ambitious and egoism.

Dharma denotes that morality and those values which are founded upon higher, i.e. metaphysical and cosmic principles and they appeal to the highest goals and yet they are related to the common life and social processes.

Dharma is learning (*vidya*), in a broader sense, which can enlighten the human beings to understand the subtle niceties of living a dignified life. The values inculcated through education included a rule of prohibition regarding acquisition of wealth or securing or fulfilling of pleasures and desires of an individual. The rule is: Reject the wealth, pleasure and desires which are inconsistent with moral law (*dharma*).

Ancient Indians also developed the concept of Yoga for disciplining the mind and the body. Without the practice of the principles of *yama* and *niyama*, which lay the firm foundation for building character, there cannot be an integrated personality. In *Yoga Sashtra* the" Right Living" is based on *yama* and *niyama*. Very simple ethical disciplines of "dos and don'ts". Sage Patanjali in his authoritative Treatise *Yoga Sutras* builds his entire Eight-fold path of Yoga on the foundation of *yama* and *niyama*. Practice of *asanas* without *yama* and *niyama* is mere acrobatics. Discipline does not arise from one's own mind. It has to be learned from outside. The word *Yama* can be broadly translated as "Selfrestraints".

9.3. Holistic Education Movement

The holistic education movement does not have a single source, a predominant proponent, or a major form of expression. Consequently, it is difficult to define holistic education. However, there are a number of values and perceptions that most schools claiming to be holistic would embrace. What gave rise to their popularity is particularly important because it is a combination of new perceptions and values which seems to be something like an international grassroots movement - a movement which rejects many of the authorities as well as the values and perceptions of the immediate past. "Whose Values?" for holistic education, is a particularly relevant question.

Holistic education reflects and responds more fully than conventional education to a new and increasingly accepted view of what it means to be human as well as to much popular social criticism. For schools to ignore what seems to be a change in humanity's view of itself is to risk having schools that try to prepare students for something they don't believe in; it is to risk having an educational system that is felt to be meaningless by the very population it wants to serve. For schools to have values and views of human nature different to those of its population is like asking a committed pacifist to attend a military academy. We see just this kind of dissonance frequently expressed in many of our schools whose populations come largely from some minority groups. These groups feel the conventional education their children are offered does not reflect their values and it ignores their views of who they feel they are. The large number of students presently disaffected with school must challenge us as educators to reflect whether these students feel a similar dissonance with the values and perspectives our schools promote.

While some advocates claim that views central to holistic education are not new but are, in fact, timeless and found in the sense of wholeness in humanity's religious impetus; others claim inspiration from Rousseau, Emerson, Pestalozzi, Froebel, and more recently Krishnamurti, Steiner, Montessori, Jung, Maslow, Rogers, Paul Goodman, John Holt, Ivan Illich, Paulo Freire. Still others feel that the views central to holistic education are the result of a cultural paradigm shift that began in the 1960's. What is clear is that the values and the vision of humanity in the holistic education movement and which it promotes are increasingly popular. There are now at least 7,500 holistic schools with more seeming to start every week. Unfortunately, the insights of this vision are often clouded by misty-eyed New Ageism, and a great deal that is valuable is dismissed because of this association.

Let us focus on developments in the 1960's and 1970's that forced some of the ideas of holistic education onto centrestage because it was these developments that made the ideas so popular. The ecological crisis, the prospect of nuclear annihilation, chemical and radiation pollution, the breakdown of the family, the disappearance of traditional communities, and the disregard for traditional values and their institutions (e.g., the church), caused many people to question the direction of the modern western world and many of its central values. The consumer society was criticised in a way that seemed to be absent in the first 60 years of this century. Even if some societies seemed able to continue their consumption from a local perspective, the earth's resources were beginning to be seen as finite; and a small proportion of the world's population consuming a disproportionate percentage of the earth's resources was seen as unsustainable and destructive - ultimately becoming a moral issue.

Mechanistic utilitarian rationality was acknowledged for its contribution to the creation of clever gadgets but blamed for uncontrolled economic and technical growth that seemed to swamp other human capacities. Because scientific thinking on its own lacked the non-rational or 'supra-rational' capacities of mind such as wisdom, intuition, appreciation for beauty and insight, it was seen as most commonly used to create brilliant weaponry or unnecessary consumer goods. The 'supra-rational' capacities were seen as increasingly important in view of what unrestrained mechanical thought was producing. *Small is Beautiful* by Schumacher and the works of Wendell Berry seemed to fly in the face of convention, yet made perfect sense to hundreds of thousands.

The professional view of human nature was also changing drastically at this time. The Skinnerian view of a person as an electro-chemical stimulus-response machine was being rejected as only a very partial view of the mind. Behaviourism seemed more of a tool for exploiting people than for understanding them in any depth. In the wake of the many explorations into consciousness of the 1960's, Freud's very compartmentalised views of the mind lost popularity while Jung's more open ended and mysterious understandings gained support. Carl Rogers, Abraham Maslow and R.D. Laing became almost cult figures, and several new forms of psychology emerged that took the science of mind further and further away from the strictures of conventional measurable science. Gestalt therapy with its slogan "the whole is greater than the sum of its parts" corresponded to the everyday common sense experience that many people had of themselves. There seemed to be too much of us that is immeasurable and non-mechanical, if not ineffable. The view of mind as machine, while increasingly popular as a model of some thinking, especially that involving computers, was seen as only a part of the mind's functioning - usually the lesser part.

Traditional nationalism and localism were also being challenged, and were seen as inadequate to meet the world's realities. The ecological crisis is not a respecter of political boundaries. The greenhouse effect, the depletion of the ozone layer, air and water pollution, radiation leaks, and the elimination of species and rain forests are perhaps national or local in origin but they are global in impact. People began to see that by serving national or local interests these problems could not even be understood, much less solved. The earth had to be seen as a whole, and Lynn Margulis' and James Lovelock's "Gaia Hypothesis" found wide and popular support.

Environmental interest went from being a gentleman/sportsman's concern for conservation to a critique of modern western thinking.

The epistemology which claims to understand things by breaking them into their constituent parts was seen as not only unable to meet the problem, it was part of the problem. Creating locally wanted conditions and looking only locally seemed often to produce problems elsewhere that eventually became unwanted local conditions. "Wholism," "whole earth ideas," "wholefoods," and "the whole child" described things that might not have always been fully examined but which seemed to many people to make sense. People began to feel they needed to look at the global to see the local. Years after the Gaia Hypothesis, educators and ecologists like David Orr and Gregory Cajete suggested that seeing the interconnectedness of all things with nature as the foundation was the basis of a new mind that the world needed for its survival, and that the creation of this mind is the first responsibility of education.

Many people began saying that looking at "wholes" was necessary to understand other things as well; the economy, human interchange, and cultures. It is not without reason that some nationalities like the French speak of cultural imperialism and find difficulty in countering a movement that is literally coming at them from all directions. The youth culture is global. The computer culture is global. Many modern cultural icons are global.

The extended seeing of wholes within wholes brought many to a religiosity that seemed inherent in the approach, and something that many holistic educators feel is fundamental to what they do. The largest whole; that which has relationships to everything; the ultimate 'more' from which all the 'less' derives was described as the absolute, the sacred or some form of ultimate order. There is remarkably little conflict amongst holistic educators on the details of this, itself an extraordinary break with tradition and something worth noting in view of the problems we have in our pluralist schools. The physicist David Bohm postulates an implicate order into which everything is enfolded and from which everything unfolds to be re-enfolded.

Many Depth Psychologists postulate a higher self which extends beyond the individual. While a few holistic educators refer to the soul or atman of traditional religions, most speak in terms of some universal order, or of common threads running through all religions, or archetypal mythologies, or what Aldous Huxley called "the perennial philosophy". These timeless and perennially re-seen insights are said to have been expressed differently in different times and places and so to have given rise to the different religions. These perennial truths are felt by some to be seen in their most unadulterated form in the religions of premodern cultures.9 Hence the popularity of rediscovering indigenous religious traditions as though this was the finding of ancient lost religious truths. These rediscovered truths echoed the truths found in other areas: the oneness of all life; the importance of a person understanding his place in the community and the community's place in the environment and in ever expanding circles to the environment's place in the full order of things; and the emphasis on self knowledge.

For many holistic educators, these perennial truths expressed in their general form rather than a particular cultural form was the key to the spirituality that they felt must be part of every education. There is little argument in holistic education that there can not be an education of the whole child if there is no education in what is transcendent. And there is also little argument that cultural expressions of transcendence have been a source of millions of deaths in thousands of conflicts in history. The three hundred years of violence in Ireland between the Catholics and Protestants is just one example.

For today's pluralist world, arguments about whose expression of 'truth' is more correct are conflictual and might be in contradiction to the very 'truths' espoused. Many holistic educators feel that all expressions of 'truth' can only be partial and remaining with the most general expressions of 'truth' not only remains closer to the original insight but helps people see for themselves beyond what is culturally bound to what might be timeless.

A sense of transcendence that remains generalised, inclusive, and therefore equally nurturing to all resonated with another pressing concern of the 1960's and 1970's -social justice. Religions had frequently been dominated by particular races, classes, castes and/or gender as were most other aspects of most cultures. Particular religions were, therefore, seen as preserving the socially unjust social order.

The focus on gender issues was only one of the ways in which relationship structures in modern society were being questioned in the

1960's and 1970's. Increased divorce, one parent families, and experiments in communal living all had people looking at what relationship meant. This questioning of relationship based on structures of meaning rather than structures of tradition was one reason why holistic education gave a central value to relationship skills. Frequently people are first interested in holistic education through the perceptions that we need to learn to live together much better and that our social ills cannot be solved without new community building skills.

In holistic education the classroom is often seen as a community, which is within the larger community of the school, which is within the larger community of the village, town, or city, and which is, by extension, within the larger community of humanity. How life is lived at the smallest level should reflect what is considered to be "right living" in the largest context. For this reason many holistic educators feel that the claims made by conventional schools to foster freedom and democracy are spurious, as most conventional schools are based on authoritarian classrooms. They feel that learning to assume responsibility, to question for oneself what is right, and to stand by one's convictions can not be accomplished by a childhood of unquestioningly obeying rules, conforming to codes of behaviour that seem meaningless, and believing that the authorities have the answers. Holistic educators feel that schools must be places where the relationships we want as adults exist for the students as much as possible — where open, honest and respectful communication is the norm; where differences between people are appreciated; where interaction is based on mutual support and not on competition and hierarchy; where the common weal is the responsibility of each individual; and where the decision making process is at least accepted by everyone. This emphasis on cooperation rather than competition often results in holistic schools giving no grades or rewards. In this view of human nature, people are seen as being more fulfilled from nurturing and helping one another than from being placed above or below one another, and competition is seen not as producing excellence but anxiety, aggression, self-centredness, low self esteem or inflated self images.

Relationships between students, between teachers, and between students and teachers are seen as both a primary source of education and a topic of education. As a source, relationships are an excellent mirror in which to see ourselves — we can learn a great deal about ourselves by seeing how others respond to us. As a topic, learning about healthy mutually sustaining relationships — how to create them and sustain them — is seen as necessary to solve many of our social and personal ills. Community building began to be seen in the 1960's as one of the principal ways of dealing with urban decay, and it remains one of the most successful approaches to problems in America's inner cities.

The commitment to school as community, and community as arena for participation, assuming responsibility and self-determination, does not usually accept that schools should be directed by governments. Most holistic schools are not. National governments, even where democratically elected, can be unresponsive to the evolving needs of individual schools each with its unique and changing population. In the 1960's and 1970's governments were being questioned, and government directed educational programmes began to be seen as more responsive to political expedience than to the needs of the individual child; and it is individual children and not undifferentiated masses that educators and parents feel are being educated.

Most political, economic, or social movements that claimed to be wholistic were decentralised, democratic, grassroots, and cooperative, and whatever the shortcomings, this was seen as a more natural human society and a more accurate reflection of human nature. These movements not only reflected values that seemed to go back to our most distant past, these movements claimed to be forums for the development and refining of wholistic values. People felt they would become more decent human beings by working in a non-hierarchical way with each other and caring for each other.

Changing the traditional structure of authority and submission in schools, and eliminating the training in uncritical acceptance normally found in schools is essential to addressing the social injustices that plague the undeveloped nations and the underclasses in the developed countries.

The respect for the individual inherent in such decentralised democracy, where people are not seen as part of a social or economic system, was linked to the religiosity mentioned before. In most holistic schools every child was seen as an expression of, an arena for, or an entity containing the transcendent, and must be recognised and treated as such. Many holistic educators expressed that the sacredness inherent in each child was not just something for the educator to be aware of, it was something that each child should discover. This led many to feel that education was only partly a process of instilling or pouring in — it needed to be mostly a process of unfolding, a leading out or bringing out.

If education is a process of discovery and uncovering, and every child is unique; how could the traditional educational judging of children be anything other than inherently wrong? How could a child be a slow learner if he was learning at a pace that was right for her/him? How could a child be disruptive if (s)he was doing what (s)he was interested in rather than what others wanted her/him to do, or were those others not in fact disrupting the child? If a child doesn't learn through words and numbers, is that child unintelligent or can that child be learning through other intelligences? Some children who are poor at words and numbers are nevertheless geniuses and terribly short changed, if not brutalised, by traditional education.

Learning takes place in many capacities of the child, not just the verbal-numerical capacities; and that this learning process is different for everyone - echoing two themes in holistic education and the holistic view of human nature. Many people felt it was not just a matter of valuing everyone, it was also important to value the different capacities that we all have; to do otherwise is to denigrate some individuals and to denigrate some aspects of each one of us.

Holistic teachers took pride in developing new methods that reflected their new views of what a child is. Research with individual learning styles, cooperative learning, critical thinking, cross disciplinary curricula and multiple intelligence theory have inspired many new initiatives in holistic classrooms. The teacher became less of an authority who directed and controlled and was more of a friend, a mentor, a facilitator, or an experienced travelling companion. Psychology talked of the dyadic response of infant learning and the importance of empathy in learning relationships, and the relevance of these seemed to extend into adulthood. Goethe's quote, "You only learn from someone you love," became almost a slogan.

Classes in holistic schools are often small, mixed-ability, mixed-age, and extremely flexible. If it becomes appropriate for a child to move to a different class, (s)he moves - regardless of the time of year or the subjects (s)he has been studying. Rigid categorisation by age and progression in large groups up some educational ladder was seen as a reflection of the manufacturing thinking of the industrial revolution when public schooling began, and not as a reflection of new thinking about human nature.

The 1970's saw some very surprising institutions proclaim respect for the uniqueness of each individual, encouraging non-conformist thinking, and decrying hierarchy. These institutions were large businesses. Several multinational corporations came to understand that traditional authoritarian structures were inhibiting the productivity of their members. They created "flat management structures" in order to foster healthier, happier, more responsive and successful organisations. They spoke of decentralising, encouraging the uniqueness and growth of all their members, and needing dialogue amongst all levels and departments of their enterprises.

That humanity's view of itself and the world has changed over the last 25 years seems incontestable. Indeed it would seem strange if it hadn't. What is in question is whether conventional schools reflect those new views and values, or whether, like many large institutions, they have a life of their own and lag behind the population they wish to serve. What does seem clear is that our traditional ways of understanding and preparing people for life have not solved our personal, social, national and international problems.

If the modern western world is changing as rapidly as some people say it is, it may be instructive to look at eastern Europe where the last seven years has seen a more obvious "paradigm shift." There the understanding of what it means to be human, the understanding of the relationship between the individual and society, the understanding of the nature of society and of their society's role in the world, have gone through a complete upheaval. The total inadequacy of most eastern European schools which still reflect old paradigms to meet people's new needs and aspirations is painfully obvious to all those involved. As one traditional Russian school commented, "I have been in education all my life, but I don't know how to educate anyone for today's world. I only know how to indoctrinate into the old." Whether conventional western schools are similarly inadequate is the question posed by holistic education.

REFERENCES

Best, R. (Ed.). 1996. *Education,Spirituality and the Whole Child*. London: Cassel.

Cajete, G. 1994. *Look to the Mountain: An ecology of indigenous education*. Durango: Kivaaki Press.

Cohen, A. 1983. *The Educational Philosophy Of Martin Buber*. London: Fairleigh Dickinson University Press.

Dudty, D., & Dudty, H. (Eds.). 1994. *Holistic Education: Some Australian Explorations. "Belconnen, ACT"*: Australian Curriculum Studies Association.

Forbes, S. 2003. *Holistic Education: An Analysis of Its Ideas and Nature*. Brandon, VT: Foundation for Educational Renewal.

Miller, J. P. 1993. *The Holistic Curriculum*. Toronto: OISE Press.

Nakagawa, Yoshiharu. 2000. *Education for Awakening: An Eastern Approach to Holistic Education*. Volume Two of the Foundations of Holistic Education Series. Brandon, VT: Foundation for Educational Renewal.

10

Environmental Education for Sustainable Livelihoods

Environmental education can play a major role in reforming educational systems owing to its interdisciplinary character and its aim of linking the process of education more closely to real life and the surrounding environment. Since the 1970s, the conceptual debate on the environment and education has given rise to a number of comprehensive theories, which are more than unbalanced, ideologically tainted approaches or behavioural doctrines. The concept of environmental education as defined by the OECD Project 'Environment and School Initiatives' (ENSI) is based upon interdisciplinary learning and the realisation of dynamic learning qualities in students by which knowledge is not passively appropriated but actively constructed. Furthermore it enables the application of knowledge to important spheres of social interaction in the environment, and social action for the environment.

In the mid-1990s, the socio-economic environmental education approach was developed in a research project conducted at the Swiss University of Technology in Zurich and tested in classroom instruction. The key elements of the socio-ecological approach are problem orientation, reference to experience and cooperation: environmental issues and sustainable development are not limited to scientific facts, but are constructed socially and context-dependent, in that they are perceived and interpreted differently by the people and social groups involved as a function of context. Existing and contextually generated knowledge is recorded, researched and reflected upon through values, value systems, conditions for action, and individual and structural possibilities for change. The concept of socio-economic environmental education rests on the assumption that learning is an active, constructive and systemically cooperative process. Learners should be able to study environmental and sustainable development issues against their own background of experiences and in specific, life-centred situations. In this way, socio-ecological environmental education discards the notion that children and adolescents should be taught environmentally friendly behaviour. In contrast to that learners should be able, through personal investigation and reflection, to develop an appropriate understanding of reality which sees and accepts the dependence on individual and collective lifestyles, personal and social framework for action, modes and conditions of action, restrictions and options, as an interactive process.

10.1. Ecologically Sustainable Development

Ecologically sustainable development stands for the long-term safeguarding of the natural bases of living. Energy supply, transport planning and also industry, trade and agriculture must be organised in a way that the resultant material cycles can be fitted into global natural cycles and adjusted to local ecosystems. Economically sustainable development aims at creating an economic system which safeguards the quality of living over the long term, geared to local conditions such as know-how, natural resources, infrastructure, and so on. Quality of living is to be understood not only as material wealth, but also as the economic (and political) self-determination and possibility of self-development for the individual and for society at large. While ecologically and economically sustainable development deal with the relation of every polity with is natural and economic environment, socially sustainable development aims at the long-term cohesion of that very polity.

Socially sustainable development implies not only internal, but also external solidarisation. A readiness to cooperate with other communities and regions, and the assumption of responsibility for global sustainable development in which disadvantaged regions can partake, are demands which sustainable social development that is viable in the future must fulfil. The sustainability debate has been criticised, particularly in the UK and Australia, for its strong orientation toward an economic market philosophy and economic growth. Industry, it was argued, would exploit nature and the environment for its own purposes and postulate solutions to problems, for instance, by monetarising nature and placing it on the same level as economic goods. This would hamper a serious consideration of alternative future strategies.

Ongoing discourse and the interplay of political forces eventually decide what is to be preserved and what not, what is to develop and what is to be left out. In the environmental debate, sustainability has often been called a master frame. Sceptics have pointed to the danger of this term being reduced to a mere catchword of the outgoing century. Fears have become loud that the consensus that was reached on the abstract aims of sustainability might be stalled in the noncommittal sphere, and that the underlying idea may degenerate into an empty shell.

Sustainable development offers a general objective and a foundation for a materially reasonable and ethically justifiable use of nature by humankind, which by necessity is formulated in relatively open terms. Therefore, a certain nondescript quality is a constituent element of this guiding idea without which consensus would be impossible. This also implies that the contradictions, moral dilemmas and conflicting targets inherent in this vision need to be constantly renegotiated in a process of discourse between the players involved in each and every concrete situation. Therefore, the consensus which is expressed in the guiding idea of sustainable development is not static, but one that needs to be re-established time and again in given situations and between different groups. The lacking precision of the term sustainable development as positive, arguing that the nondescript nature of the term can delineate an extremely creative, manifold and dynamic field, which is nevertheless oriented towards one direction.

According to de Haan and Harenberg, environmental education after the 1992 Rio Summit has been conceptualised as education for sustainability. Apart from ecological matters proper environmental education is determined by the idea of fair and equitable global distribution. A new configuration of ecological, economic and social components emerges.

In this way, education for sustainability can become a trailblazer for general educational reform. This would imply for instance:

— to address constructivism as a general scientific outlook (all statements on nature, humankind etc. are subject- and culture-dependent);
— to examine guiding principles which bundle the hopes, wishes and aims of societies and thus have a motivating, orientating and coordinating function;
— to understand the environment and equity issue as a corollary of an economic system that is based on competition and exploitation;
— to consider inter- and intra-generational equity as a core theme of the educational discourse;
— to better observe the process of individualisation; and at the same time
— to recognise the need for participation and sharing.

Sustainable development as a guiding principle for a policy programme. Its implementation in specific social contexts, which are controversial as a rule, is a task for the entire society which requires cooperative, communicative and creative skills from all players. Learning in terms of sustainable development means addressing the question, in concrete fields of action, of how to shape the future with a view to sustainable development. This form of learning includes an analysis, evaluation and shaping of a given situation in terms of non-conventional, creative and cooperative solutions.

Owing to its interdisciplinary nature and its present and future relevance, the study of issues relating to ecological, economic and socially sustainable development offers a starting point for innovation in schools. It is of utmost importance to address the twofold challenge of the vast complexity which results from sustainability and related uncertainties in order to retain a capacity for action with out lapsing into simplistic dogmas.

While sustainability issues are used as a vehicle for innovation by these initiatives on the one hand, they are also meant to trigger concrete sustainable social development processes on the other hand. In the 'school development' context, environmental education culminates in the concept of an ecologically oriented further development of school as a place of teaching and learning. The school development process, which is prompted by environmental initiatives, is called the ecologisation of schools. Ecologisation is targeted at awareness and behaviour, at social structures and impacts on environmental quality that can be observed and quantified.

The ecologisation of schools is the environment-oriented design of work, teaching and learning at school and the school environment on a human scale which involves all players (pupils, teachers, school head, non-teaching staff, parents, citizens). It implies an opening of the school towards the outside world (development of new forms of teaching and learning, school development as a culture of communication, cooperation, conflict and decision-making), as well as towards others (the local community as a place of teaching and learning for school, being a cultural centre in the community).

Ultimately, pupils are to be empowered in a narrower sense to make an active and constructive contribution to sustainable social development; in a broader context, the ecologisation of schools is to contribute to safeguarding the quality of living on a lasting sustainable basis. For this, it is imperative that knowledge and the enormous wealth of information are used critically and reflectively, and that dynamic skills are developed. Moreover, teachers need greater willingness and ability to handle learning processes which are not a priori structured. This regards a capacity to tolerate complexity and contradictions while remaining capable to act, to accept existing achievements and accomplishments while being critical, and to engage in cooperation while acting self-reliantly.

10.2. Education for Environmental Protection

Modern environmental education deals with matters such as lifelong learning, sustainability and international dynamics, i.e. contexts other than formal teaching. This is a step forward when compared with its past focus, which has made it of interest to few people and relatively innocuous from a political perspective. Despite their different roots and profiles, there has to be acknowledged the existence of a number of common features related to the methods and approaches through which industrial ecology and environmental education may be pursued. The analysis of such common features may be helpful towards a better understanding of environmental issues and in solving environmental problems. After all, their basic goal is the same: to contribute towards a better man-environment relationship and towards improving the quality of life. The contribution of industrial ecology and environmental education to sustainable development. However, there are still some areas of divergence among industrial ecologists. According to the opinion expressed by various authors, the majority of discussions of industrial ecology tend to agree on the following elements.

— industrial ecology is a systems approach drawing upon methods for analysis and synthesis from systems science
— it seeks to redesign industrial activities to reduce the ecological impact of human activity to levels natural systems can sustain
— it is interdisciplinary, linking the research and planning of many fields, including ecology, engineering, economics, business management, and public administration and law, among others
— it studies the flows of materials and energy through the economy, ranging from those of an industrial or public facility to the planet itself and seeks strategies to increase the efficiency and reduce the impact of these flows
— it enables local decision making with awareness of broader regional and global impacts.

There are many within the industrial ecology community who defend the view that industrial ecology is a means of balancing environmental protection with economic and business viability. This balance, it is often argued, must be dynamic, adapting to new knowledge about industry's impacts and nature's responses. Concern about the relationships between industrial ecology and sustainable development is easy to spot. The concept of industrial ecology as it relates to environmental education per se and the long-term goal of sustainable development are: the search for solutions to environmental problems sometimes ignore the magnitude of social and political concerns. The usually short-term goals of industry sometimes prevent the implementation of measures leading to longer-term benefits, solutions with immediate impacts being preferred.

1 *Awareness*: to help individuals and social groups acquire an awareness of a sensitivity towards the total environment and its allied problems.

2 *Knowledge*: to help individuals and social groups acquire a basic understanding of the total environment, its associated problems and humanity's critically responsible presence and role in it.

3 *Attitude*: to help individuals and social groups acquire social values, strong feelings of concern for the environment and the motivation to participate actively in its protection and improvement.

4 *Skills*: to help individuals and social groups acquire the skills for solving environmental problems.

5 *Evaluation Ability*: to help individuals and social groups evaluate environmental measures and education programs in terms of ecological, political, economic, social, aesthetic and educational factors.

6 *Participation*: to help individuals and social groups develop a sense of responsibility and urgency regarding environmental problems to ensure appropriate action to solve these problems.

Some further common features of industrial ecology and environmental education reside in the fact that both are:

— interdisciplinary: both areas cannot be effectively be worked out without the body of knowledge from related fields such as ecology (per se), economics, mathematics, sociology, etc.

— integrative: both areas try to encompass information deriving from different sources, from different fields, which they then assimilate and integrate as part of their own profile.

— focus on sustainability: no matter the angle one looks at in both areas, their ultimate focus is the search for ways through which sustainability may be pursued.

— participatory: industrial ecology and environmental education rely on the active input of individuals in pursuing their goals and aims and in their participation in influencing ever-changing scenarios.

Last but not least, both are continuously going through a process of change. Such a change, albeit not always dramatic, is indeed a common element of both areas and enables them to evolve along within society, as society itself is going through its own changes. In addition, the areas where the different approaches are mutually complementary may include four main domains: the views adopted, the objectives, the approach used and their target groups

Industrial ecology looks at things from a critical, systemic perspective, angles which environmental education tends to ignore. Environmental educatio weeks to foster awareness on environmental matters and as a result, catalyse active participation in environmental action. Industrial ecology works intensively via incremental improvements in environmental management with a view to improving the efficiency of industrial activities.

Environmental education, in its turn, tries to develop a sense of commitment towards the environment and prevent the exarcerbation of environmental problems by working at the conscience level. Industrial ecology will primarily focus on those whose activities are directly related to industrial practice, while environmental education—be it performed in formal or informal teaching—aims at all individuals since it works on the assumption that every person has an impact on the environment.

Industrial ecology may be seen as a combination of a scientific field and a sector where environmentally sound processes may be tested and implemented. Environmental education is often seen as a process by which educational approaches and methods are put to use in order to raise better awareness on environmental matters. It focuses on soil, water, air, plant and animal life, forests and other ecosystems. It incorporates not only education per se, but also, land-use planning, the concept of shared decision making, and the use of information systems.

Environmental education also addresses renewable and non-renewable natural resource use in urban and rural settings. It involves people, communities, and organisations in experiences that apply appropriate technology to everyday problems.

Reliance on scientific methods and principles enables educators to deliver objective information, even if issues are emotionally charged. This illustrates how complementary both areas are and the usefulness of approaches aimed at integrating them. The goal of integration can be achieved by various ways, such as:

- via the design of projects where attention to both matters are paid
- via case studies in which industrial ecology is combined with educational approaches such as, for example, industry-based environmentally-focused training programs
- by means of projects in which the development of analytical skills is combined with environmental problem solving efforts
- by developing competence among staff working in industry in relation to environmental dialogues so as to enable them to deal with the public
- by integrating principles of environmental communication and information as part of the normal business practice in industry.

Since the degree of development of industrial ecology among countries varies and so does environmental education's, the choice of which approach to use and the extent to which a certain area is favoured—as opposed to others—may vary according to local contexts.

There are of course some particularities which not only limit the fields of action of environmental education and industrial ecology but may also—potentially—restrict joint applications. First of all, the focus of industrial ecology is obviously the industrial sector. Second, there is a natural inclination of environmental education to concentrate on formal teaching. This is because, in this area, the 'educationalists' (professionals of the environmental education sector with an educational background) exist in far greater numbers than the 'environmentalists'.

In addition, changes in the field of environmental education are progressive, focusing on improvements in attitudes and behaviours over a period of years or decades. Industrial ecology, due to its own nature, works on shorter time spans. Another problem to be addressed in moves towards the closer integration of industrial ecology and environmental education is the issue of perception.

Traditional environmental educators go a long way towards avoiding specific reference to industry-related issues out of sheer ignorance about details related to them. Historically, industry has always been seen as a negative entity, the cause of various environmental problems and the root of all sorts of ailments to both people and the physical environment.

Industrial ecology, already closer to the hearts of environmentalists due to the suffix 'ecology', tend to see environmental matters under very specific angles, being bound to be problem-oriented, without always paying attention to the benefits awareness-raising components may bring about. Other perceptual problems are:

— the technicalities of industrial ecology (e.g. management, production) are seen as too complex for educators
— the principles of education and pedagogy (e.g. motivation, awareness-raising techniques, role-play) are judged as too vague by industrialists
— the lack of tradition of joint ventures between the two sectors
— the nature of education which, as a process, only produces results in the medium and long term, while in the industrial sector, emphasis is given to immediate results.

In the same measure, responsible industrialists know that although some degree of tolerance in relation to the environmental consequences of their activities may be found, they will not be allowed to cause unreasonable damage to the environment. Few would dispute the fact that, in the context of industrial activities, emissions and wastes should be reduced and recycling should be practised. Yet, prior to making such items a reality, there is a need for the re-orientation of industrial activities towards more ecologically-acceptable standards, a goal industrial ecology aims to pursue. It is here where the heart of the problem lies: the need to differentiate industrial ecology from industrial activities per se and emphasise its 'good' environmental side. Industrial ecology and environmental education may also be integrated by focusing on issues of global concern, such as:

— Air, land, and water quality.
— Citizen understanding and responsibility for public policy and environmental justice.
— Conflict management and other social-process skills.
— Ecologically sensitive approaches to land use.
— Ecosystem management, biodiversity, and threatened and endangered species protection.
— Energy alternatives/conservation.
— Environmental hazards, risks, and liability minimisation.

- — Human interaction with natural resources and ecosystems.
- — Integrated resource management.
- — Pollution prevention/clean-up.
- — Solid, hazardous, and animal waste management.
- — Sustainable production and efficient use of goods and services from natural resources.

As the 21st century begins, world attention is focused on how to make sure the environment and natural resources are sustainably used. Global trends and concerns are often expressed through community level actions. However, policy makers and industrialists in urban and rural communities are the ones making most decisions about the use of energy and forest products, which, if not carefully taken, invariably lead to problems such as overflowing landfills or poor air quality, to name but a few.

Industrialists and educators alike want to protect wildlife habitats and open space, they want to understand global change and to address dozens of other environmental questions. They can do this better by changing the ways environmental issues are usually handled. Policy makers' actions, resulting from thousands of decisions, collectively influence the sustainability of our natural resources and our environment.

Making intelligent decisions about environmental issues is critical, but it is not always easy. The amount of environmental information available is astounding and includes both fact and fiction. Some experts tend to emphasise the tangible benefits to society through harvesting natural resources. Other sources may highlight environmental health as the only relevant consideration for natural resource management decisions.

The most accessible information may not be the most useful and the job of searching for particular knowledge may be overwhelming. Teaching people how to make intelligent decisions about the use and management of natural resources is our best insurance for sustaining the production of goods and while protecting the natural resources on which we depend. There is a perceived need to help people to acquire the knowledge, skills, and tools they will need to make informed decisions about natural resources and the environment. This also applies to the industrial sector.

By integrating industrial ecology with environmental education and other programs, millions of people can learn more about the relationships between natural resources, environmental sustainability, and human well-being. This knowledge, accompanied by appropriate action, is necessary to maintain not only our natural resources, but also our way of life. Industrial ecology and environmental education thus need to reach for closer cooperation and more involvement in expanding their combined effect.

10.3. Education for Sustainable Livelihoods

In 1990, the Jomtien Conference reoriented the attention of international organizations concerned with education towards meeting basic learning needs as a global goal. Advanced knowledge development and technical/scientific education and training are no less important to the development of human resources in these swiftly changing times. But to continue to neglect the fundamental task of education for all, and to provide educational opportunity at least through primary school, for every child worldwide, was to short-change development at its base. Jomtien reminded the education community of several important principles: to look beyond mere enrolment as a measure of educational success to assess what is actually learned; to focus not only on learning substance, but also on developing continuing capacities to learn; and to place basic education higher on national agendas. Now, almost eight years after Jomtien, the record is mixed. A mid-decade review reported in Amman in 1996 produced evidence of some increases in primary enrolments, little evidence of improved quality, and (with conspicuous exceptions in some regions) a growing gender gap.

The Paris (September 1997) meeting of the International Consultative Forum on Education for All (EFA) noted two particular deficiencies, one at each end of the basic learning continuum. Firstly, evidence is steadily accruing for the importance of nutritional, cognitive and social development in early years for successful maturation. Thus human development strategies, especially those addressing poverty, must pay more policy attention to this issue. Second, basic learning needs of adults remain largely unmet in less developed countries.

Rapid changes are occurring in working environments, basic literacy and numeracy have been transcended as basic requirements for obtaining formal sector employment, and much of traditional basic education curricula lack relevance to actual livelihood strategies of those living in poverty.If the two ends of the continuum exhibit shortcomings, the middle (public formal and non-formal education at basic levels) is weak too. Teachers are often not present, and when present are sporadically paid, and often underqualified. Yet there are encouraging examples too, for instance where communities are closely involved in the basic educational process.

In a recent EFA meeting of the nine largest pop lation countries in Islamabad, among the key future challenges noted for Indian education were: sustaining community interest, motivation and participation, community ownership, strengthening decentralization, and nurturing community-based innovations. Emphasis is on tapping the creative energies of each community into the basic education effort. This takes deep involvement of people, and above all, close relevance of the basic educational experience to peoples' lives and livelihoods. 'Livelihood' is a timeless term, but has been brought into new prominence in development strategies by UNCED and Agenda 21, and most recently by the Social Summit Declaration at Copenhagen in 1995. Before reviewing the knowledge streams which intersect on the relationship between education and livelihood. Robert Chambers, who brought forward the idea of livelihood for new and intensified discussion in the development community, also was candid in his concern about the use of the word. He acknowledges "livelihood" in the evolution of ideas about rural development but cautions that it may mean "desirable change in rural areas" and that what is considered desirable differs by country, region, person and over time. According to Chambers, definitely not. It is important to note here what livelihood does not include and the importance of these exclusions.

Livelihood "can include food, health, a strong family, wealth and income. It can be described as a level of wealth and of stocks and flows of food and cash which provide for physical and social well-being and security against impoverishment. To this may be added access to basic goods and services, but while these are important, for the poorest they may only come second to subsistence and security. There is also the quality of living and experience...the value people set on the familiar, on being needed, on a purpose and role in life, on love, on religious observations, on dancing and song, festivals and ceremonies, on things in their seasons, and bringing in the harvest. Perhaps the most one can say is that for the full enjoyment of these, secure and decent livelihoods may be necessary but not sufficient on their own. "

Livelihoods, however, are necessary, and if the poor are to be put first, then the growing interest in sustainable livelihoods is an important step in the right direction. It is at this point a working hypothesis "to be confirmed or refuted case by case" but the cases are accumulating in favour of using this concept. Chambers moves to a sharper definition of livelihoods in relation to jobs and employment.

The concept of 'job' has emerged as a central element in human resources strategies and policy. Education systems are expected to be able to prepare people for jobs, individuals make job choices, media publish job opportunities, statistical systems count jobs and currently, job creation is high on the priority list of governments worldwide in both the north and the south.

Paradoxically, even modern sector employment is no guarantee of an adequate livelihood for a single wage-earner supporting a family. Livelihoods systems and strategies (coping and adaptive) are suggested by Chambers as a more useful concept than employment per se for those living in poverty. Livelihoods have been recently defined by UNDP (in terms of a development goal, as "the activities, means and entitlements by which individuals make a living" and "sustainable livelihoods are derived from people's capacities to exercise choice, and to access opportunities and resources, and use them for their livelihoods in ways that do not foreclose options for others to make their living, either now, or in the future".

"Livelihood systems" are the "sets of economic, social and physical elements and interrelationships which form the basis of livelihood decisions." Learning about livelihoods is best done by talking to and observing the people who own those livelihoods.

There are educational elements in all of the above, and the 'northern' or 'western' bias is readily acknowledged, so feedback from the working group is openly solicited. The strategy is to approach traditional learning/education areas through a review of relevant literature on development, sustainable development/environment/ecology, and economics.

The aim is to identify, briefly, key concepts which link learning, schooling and education in relation to sustainable livelihoods, rather than any in-depth review. Livelihood has long had an economic connotation and it is from within the fields of economics and economic anthropology as well as from development philosophers, that the real backlash has come against thinking of livelihoods as having a purely market-oriented connection.

Economic anthropologists such as Gudeman have argued that economies and economic theories are "social constructions" and that the central processes of making a livelihood are culturally modelled. In this view, the activities of livelihood are taken from a symbolic scheme drawn from features of the social world, while western models of livelihood have used logical and mathematical schemes.

The differentiation that Gudeman describes has important implications for the bases of development, particularly in the connections to participatory development and learning. In 1944 the economist Karl Polyani proposed the concept of an economy as a "material-means-provisioning process" for society.

Many economists who believe that growth is generated in the "real sphere: more people, more wishes, technological development, new markets determine economic activity". The financial sphere, according to this mode of thinking, simply follows or facilitates what is happening in the real sphere. A British economist, James Robertson, proposes "decoupling the work people can do from what employers can provide, and decoupling local economic activity from what the national economy can provide". In practice Robertson envisions this decoupling as leading to changes in perception and values and changes in government policies. On such change, he says, would be that the "aim of education will be to enable people to manage their own lives, including their work lives, rather than preparing them to work for employers".

Relevant to learning and education, Daly states that "an economy in sustainable development adapts and improves in knowledge, organization, technical efficiency and wisdom; and it does this without assimilating or accreting, beyond some point, an ever greater percentage of the matter-energy of the ecosystem into itself....." An aspect of the economic development equation now receiving increasing attention is "globalization". This too has important ramifications for learning, schooling and education.

There are a variety of faces of globalization, according to Korten. "One face is a globalizing civil society. Another is an emerging global consciousness of our mutual dependence on the life support systems of a small planet. A third is the globalization of communications. A fourth is the globalization of the consumer culture. A fifth is economic globalization...the erasing of economic borders to allow the free flow of goods and money". It is economic globalization which is causing the most controversy.

"Sustainable livelihoods" is described as taking a systems approach, "looking for impacts on social and gender equity, patterns of resource use, and the creation of opportunities that do not involve cost-shifting and that make people's lives better without impoverishing others or the next generation".

Use value production takes place outside of market exchange both in the household and in the subsistence sector. It generates "social relations between people" and therefore forms part of the "categories of economics. Because it does, states Beneria, use value production, often the labour of women, should be a part of the definition of "active labour".

"Learning", "Schooling" and "Education" are charged words. The anthropologist Mary Catherine Bateson has mused on their meaning and found herself drifting into "the insidious equation of learning with education and, more narrowly still, with schooling":

" Trying to understand learning by studying schooling is rather like trying to understand sexuality by studying bordellos. Certainly schooling is part of the spectrum of learning in human lives, but it is not the model for all learning, only one of the byways. Learning and teaching are both fundamental for human adaptation, but not all societies segregate them from the flow of life into institutional boxes."It is interesting that the differentiation among learning, schooling and education is so similar to the clarity now being sought among "livelihoods", "jobs", and "employment".

Sustainable livelihoods would seem to have closer kinship to learning. Bateson notes that "preoccupied with schooling, most research on human learning is focused on learning that depends on teaching or is completed in a specified context rather than on learning that takes place spontaneously because it fits directly into life."

Schooling and education are, however, part of the "byways" of learning and cannot be ignored but paying greater attention to the myriad learnings that occur outside of institutional contexts fits nicely with the concept of sustainable livelihood.

Miller perceived four educational implications of a broader conception of development:

1. Education must become less formal.
2. Education must be freed from system restrictions and be developed through a variety of specific projects on a smaller scale.
3. Education projects must be recognized as experimental and must be monitored so that we may find out what works in specific situations.
4. Education must become more of a service within a complex of development efforts and less of an instructional program for the sake of instruction."

Any education that is mainly about economic utility is far too limited to be useful, and, in any case, so diminishes the world that it mocks one's humanity. At the very least, it diminishes the idea of what a good learner is. Howard Gardner is another important American educator whose views can link with the concept of sustainable livelihoods. His pioneering research on "multiple intelligences" outlined in his early book Frames of Mind provides one such linkage. He has theorized that all human beings are capable of at least seven different ways of knowing the world (seven intelligences).

These are language, logical-mathematical analysis, spatial representation, musical thinking, the use of the body to solve problems or to make things, an understanding of other individuals, and an understanding of ourselves. Where individuals differ, states Gardner, is in the strength of these intelligences. These differences challenge an educational system that assumes everyone can learn in the same way, and that a uniform, universal measure is enough to test student learning.

Notwithstanding the fact that increasing evidence from early childhood development research shows the importance of infant nutrition and stimulation in brain development, the first years of schooling are critical. For the majority of children in the world's poorest regions, a few years of primary schooling may the most formal education they get.

Basic education is thought to increase productivity in the informal, non-farm sector but there have been few definitive studies on this linkage. Education has been found to lead to an increase in the duration of labour force participation among women. Many of the private and social returns to education are attributed to non-market benefits that are both intra- and intergenerational. These include improvements in life expectancy, family health and nutritional status, as well as decreased fertility rates for women.

The social benefits attached to education are "especially profound" when girls gain access to schooling" and a number of studies are outlined to confirm specific benefits. Because many of the effects of basic education are intergenerational, the inequities of one generation are visited upon the next. Maternal education benefits sons and daughters alike. Literacy is closely linked to strong school completion rates. Education may assist in the redistribution of income, the relationship between attainment and earnings is very complex. Education alone is seen to be insufficient as a distributive measure.

10.4. Adult Education for Sustainable Development

Adult education offers a hospitable environment for sustainable livelihoods thinking. Learning in adult education rests on a set of assumptions known as andragogy first described by Malcolm Knowles. These assumptions are:

— "Adults both desire and enact a tendency toward self-directedness as they mature, though they may be dependent in certain situations;

— Adults' experiences are a rich resource for learning. Adults learn more effectively through experiential techniques of education such as discussion or problem-solving.

— Adults are aware of specific learning needs generated by real-life tasks or problems. Adult education programs, therefore, should be organized around "life application" categories and sequenced according to learners' readiness to learn.

— Adults are competency based learners in that they wish to apply newly acquired skills or knowledge to their immediate circumstances. Adults are, therefore, "performance-centered" in their orientation to learning. "

Experiential learning techniques are highly participatory and therefore complement the sustainable livelihoods concept. Participatory training techniques are employed worldwide with adults through a wide variety of nonformal education, life-long education, and community-based education activities.

Community education has as its ultimate goal the transformation of our society. The always sensitive field of educational evaluation has developed a remarkable breadth and depth over the past decade. It nevertheless is difficult to escape the testing mentality for education. For nonformal and adult education programs, needs assessments are now conducted through the techniques embodied in RRA (Rapid Rural Appraisal) and PRA (Participatory Rural Appraisal). At a higher level of impact monitoring and evaluation, there has been a move away from trust of international comparisons of school effectiveness and a move towards more qualitative types of monitoring and evaluation which do not directly look at pupil achievement. The latest perspectives on evaluation now discourage generic school effectiveness studies outside the context of a particular country.

Poverty eradication must become an explicit and priority concern for those involved in design and implementation of basic education programmes. That it has not been in the past, even in the world's poorest regions, is testimony to the systemic distortions which can perpetuate poverty by maintaining exclusionary attitudes and values.

'Poverty in the past has been treated as too economics-specific a problem for educational action except in an indirect way, and subsumed under the more general category of 'educational disadvantage'. The belief dies hard that education cannot have anything directly to do with a hard core, economic problem like poverty, and that it can, at best, only play a secondary or marginal role.... [requiring] the conscious pursuit of empowerment of the poor as an overt objective of all basic education programmes'.

Educating for 'jobs' while often controversial in the past, is today increasingly challenged by the need to build human capacity not only for employability, but for broader lifelong learning as well as for adaptive and 'coping' livelihood strategies in a fast-moving and complicated world.

HRD supply systems in the poorest countries, particularly formal education at the basic levels, are still designed primarily to prepare people for further education and for modern sector 'jobs' in contradiction to clear empirical evidence which shows that small fractions of primary school intake go on to secondary, and much smaller fractions to higher education and/or employment in the formal sector.

Few opportunities now exist for adults, especially those with low formal skills, to recycle through education institutions, even though the need may be great. More effective linkage between education and sustainable livelihoods across a lifetime therefore becomes a central issue in social development and poverty eradication strategies.

Such entrepeneurial educational efforts are increasingly needed at grass roots levels if formal education systems of the future continue only to empower relatively few people in poor communities. Accordingly, in India, 'lokshala' (local community) efforts are being supported in meeting the basic learning needs of poor children and adults.

UNESCO and UNDP have suggested that integrating other basic social services with education at the community level can contribute to improved health, nutrition, hygiene and sanitation. Awareness and knowledge bases of households can be substantively increased, potentially unifying parents, children and teachers around common problem-solving goals for community improvement.

The Human Rights education effort has provided some experience base on which to initiate these kinds of approaches, as well as pointing up some of the difficulties. There is new evidence from North America that the number of people who regularly access the

Internet through points other than home, office or school has nearly tripled in the last year.

This growing phenomenon of "alternative points of access" such as libraries, museums and civic organizations, illustrates the heightened need for access to this medium, and suggests a burgeoning democratization of the INTERNET from personal to community life. The rapid spread of INTERNET cafes and parabolic antennas in peri-urban, even rural areas in Morocco is one indication of the speed at which these technologies are permeating developing countries.

A major brake on this process is insufficient rural electrification, solutions to which may of course pose further threats to fragile environments. UNDP through its Sustainable Development Networking programme has provided INTERNET access for several developing nations, and through its LISTSERVS in connection with the Social Summit, Beijing and Toronto Conferences has opened up UN deliberative mechanisms to the nascent democratization and new ideas implied by this fresh and more participatory access.

UNDP is also exploring with UNESCO and NGOs such as the International Council for Adult Education alternative means for bringing educational materials to remote areas through landbased or satellite communications, and for linking island nations and communities through INTERNET for example in the Caribbean region. These newly available methods can bring information out to people where they live.

10.4.1. Environmental Education for Adults

The Fifth International Conference on Adult Education provided a unique opportunity to create a dialogue between policy-makers, educational planners, practitioners, and between governments and NGOs. The workshop was jointly organised by the International Network for Sustainable Energy (INFORSE), the Learning for the Environment Programme (LEAP) of the International Council for Adult-Education, the University of Lüneburg and the UNESCO Institute for Education, Hamburg.

According to a working definition provided in 1992 by UNEP/ UNESCO/ OECD Paris, environmental education is "a permanent process in which individuals gain awareness of their environment and acquire the knowledge, values, skills, experiences, and also the determination which will enable them to act individually and collectively to solve present and future environmental problems... as well as to meet their needs without compromising those of future generations."

Adult environmental education should disseminate knowledge about the environment's direct and indirect physical and related social impact. It should also transmit knowledge on the interaction between local activities and their effects which may occur further away. Direct impacts, such as deforestation and diseases caused by polluted water, are visible and tangibly affect daily life. Solutions to them can be found in the short term if appropriate measures are taken.

Indirect environmental impacts may include increased soil erosion, a disproportionate workload for women, general depletion of resources such as food, animal fodder and water, reduction of numbers and diversity of wildlife and increased risk of bush fires and flooding. Indirect effects take longer to be felt. They occur over a wider geographical area. Their solution requires long-term planning, commitment and global approaches Adult education has often included a political and socially transformative perspective.

The environmental factor is now becoming increasingly important and can hardly be ignored in education efforts committed to social and political goals. With the links between changes in the physical environment and current social and political problems becoming more evident, environmental education is assuming an important social function. It is developing into a more holistic education project similar to the education envisaged by Freire.

However much remains to be done. Much environmental education is still purely science and technology oriented rather than addressing environmental and social issues in an integrated way. Linking environmental and social issues and locating environmental problems within the context of our daily lives and action are important challenges for adult environmental education.

Current adult environmental education is experimenting with different ways to bring about change and initiate action. Such projects go beyond creating understanding and awareness. They aim at developing skills, creating a sense of commitment and stimulating individual and collective action.

Environmental education has the potential to bring about action at individual, community and governmental levels. However, environmental activists and educators are becoming aware of the kinds of situation that create barriers to participatory action for the environment, such as:

— Situations where marginal communities face grave economic and social problems.

— Where there is a lack of environmental awareness and of commitment to environmentally friendly policies among governments and industry.

— Where local initiatives do not achieve their aims because of lack of support from the institutional sector, and because of lack of co-ordination with other initiatives.

Adult learning is a central tool in the process of raising environmental awareness and promoting environmentally supportive action. Many environmental organisations disseminate information, organise community initiatives and practise non-formal adult education.

Environmental educators and activists recognise the need to strengthen and innovate this educational dimension of their work. Environmental groups often seek the collaboration of adult educators, and in this sense they are trying to change their educational work from mere information sharing to more participatory and creative ways of learning.

Environmental issues are becoming more and more important for other fields of adult education too. Given the negative effects of environmental degradation and pollution on people's health, environmental questions can be dealt with in health education programmes.

Environmental topics can also be an important component of community education programmes. Such programmes can provide a frame for linking environmental issues with social and political problems of the community.

In a community education project in Northern Ontario, the two most important issues identified by the community were youth violence and soil erosion. At first sight it seemed doubtful how such apparently disconnected issues could be linked to each other. However it soon became clear that the two problems had a lot to do with each other. Collaboration between environmentalists and adult educators should be strengthened. They could, for example, join efforts in planning and implementing activities at the community level and promote local capacity building.

At the same time adult educators and environmentalists should work together in influencing policy, at both national and international levels. National and international NGOs can be important partners in this process. The integration of the environment into general and vocational adult education can provide a range of new opportunities for an environmental education which is more relevant to learners' concerns. This is particularly important for developing countries which are today experiencing serious environmental problems that directly affect people's lives.

Environmental education, if it is to be meaningful to adults in their daily lives, needs to address ecological questions in terms of the social, political and economic factors involved. In industrialised regions, for example, environmental education entails dealing with the crisis of modern production systems and their consequences for employment.

In developing regions, on the other hand, it deals with issues relating to global production structures, national economy, international trade, local agriculture, development aid and foreign debt. One of the big challenges for environmental adult education is to change the widespread belief that what happens to the environment is not caused by our own actions, but by someone somewhere else.

Yet adult educators are aware of the fact that, although community action is a powerful tool, there are clear limits to what can be achieved at this level, especially when local political and social conditions are taken into account.

Kutch Mahila Vikas Sangathan (KMVS) is an organisation of rural women living in the arid border villages of Kutch District, Gujarat. The organisation, which was founded in 1989 and includes more than 1200 members, provides a range of projects aiming at supporting rural women, articulating their concerns and initiating new action to improve their lives and economic situation.

A major focus of KMVS is ecological degradation and income generation. In Kutch, women are most affected by the negative consequences of ecological degradation. There is water scarcity and soil salinity. KMVS has initiated an education programme including a water harvesting programme. The programme met with serious resistance from the men of the village. Women are traditionally responsible for fetching water, while resource management is a male task. Addressing water scarcity resulted in a complex situation where the women also had to deal with the question of rights to land holdings. This is a politically sensitive and touches on issues of caste and gender.

Although the negative effects of modern production and agricultural techniques on soil fertility, for example, are beginning to be recognised by many governments and aid agencies, yet there appears to be a continuing contradiction between the interests of economic growth and sustainable resource management.

Technological progress is still considered a positive factor in economic development, even though it has many negative consequences for the natural environment.

Tambuyog Development Centre (TDC) has developed an environmental education and training programme for coastal communities. Fishermen and women learn to understand the political, economic and biological factors which lead to the growing destruction of the marine ecosystem. Several factors are involved:

— the exploitation of resources through the fishing industry;
— the fact that the fishermen and women have no property rights over the sea and the mangrove areas;
— the support given by power structures to the fishing industry;
— the deteriorating income of fishermen and women;
— the use of dynamite to catch fish.

The project helps fishermen and women to understand their own complex situation. At the same time it provides them with the necessary insights into the existing power structures. It creates an awareness of the effects of the use of dynamite on fishing resources and the status of the mangroves.

TDC's environmental education project includes holding workshops and the use of educational comic books to reach a larger public. But awareness-raising activities alone cannot lead to sustained change. TDC is now providing resource management training for the fishing community, helping them in establishing local organisations and supporting alternative fishing techniques.

In poor and marginalised communities, environmental education is often regarded as a luxury. Even in many industrialised countries, environmental issues are being given less attention than, say, 10 years ago. Very few countries are willing to experiment with radically new political solutions.

In view of the present unemployment situation, solutions which aim at transforming the economy towards more ecologically sound patterns of production and consumption often clash with policies for short-term economic growth. Environmental adult education often suffers from this mistaken conflict between economic growth and sustainable development.

At times when economic needs are a priority, it might seem absurd to propose the integration of environmental dimensions in to educational programmes. Yet this is a concern of many educators, social workers and development workers, in both developing and industrialised countries.

Environmental education has the urgent task of overcoming such misconceptions. It needs to stress that environmentally friendly technologies can be an opportunity to modernise and improve production systems. More importantly, such an education needs to reveal to its participants that an ecologically sound production strategy does not automatically imply higher costs and lower revenues.

Many women's groups and environmental organisations focus their work on household production and consumption, as this affects the lives of women directly. One of the main issues that women's projects address is the consumption of fuel, principally wood, for cooking and heating.

Some projects are promoting a combination of methods of food preparation, cooking, heating and fuel substitution. Since women are often the primary collectors of wood and do most of the cooking themselves, many initiatives in this area focus on lowering their workload and improving their situation.

At the same time they promote the use of environmental-friendly energy resources for the whole community. The use of firewood or charcoal for cooking and heating is widespread. In many communities in Africa cooking is traditionally done on large fireplaces which consume great quantities of firewood. These traditional hearths can also lead to serious health problems, because women inhale large amounts of smoke as a result of spending many hours of cooking at the hearth daily.

The use of wood also seriously depletes local forests. The resulting soil erosion has a negative impact on local agricultural production. However, as people seldom have an alternative to firewood, they continue to rely on wood despite their awareness of the negative consequences of wood cutting.

In Uganda, a local organisation has developed an education programme to introduce clay stoves in the villages. It aims to equip communities with the skills and knowledge needed to manage their natural resources in a sustainable manner. People are also trained in new methods of charcoal production which use considerably less wood than traditional methods.

Moreover, the production and sale of charcoal provides families with an additional income. Many local associations and NGOs are promoting the use of fuel-efficient stoves. These come in many different designs and use different materials. Solar cooking and heating are also being promoted. The savings in fuel consumption range from 0% to 40% depending upon the quality of the project, funding, the extent of local initiative and participation as well as on cultural acceptance of the innovation.

In some places people are supplied with supplementary fuels, the consumption of which is less damaging to the natural environment than wood. Among the substitutes being tried are charcoal, peat, crop residues, kerosene, bio-gas and carbonaceous briquettes. Projects, such as the one from Uganda, often combine the introduction of energy conservation methods with strategies to protect and restore trees and other vegetation.

Firewood consumption is a crucial problem in Uganda. For the fishing community in the Philippines the biggest issue is the state of the mangroves and over fishing. In arid and semi-arid regions of Senegal, access to water is the major environmental problem. While community initiatives are vital, it is evident that the local level cannot be the only focus of change. It is also necessary to create greater awareness of global environmental problems, through networking, advocacy and lobbying at all levels, from government to the factory floor. Because of the global dimensions of current problems, environmental education for one region must include environmental education elsewhere. For example, environmental education for Africa must start with educating people in the North, because as long as industrialised countries continue to take large quantities of timber from Africa, Asia and Latin America, deforestation and desertification in these regions cannot stop. At the same time environmental conditions—water, energy, climate and soil - are different in each region and each local context.

Educational tools therefore need to take into account the specific cultural, political and environmental contexts. Environmental learning encourages participation. It builds a vision in which the contributions of women, men, persons of different colours, abilities and creeds, indigenous people, the young and the old are equally respected.

Environmental education explicitly draws from the knowledge of indigenous people and those who are closest to the land. The need to promote and build on local knowledge and indigenous traditions has been repeated time and again. That communities often possess immensely valuable knowledge and mechanisms for coping with often harsh environments is widely known and acknowledged.

The expertise of the learners, who have a first-hand experience of the changing environmental balance, is regarded as an important source of knowledge. Similarly, the role and authority of local communities in protecting their own environment is stated in many policy papers and reports. But in reality many indigenous populations today have been deprived of their rights, including property rights over the land they inhabit. Backed by national governments, international companies make enormous profits by exploiting national resources on a large scale. In Malaysia, for example, communities' livelihood is seriously threatened as their lands are being destroyed by logging and plantations.

Traditional knowledge, which functioned as part of a system of governance, no longer exists. It is often claimed that environmental education needs to include traditional knowledge and has a specific responsibility to revive and promote such traditions. However, in a context which is characterised by economic exploitation and political domination, local systems of preservation, which rely on local authority and control over resources, may no longer be effective. It is nevertheless possible and even necessary to use traditional knowledge in environmental education, provided that local traditions are reassessed in the context of the present conditions.

Following are the number of problems facing current adult environmental education.

— Government and donor policies with regard to adult environmental education are in a precarious state.

— Environmental education is less developed in adult and non-formal sectors than in schools.

— Teaching practices in environmental adult education often tend to be limited to the transmission of knowledge rather than to promoting a critical examination of environmental problems.

— Practical solutions are seldom promoted in environmental education for adults.

— Environmental education is seldom linked to the immediate environment of the participants.

— There is often a bias towards promoting 'expert' knowledge and scientific and technological approaches.

— There is still the pervading notion that science is neutral, progress linear and growth unlimited.

In other words, rather than critiquing dominant models of development and economic growth, adult environmental education remains locked within ideologies which have caused many of our contemporary environmental problems. In addition to discussing the many difficulties facing the current adult environmental education, the workshop proposed a range of possible solutions and approaches.

References

Gruenewald, D.A., 2004, A Foucauldian analysis of environmental education: toward the socioecological challenge of the Earth Charter, *Curriculum Inquiry* 34(1):71-107.

Malone, K. 1999, Environmental education researchers as environmental activists, *Environmental Education Research* 5(2):163-177.

Palmer, J.A., 1998, *Environmental Education in the 21st Century: Theory, Practice, Progress, and Promise,* Routledge.

Science (ed.), 1997, Overhauling environmental education, Science, 276:361.

Smyth, J.C. 2006, Environment and education: a view of a changing scene, *Environmental Education Research* 12(3,4):247-264.

Roth, Charles E. "Off the Merry-Go-Round and on to the Escalator". In *From Ought to Action in Environmental Education,* edited by William B. Stapp, pp. 12–23. Columbus, OH: SMEAC Information Reference Center, 1978. Ed 159 046.

Bibliography

Andreopoulos, George J. and Richard Pierre Claude, Eds., 1997. *Human Rights Education for the Twenty-First Century*, University of Pennsylvania Press.

Banks, James A. 1997.*Educating Citizens in a Multicultural Society.* New York: Teachers College Press.

Best, R. (Ed.). 1996. *Education,Spirituality and the Whole Child.* London: Cassel.

Boulding, Elise, 1988. *Building a Global Civic Culture: Education for an Interdependent World*, Teachers College Press.

Bower, William C. 1952. *Moral and Spiritual Values in Education*, Lexigton, university of Kentucky Press.

Bowler, I.R., Bryant, C.R. and Cocklin, C. (eds) 2002 *The Sustainability of Rural Systems: Geographical Interpretations* (Dordrecht , Kluwer.

Budhanda Swami. 1983. *How to Build Character A Primer* : Ramakrishna Mission, New Delhi.

Cajete, G. 1994. *Look to the Mountain: An ecology of indigenous education.* Durango: Kivaaki Press.

Clarke, J. 1975. *Beginning Values Clarifications*, Pennat Press.

Chambers, N., Simmons, C. and Wakernagel, M. 2000. *Sharing Nature's interest: ecological footprints as an indicator of sustainability* Earthscan, London .

Cohen, A. 1983. *The Educational Philosophy Of Martin Buber.* London: Fairleigh Dickinson University Press.

Core Group, Govt. of India . 1992. *Value Orientation Education*, New Delhi.

Damon, William. 1988. *The Moral Child: Nurturing Children's Natural Moral Growth.* The Free Press, New York.

De Souza, G. and Gebremedhin, T. 1998 *Sustainability in agricultural and rural development.* Ashgate, Aldershot .

Department for Education and Skills (DfES). 1999 *A better quality of life: a strategy for sustainable development for the UK.* HMSO, London .

Diaz, Carlos, Byron G. Massialas, and John A. Xanthopoulos. 1999.*Global Perspectives for Educators.* Boston: Allyn and Bacon.

Downey, M and Kelly, A.V. 1978. *Moral Education: Theory and Practice*, Harper and Row, London.

Dudty, D., & Dudty, H. (Eds.). 1994. *Holistic Education: Some Australian Explorations. "Belconnen, ACT":* Australian Curriculum Studies Association.

Elliott, J.A. 1999 *An introduction to sustainable development.* Routledge, London .

Fisk, Larry and John Schellenberg, 2000. *Patterns of Conflict: Paths to Peace*, Broadview Press.

Forbes, S. 2003. *Holistic Education: An Analysis of Its Ideas and Nature.* Brandon, VT: Foundation for Educational Renewal.

Frankel J.R. 1977. *How to Teach About Values*, New Jersey, Persstince hill.

Galbraith, R.E. and Jones, T.M. 1976. *Moral Reasoning: A teaching handbook for adopting Kohilberg to the class-room*, Anoka, Minn Green Haven Press.

Gruenewald, D.A., 2004, A Foucauldian analysis of environmental education: toward the socioecological challenge of the Earth Charter, *Curriculum Inquiry* 34(1):71-107.

Gupta. N.L. *Value Education, Theory and Practice*, Krishna Brother, Ajmer. 1986.

Hiriyanna, M. 1960. *The Mission of Philosophy*, Mysore, Kavyalayas Publishers.

Harmin, M. Kirschenbaun M. and Simon S.B. 1973. *Clarifying Values through Subject Matter*', Minneapolis Winston Press.

Hall. R.T. and Davis J.U. 1975. *Moral Education in Theory and Practice*, Buffalo, N.Y. Prometheus Books.

Hawley R.C. 1975. *Value Exploration Through Role Play,* New York Publishing Company.

Kirschenbaum, M. 1977. *Advanced Value Clarification*, California University Associates.

Lulla, B.P. *Values-oriented Teacher Education*, Bombay Teachers Training College, Bombay.

Lynch, James. 1989.*Multicultural Education in a Global Society.* London and New York: Falmer.

Malone, K. 1999, Environmental education researchers as environmental activists, *Environmental Education Research* 5(2):163-177.

Martin Purvis and Alan Grainger (editors). 2004. *Exploring Sustainable Development: Geographical Perspectives.* Earthscan, London .

Mascranahas, M. A and Justa M.R. 1989. *Value Education in schools and other essays,* Konark Publishers Private Limited,

Meyer J. Burnham B. and Choilvat. J. 1975. *Values Education. Theory, Practice, Problems and Prospects,* Waterloo, Ontario, Wilfred Lauerer University Press.

Miller, J. P. 1993. *The Holistic Curriculum.* Toronto: OISE Press.

Nakagawa, Yoshiharu. 2000. *Education for Awakening: An Eastern Approach to Holistic Education.* Volume Two of the Foundations of Holistic Education Series. Brandon, VT: Foundation for Educational Renewal.

O'Riordan, Tim, ed. 200. *Globalism, Localism, and Identity: Fresh Perspectives on the Transition to Sustainability.* Sterling, Va.: Earthscan.

Palmer, J.A., 1998, *Environmental Education in the 21st Century: Theory, Practice, Progress, and Promise,* Routledge.

Parker, Walter C., ed. 1996. *Educating the Democratic Mind.* Albany: State University of New York Press.

Power, F.C. . Higgins A. and Kolnberg L. 1989. *Approach to Moral Education,* Columbia University Press, New York.

Rama Rao, K. 1986. *Moral Education: A practical approach,* Ramakrishna Institute of Moral and Spiritual Education, Mysore.

Rath, R.E., Harmin. M. and Simon, S.B. 1978. *Values and Teaching: Working with values in Classroom,* Columbus, Charles E, Merrill.

Ray, Douglas, Ed., 1988. *Peace Education: Canadian and International Perspectives,* London: Third Eye Publications,.

Reddy, N.Y. 1980. *Values and Attitudes of Indian Youth, Light and Life* Publication, New Delhi.

Reid, D . 2004. *Sustainable development: an introductory guide.* Earthscan, London .

Roth, Charles E. "Off the Merry-Go-Round and on to the Escalator". In *From Ought to Action in Environmental Education,* edited by William B. Stapp, pp. 12–23. Columbus, OH: SMEAC Information Reference Center, 1978. Ed 159 046.

Ruhella , S.P. *Education, Human Values and Education,* Sterling, New Delhi.

Ryan, Kelvin and McLean G.T. 1987. *Education, Character Development in Schools*, Praeger, New York.

Saraf, Som Nath. 1995. *Education in Human Values: A handbook on programme implementation* . Apeejay Education Foundation.

Science (ed.), 1997, Overhauling environmental education, Science, 276:361.

Sheshadri, C., Khader M.A. and Ddhya G.L. 1992. *Education in Values: A source book*, NCERT, New Delhi.

Smith, David C. and Terrance R. Carson, 1998. *Educating for a Peaceful Future*, Kagen and Woo, Ltd..

Smyth, J.C. 2006, Environment and education: a view of a changing scene, *Environmental Education Research* 12(3,4):247-264.

Tye, Barbara Benham, and Kenneth A. Tye. 1992. *Global Education: A Study of School Change.* Albany: State University of New York Press.

UNESCO, 1997. *UNESCO and a Culture of Peace: Promoting a global movement*, UNESCO Publishing.

Wakernagel, M. and Rees, W.E. 1996. *Our ecological footprint: reducing human impact on the Earth.* New Society Publications, Toronto.

Index